Kids and School Reform

Patricia A. Wasley
Robert L. Hampel
Richard W. Clark

Kids and School
Reform

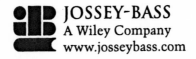

JOSSEY-BASS
A Wiley Company
www.josseybass.com

Published by

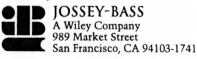 **JOSSEY-BASS**
A Wiley Company
989 Market Street
San Francisco, CA 94103-1741

www.josseybass.com

Copyright © 1997 by John Wiley & Sons, Inc.

Jossey-Bass is a registered trademark of John Wiley & Sons, Inc.

"If We Must Die" by Claude McKay in Chapter Two from Burnet, P. (ed.). *Penguin Book of Caribbean Verse in English.* New York: Penguin Books, 1986.

The Nine Common Principles in Appendix A reprinted with permission from the Coalition of Essential Schools.

Jossey-Bass books and products are available through most bookstores. To contact Jossey-Bass directly, call (888) 378-2537, fax to (800) 605-2665, or visit our website at www.josseybass.com.

Substantial discounts on bulk quantities of Jossey-Bass books are available to corporations, professional associations, and other organizations. For details and discount information, contact the special sales department at Jossey-Bass.

We at Jossey-Bass strive to use the most environmentally sensitive paper stocks available to us. Our publications are printed on acid-free recycled stock whenever possible, and our paper always meets or exceeds minimum GPO and EPA requirements.

Library of Congress Cataloging-in-Publication Data

Wasley, Patricia A., date.
    Kids and school reform / Patricia A. Wasley, Robert L. Hampel, Richard W. Clark. — 1st ed.
       p. cm. — (The Jossey-Bass education series)
    Includes bibliographical references and index.
    ISBN 0–7879–1065–1 (cloth : acid-free paper)
    1. High schools—United States—Sociological aspects.
2. Educational change—United States. 3. Education, Secondary—Aims and objectives—United States. 4. School management and organization—United States. I. Hampel, Robert L. II. Clark, Richard W. III. Title. IV. Series.
LA222.W35 1996
373.73—dc21   97–21058

FIRST EDITION
HB *Printing*   10 9 8 7 6 5 4 3

The Jossey-Bass

Education Series

Contents

Preface

When we began this work in 1990, we felt that although many journalists and educational researchers were writing about the plight of our high schools and about the measures taken to reform them, no one seemed concerned with the stories of the students involved. In the 1980s, many good books profiled teachers, and a number of teachers themselves wrote revealing stories about the challenges they faced in their schools in light of the significantly changed social conditions that surrounded schools. Studies of and by administrators also were plentiful. But stories about the kids were missing. Because reform of our nation's high schools is undertaken on behalf of our students, their silence seemed particularly troubling.

So we set about the task of listening to students. They came from a particular cluster of high schools, those associated with the Coalition of Essential Schools (CES), a network of more than one thousand schools here and abroad. CES stemmed from the ideas set forth by Theodore Sizer in *Horace's Compromise* (1984), elaborated in *Horace's School* (1992) and *Horace's Hope* (1996). All three books advocated lively, flexible schooling—student-centered classrooms with interdisciplinary projects to challenge all ability levels, teachers working in teams to engage students in important contemporary problem solving, newly developed master schedules with reduced student-teacher ratios, and leaner curriculum with clear standards for student accomplishment that would promote intellectual intensity. The fragmentation, impersonality, and tedium of most American high schools would give way to a more joyful, yet thoughtful atmosphere.

Sizer's ideas are no longer unique to CES schools. Thousands of schools unaffiliated with CES are hard at work on the same goals. A trimmer curriculum, lower student-teacher ratios, less teacher talk, new authentic assessments for students to show what they know and can do—all those aspects of CES ideology, unfashionable a decade ago, now permeate the national conversation about improving high schools. As a result, colleagues from around the country who are in reforming schools not affiliated with the Coalition have suggested that the findings reported here may well reflect what is happening in a majority of reforming high schools around the country.

Kids and School Reform spotlights students in five CES high schools that were undertaking ambitious reforms in the early 1990s. Above all, we want to answer this question: When the adults in American high schools make far-reaching changes, what differences ensue for their students? Teachers can use new instructional methods, rearrange the blocks of time during the school day, devise new forms of testing, or adopt other innovations—but when do these changes truly improve student learning? And when do they yield little or nothing for kids?

In Chapter One, we introduce Sally, Tommy, Alicia, Sean, Hakim, and Diego. Sophomores all, they exhibited the full range of adolescent ups and downs, successes and setbacks. Through them, we got to know dozens of their classmates, their teachers, their administrators, and many of their parents. And we watched them for clues about when school reform strategies made a difference for them.

In Chapters Two through Five, we discuss four *sets of connections* that seemed critical to making genuine differences in kids' performance. We learned that school reform requires dynamic interplay between *sets of conditions* that are too often pursued in isolation. For instance, a school with *high expectations* for serious academic work from all students gets better performance of those expectations when *caring* for students gets equal attention. Traditionally, many teachers struggle between two extremes: they either care deeply for students and allow their compassion to override their expectations for strong academic performance, or they set high academic standards and express caring only for the select group of students who are readily able to meet those standards. The study schools worked to achieve the connection between caring and expectations—a difficult objective but one they knew would yield greater gains for kids than either would garner in isolation from the other.

Following the discussion of the four connections, we conclude in Chapter Six with an in-depth look at our six students, now seniors. Although they appeared throughout the other chapters, here we revisit them at length to review how the four connections enhanced their education. We believe that *Kids and School Reform* will interest readers who want to know more about high school reform. We hope that the voices of these students will provide valuable insights for education professionals and for parents and taxpayers who want to understand the kinds of school reform efforts that will help our youth realize their greatest potential.

July 1997

Patricia A. Wasley
New York, New York

Robert L. Hampel
Newark, Delaware

Richard W. Clark
Bellevue, Washington

Acknowledgments

We are grateful to many people who contributed to our thinking as we were writing this book. We owe a particular intellectual debt to Theodore Sizer, chairman and founder of the Coalition of Essential Schools (CES), for his faith in this project and for his gentle but persistent prodding in early versions of the manuscript.

The study was only possible because of generous contributions from three foundations. We gratefully acknowledge the contributions of Ed Ahnert and the Exxon Educational Foundation, Donna Dunlop and Carla Asher and the DeWitt Wallace–Reader's Digest Fund, and Patricia Patrizi and the Pew Charitable Trusts.

An exceptional group of research associates joined us on every site visit. This book could not have been written without the observations and interviews done by Judy Bray, Laraine Hong, Donna Hughes, Janet Miller, Vickie Murray, Barbara Powell, and Neill Wenger. We also benefited from the wise advice of Ann Lieberman, Art Powell, and Seymour Sarason, our advisory board.

There are many in the study schools to whom we owe deep debts—individuals who invited us into their spaces, shared their successes and struggles, and helped us understand their work more clearly. Of these many, we particularly want to acknowledge the following teachers and principals who helped coordinate the information gathering: Sherri Abma, Frank Arcuri, Bruce Bowers, Linda Brown, Vicki Catlin, Karen Delguercio, Deidre Farmby, Bob Fecho, Eddie Gutierrez, Julie Henderson, Natalie Hiller, Marilyn Hohmann, Sherry King, Bob Kuklis, Chris Louth, Kathy Mason, Andy Rendon, Jean Stratton, Jim Streible, and Doug Wildesen.

We benefited from the input of many of the staff of the Coalition of Essential Schools, including Rick Lear, Joe MacDonald, Ginny Pires, Jessica Towbin, Ruth McCutcheon, and Susan Fisher. We were fortunate to receive helpful critiques of early manuscripts from a number of the people we have already mentioned and from Carl Clickman, Ruth Holmes, Abi King, Deborah Meier, Lynn Miller, Jackie Powell, and Erin Schnieder. Many other people helped clarify for us the difficult nature of school change—in the district and state offices, at conferences such as CES fall forums, and at the American Educational Research Association, where we tried out our ideas and obtained valuable feedback; and the editorial staff from Jossey-Bass with whom we have worked in completing this book.

From Pat: Thanks to my Oak Hill research team, Donna Hughes and Barbara Powell, my coauthors, Dick Clark and Bob Hampel, my husband, Rick Lear, and my dear friend Seymour Sarason, all of whom prompted and prodded me throughout this project and provided me with excellent company.

From Bob: I regret that my better half, Michael Sullivan, did not live to see the completion of this book. Mike was my essential connection, my link to love, laughter, and everything else that can be shared in nine years together.

From Dick: Thanks to my wife, Rosemary, whose support is always a help. Appreciation is due to our son Cameron and his wife Shannon, and to our daughter Melissa, her husband Brian, and their three boys—Bradley, Christopher, and Jamison—each a reminder of the reason for school reform.

P.A.W.
R.L.H.
R.W.C.

The Authors

Patricia A. Wasley started her career as a public school teacher and administrator after earning a bachelor's degree (1972) and a master's degree (1982) in literature at Western Washington University. She received a doctorate in educational policy and administration from the University of Washington in 1989. She has worked as a researcher for the Puget Sound Educational Consortium at the University of Washington, at the Coalition of Essential Schools, and at the Annenberg Institute for School Reform at Brown University. The focus of her research has been on the improvement of public education and school change. She is the author of numerous articles and books on school reform, including *Teachers Who Lead* (1991) and *Stirring the Chalkdust* (1994). She has lectured all over the United States, in Australia, and in parts of Asia on changing schools and the implications for teachers' roles. She is currently dean of the Graduate School of Education at Bank Street College in New York City.

Robert L. Hampel is professor of education at the University of Delaware. He received his bachelor's degree (1972) from Yale University in history and his doctoral degree (1980) from Cornell University in American political history. His research focuses on the politics of school reform and the history of high schools. Before joining the University of Delaware faculty, Hampel was a research associate with A Study of High Schools, an inquiry into American secondary education chaired by Theodore Sizer. For the study,

Hampel wrote *The Last Little Citadel: American High Schools Since 1940*, published in 1986.

Richard W. Clark is a senior associate with the Center for Educational Renewal, College of Education, University of Washington, and a senior associate with the Seattle-based Institute for Educational Inquiry. His focus is to help obtain the simultaneous renewal of schools and the education of educators. Clark has been a teacher, assistant principal, principal, and deputy superintendent for the Bellevue, Washington, public schools. He has taught at three universities and has consulted throughout the United States and in Canada on school-based management, evaluation of teachers, and evaluation of reform efforts. He has written language arts textbooks as well as articles and book chapters on curriculum, professional development, school-university partnerships, educational finance, and program evaluation. Clark received a bachelor's degree (1957) and a master's degree (1961) in speech and a doctorate (1970) in education from the University of Washington.

Chapter One

Connecting Kids to School Reform

The halls of our nation's high schools are deafening places in the early morning half hour before classes start. A blue jean sea. A Walkman's rock music wail. Voices on voices shouting greetings, shrieking, guffawing, whispering. It is intimidating nowadays for us as adults to walk amid waves of young people: some look like the kids next door; others look ominous, with pierced noses and belly buttons, green hair, heads shaved in patterns or completely bald. Tattoos. Jeans ripped, torn and hanging precariously—are they going to fall off? Baseball caps—forwards and backwards and sideways. Alarmed adults quake, "What does that mean? A gang? If so, what do we do about it?"

We hear their language: "Shit, man! What kind of foolishness are you talkin'?"

"Don't give me any crap!"

"Marci, your overalls are so *bad!* Where did you get them?"

"It was so, like, cool. You know what I mean? I mean, like, everybody who was there really felt it. Way cool."

"Avery, what math class are you in? I hope we're together."

"Fuck you, man. So you can cheat off me again?"

Fuck and *shit* seem to have different meanings to them than they do to adults. And from what we saw, there is no fear that we might hear. This is their time, and we are not adults known to them. We grumble, remembering only the swear words, to us the flotsam in a sea of conversation.

In hall after hall, lockers bang, noise escalates, quiets, and escalates again as walls of students greet one another, stow coats, grab books, slide to the floor for a brief conversation, clutch one another, kiss, fondle, touch, punch, glance surreptitiously, attempt to embody cool, perform for those who are not in their group but are near enough to notice, to see. They confide, tease, argue, expound, harass, sing, dance, rap, belittle. And they watch. In the midst of all the furor, most significantly, they watch one another, always with an eye to themselves, always thinking: Where do I stand in relationship to her? What is he really like, anything like me? And they hope—not too much, for fear of disappointment—for friends, for recognition, to be ignited with interest, to be successful.

Seeing them like this or in classes or at games, it is easy to think about them as a group. Teenagers today—so different from us. Tougher, rowdier, less respectful. But are they really? Is this just the latest manifestation of the generation gap? Even given that, they seem more extreme than we did at that age, and the statistics that predict what they can expect are so daunting. Many will drop out. Many will experience violence. Many will have babies out of wedlock before they finish school. Many will pass through these halls unaffected. Or will they?

When adults see youngsters en masse, solutions to the problems of public high schools seem straightforward: The answer is to get tougher. Kick them out if they don't want to be here. Or: What was good enough for me is good enough for them. I got a good education out of my high school—let them get the same. If they drop out, herd them back in. That's what the police are for. Or: We need metal detectors, tougher standards, more tests.

Recently, we spent three years in five schools where students, faculty, parents, and community members took a different tack. They decided that they wanted higher standards, that they needed to get more from kids. They believed that to get to higher standards, they had to change long-held traditions, structures, classroom practices. They made a long-term commitment to a reassessment of their work so that they could capture, hold, and hone the energy of these kids. The faculty wanted the kids to pop and sizzle, not just physically for one another in the halls, but intellectually in their classes.

All of the schools are members of the Coalition of Essential Schools, a school reform partnership between Brown University and 1,299 schools (as of spring 1997) around the country. The Coalition formed in 1984 in response to three major studies that revealed troublesome conditions in America's high schools. The findings from these studies were reported in three highly publicized and well-respected books, *A Place Called School* by John Goodlad (1984), *High School* by Ernest Boyer (1983), and *Horace's Compromise* by Theodore Sizer (1984). In *Horace's Compromise*, Horace, an English teacher, made the problems that plague our high schools clear. School practices have solidified into unworkable structures that compromise students' education: teachers have too many students and too many classes to get to know kids well or to give them adequate feedback on their work. One subject area is disconnected from another, and little time is available for teachers to help students make sense of it all. There is no time for the adults in schools to work together to solve problems or to forge common goals for their students. And more. Horace's ability to educate his students is undercut so significantly that there are days when he wonders whether it is worth the effort; he is bolstered only by his love of kids, and by his commitment to their education.

In order to undo these unfortunate compromises, Coalition schools share a common goal: they hope to redesign their practices using what the Coalition calls the Nine Common Principles, a set of philosophical and practical guideposts, in order to increase students' capabilities. The Nine Common Principles emerged as a set of recommendations about how schools might reorganize themselves to accomplish better the task of educating students. They come out of A Study of High Schools, a five-year inquiry (1979–1984) on American secondary education conducted by Theodore Sizer and colleagues. The principles suggest a particular reform approach. Schools and their communities are encouraged to use the principles as tools to help them redesign school practices in keeping with the particular hopes, values, and interests of the local community. Thus, no two good Coalition schools should ever look just alike, and the intellectual work of figuring out what needs re-designing falls specifically to the local community. The principles, which at first may appear simple and straightforward, challenge the traditional American high school in profound ways. As such, they stimulate healthy controversy both in schools and out. (The nine principles are outlined in Appendix A.) The strategies these schools adopt to bring these principles to life have become common to many reforming schools, members of the Coalition or not. Key strategies include reducing the number of classes that students attend per day and lengthening class periods so that both teachers and students are less rushed and better able to dig in to meaty work; instituting advisory programs so that all students have one adult who is interested in their academic welfare, which reduces the likelihood that any student might pass through the system unknown and ignored; establishing team teaching, whereby teachers join together to teach two subjects in integrated combination; using authentic assessments, tests that require students to demonstrate that they know the material and have the skills they have been working on and that they can use both; establishing new graduation requirements, again, meaningful final tasks that require students to stand before a panel of judges, which includes community members and educators, and demonstrate their overall academic competence via a complicated task. It is these kinds of changes and others like them that these schools have been undertaking (see Tables C.2–C.6 in Appendix C).

The schools are representative of the spectrum of American high schools.[1] Lincoln is part of a large mid-size American city system, but it is located on the rural fringe. The fields and white fences that surround it make it easy to forget that the school is constantly buffeted by mandates for change from the school district's central office and from the State Department of Education. At the time that the study started, it housed 1,120 students, mostly white, with a small African American population bused in from downtown every day. The top students in the city system were skimmed off to special high schools called magnet schools and geared for the academically talented, so Lincoln drew on a less academically motivated student population.

Oak Hill is a small suburban school with 350 students. Fifty years ago, it served a quiet but resilient blue-collar community. In recent years, however, it has changed, its socioeconomic status becoming more white-collar, as concerned parents have fled the nearby major urban center. As the educational background of the parents has increased, so have the expectations for Oak Hill students. Eighty-nine to 93 percent of the students go on to some form of tertiary education. Like many suburban schools, its student population is mostly white.

Marshall and Forest Park are both part of a large inner-city school system that housed 2,060 students and 800 students, respectively. As is the case in Lincoln's district, this school district also sends its academically talented students to magnet schools, leaving neighborhood schools with students who typically have had less success in school. Facing issues of poverty and violence, with high dropout rates, these two schools were desperate to find better ways to serve their students. They were both part of a citywide drive to dismantle large, impersonal high schools. As a result, both were in the midst of reorganizing into a number of smaller *mini-schools* within their original buildings. In each mini-school, teachers worked as a team to determine a focus for their unit that might hold and serve its students better. We frequently use the term *mini-school* rather than the often-used term *charter school*, which means many different things across the country, as charter legislation grows state by state.[2] In its original sense in this district, the mini-school was designed simply to break the larger high schools down into smaller subunits so that students would be better known and so that there might be stronger links between families and schools. These subunits existed within the walls of the original school, though they might have had an identifying wing or hallway around which all of the classrooms were located. Each of the mini-schools was coordinated by a head teacher, and all of the mini-schools in the building were joined under the leadership of a single principal.

Crossroads was the second high school established in a small but booming city in the Southwest. Opened in 1988, Crossroads always intended to be a school that made a difference for its students by creating different structures and fresh practices. It served 1,100 students, 73 percent Hispanic, poor, from single parent families or recent immigrants. One of the biggest challenges for Crossroads was the terribly low wages for teachers and administrators, which made it hard to keep staff for any length of time. There was such a disparity between teacher salaries and the cost of living that teachers could not afford to live in the community. As a result, up to one-third of the staff turned over every year. (For more thorough descriptions of the schools and the changes they are making, see Appendix C and Tables C.2–C.6.)

These schools were dramatically different from one another. The context in which they operated included differences in race, social class, ethnicity, cultural values, and religion, to mention just a few. They were similar in that all of them were committed to changing their practices and had been doing so for a minimum of seven years by the time we completed our work with them. It was their experience in and commitment to doing more for kids that made them—for all their differences—appealing to us. We wanted to see, as they did, if the efforts the adults were making were, in fact, making a difference for their students.

The Kids

As we watched the kids in these schools, our sense of them as groups of kids dissolved, almost imperceptibly, as happens in real life as well as in movies. Individual kids began to emerge. It was not because they were standouts or that they demanded extra attention. It was just what happened over time: individual personalities asserted themselves; patterns asserted themselves—friendship groups, styles, interests, distinguishing characteristics. It was as these individual youngsters emerged that the real challenge of improving schools became much clearer.

Sally

Sally Hempstead is a sophomore at Oak Hill High School. Leaning against a locker in a cluster of friends, she is five feet seven inches tall and a knockout redhead. She looks confident, affluent, slightly arrogant. Fanciful possibilities of her future come to mind. On the Concorde to Paris for a magazine shoot? In law school, carrying a stack of books, her reading glasses perched to control her magnificent mane? Eventually, we begin to see that her cultivated aloofness is a self-protective shield, that in reality she is a little lost. She confides that she feels most confident when playing softball: "It's the one place where I feel coordinated, like I know what I am doing. I go out there and it all comes together." In her classes, her teachers do not seem to see her. Somehow, she does not stand out, and no one seems to be watching out for her, looking for her particular strengths.

Her parents divorced when she was in the fifth grade. She stayed with her dad for three years because he stayed in the house. "My mom had no idea where she was going when she left. Even though she just moved down the street." Her father comes from a very large family, and Sally found it difficult to get along with them. Eventually, she moved back in with her mother. Both of her parents are remarried, and she now has two little stepbrothers in addition to a brother twenty-three and a sister twenty-one. Her mom is a dispatcher. Mom's new husband is with IBM. Sally's father is a lieutenant in the fire department, and her stepmother works with emotionally disturbed kids. "I don't hear from my dad much—just once in a while. He doesn't remember to call on birthdays and stuff. That only hurts when I think about it."

Lounging with her friends in a class that does not seem to require much, Sally confesses that she hates school. Really hates it. It is boring. Like this particular class: they have lots of work to do, but the teacher does not care whether they do it in class or not, and they do not have to do much of it in order to get a C, a decent grade in Sally's mind.

She rolls her eyes, that highly irritating, fifteen-year-old-girl thing that indicates that *all* adults are stupid when they ask why school is boring. To explain why would require that she think, find examples. Such an effort would create a significant pull against the practice of noneffort that she has slipped into over time. She describes a climate of repetition and sameness, where interest evaporates almost instantly. She has been "messing up" this year—not doing her work, missing some school. Her sister and her mother both said that the school was great when they were there—full of school spirit, but none of that seems evident and Sally is disappointed. She blames much of this on the principal, "who isn't helping *at all!* She is so intent on getting everyone a good education and stuff. All the teachers are, like, work, work, work. No joking around. They are cracking down on everything. The other day the principal said to me, right in class in front of everybody while I was listening to my Walkman, 'How can you concentrate when you are listening to that?' My best classes are classes where I can listen to CDs while I work, like art."

There are advantages to being in high school, however. Cars for one. Sally will get her license next year. More freedom. Her boyfriend who is older, working. The fact that everybody is friends. School will be over soon.

Hakim

Tall, stocky, and talkative, Hakim hangs out inside his advisory teacher's classroom before school with several other kids. It is safer here because they do not know everybody else in the school. His school is much larger than Sally's—2,000 kids as compared to 350. Hakim arrived at Marshall High School and was assigned to Marshall's Overland mini-school after being pushed out of another city school. He received a letter telling him that because his grades were not satisfactory, he would be attending his neighborhood school. Boom. Just like that. "I didn't have anyone who was really there for me in the ninth grade. I was on my own, because my mom had just died that year, right before I went into high school." Once at the neighborhood school, he joined the peer counselors for younger students so that he could help younger kids avoid the circumstances in which he found himself. He also found teachers who were on him and stayed on him in the Overland mini-school—one of the smaller units in his school. He took most of his classes in Overland.

Hakim was currently working on a homework assignment for English and social studies for which he interviewed a homeless person in his neighborhood. This seemed intensely real and personal to him, as he knew many of the homeless men that hung out on the corner of his block. He conducted an interview on the street with a tape recorder, and then he took his subject out for dinner. He described his class presentation:

> I dressed up like the homeless guy on video and for Mr. Marshall, the lead history teacher in my charter, and in class. I sounded like him cause I'm good. I do voices. But I mainly focused on the down part of the community. Cause where I live, it's a lot of people shooting and gangs. But most of the gang kids I grew up with. They aren't much older than me, and we all played football in the street together when we were young. But you know, their life turned that way, and I went this way as far as schoolwise. There's a lot of winos that respect me from when I was a kid. They knew my dad and respected him. My dad owns a boxing gym on Boxner Street. That's how I know a lot of the older men, thirty, forty, fifty, that stand on the corner and drink. That's how I got a lot of information from them that helped with my report.

He thought about the kids who had dropped out of school and his relationship with them. "It's like they're not gangs, but it's just that they all hang together. But it's just they do things that I don't want to be around. You know. Selling the drugs, shooting at people, back and forth. But when it's nice outside and I come from school, you know, they're sitting on the steps, and we all start talking about football and stuff. But I don't stay too long. I don't want that path. No way, man." Hakim gets ideas from the school about things he could do that would make a difference and that make him feel good.

Alicia

Alicia, a sophomore at Lincoln High, a school of 1,120 students in the Midwest, is beyond effusive about her school:

> I don't like it; I love it! This school is something else! The teachers, they're friendlier, they're easier to work with. If you need help, they'll bend over backwards to help you, if it's after school, before school, anything—they'll do it. I know just about every teacher here. I'm a really friendly person. And they're wonderful. I wouldn't trade them for nothing. I loved eighth grade, but that does not compare to Lincoln. I mean you would not believe it. This school is so dedicated. That's the word, dedicated, that's what this school is to their students. They would stop what they're doing to help you. This school cares about their students.
>
> Last year, we had a spring festival. It was called the Keystone Team Spring Festival, just like the one our city has. We had our own races, we cooked out too. You never know what to expect. You don't know if you're going to the library, or outside. It isn't like a teacher, a chalkboard, turn to page blah, blah, blah, and do your work. We do more group work. We are really into social skills.
>
> Everybody is just so friendly here. If I had a problem, I could tell anybody, and I would have no problems talking to them whatsoever. Mr. Stewart is like a dad to me; if I need something, he's there. I don't call him Mr. Stewart; I call him Stu.

Alicia's enthusiasm for school is fueled by the problems she faces at home. She has a deeply troubled relationship with her mother, who is an obese woman. "Practically her first question every day is what did I eat at school!" Her mother tries to buy Alicia's affection with presents and new clothes and then later tells Alicia that she wishes Alicia were dead. "If I were not in this school right now, I would be in a group home. This is the only reason that I'm trying to work things out with my mom, cause I got so much going on here."

Alicia is proud of her school, "They don't teach the way other high schools do. I can ask a question ten, eleven, twelve times, and they will still be there without getting hostile. They're not like, 'Why haven't you gotten this through your head by now?' They'll go, 'Why don't we try it a different way?'"

Alicia burbled enthusiastically about her work, "We're studying DNA in biology, and I saw a soap opera where they used DNA to ID the killer, so I'm writing a current events report about the soap opera. And I got D's and F's in math in middle school, and now I'm getting A's and B's. My dad said to me the other day, 'I cannot believe you're making A's in math. You've got me amazed. I think they've got the wrong girl.' I think I'd like to be a teacher someday—especially if I could teach here!"

Tommy

A steady stream of parents, teachers, and kids move in and out of the main office at Oak Hill, Sally's school in a northeastern suburb. Two secretaries answer phones and deal with the lines of people in front of them: "I understand that Nathan needs to leave for a dentist appointment at 1:10 and that your sister will be picking him up. Thank you for calling, Mrs. Ord."

One of the secretaries moves from the phone to the front counter. "Good morning. How are you Cathie? You must be Cathie's mother."

The woman, red faced, dispenses with pleasantries, "I got a note saying Cathie is ineligible for soccer. I want an appointment to talk to the teacher who was responsible. Her grandparents are coming to watch that game."

One mother is waiting to see the principal and a counselor. She describes her son, "I am so worried about him. He's a sophomore this year, and school is definitely not his thing." She is attractive, beautifully dressed, and is a mom with a career, commuting several days a week into the nearby city. She continues:

> He was doing fine until fourth grade when it was apparent that he had a language and a learning disorder. He *hates* to write. It is incredibly difficult for him. We put him in resource room in fourth grade, and when he came to high school, he decided that he wanted to be in regular classes.[3] He struggled last year, but made it, but not with great grades. My daughter graduated from here two years ago. She was at the top of her class, very academically oriented. Tommy is so different. He's very emotional, real highs and lows. He's in therapy; we hope that is helping. We don't care about high academic achievement for him. We just want him to feel good about himself. It would be great if he could find a few things that he is really good at. I understand that the school is trying to change, and I am supportive because I was convinced by the principal, who is now the superintendent. She is really something. Have you met her yet? I hope the school changes enough to build as much strength in a kid like Tommy as it did in Elizabeth. Of course, most schools serve kids like Elizabeth well, but not kids like Tommy. He has the capacity to get into a lot of trouble here.

She points him out. He is in the hall with a circle of friends, all of whom sport baggy jeans hanging on the lowest possible point, so much so that his mother worries that the pants will simply drop to reveal all. The boys are arguing about the principal, who is new this year and very friendly and spends a lot of time with students. The kids debate whether the guy is sincere or just some kind of desperate dork. Too soon to tell, they decide.

Diego

A crash. A bang. Two tall sophomores slam each other into one locker and then another as the kids around them open a clearing to get away from them. The moment seems frozen: Will they fight?

One moment stretches on interminably as they recoil, move away from each other, and are swallowed by the other kids who begin to move again. Another hallway, another school, this one in the Southwest. It becomes apparent that there are a number of groups of kids that are moving together, jostling one another, but yet seem separate from one another. One group is Hispanic and affluent. These are kids who have been in the United States for some time. Another group, poorer, have recently immigrated here from Mexico. Diego is in the midst of this group but stays away from the center where there is danger of getting into trouble. Short, thin, with dark hair and complexion, Diego is in his second year at Crossroads High, a majority Hispanic school of 1,100 students. His family moved to this country to find better work, a better life, and an education for their children. Though he is a native Spanish speaker, he is quickly learning English and is doing very well in school. He is shy and keeps his eyes lowered, glancing up only occasionally to check the reactions of those to whom he is speaking. There is a quiet sweetness about him. "I want to do well in school, and I work hard to please my parents. They want me to get an education. I will be the first in my family to graduate from high school." He wants to go to the local community college when he completes high school and then to a four-year college to get a degree related to his interest in technology and industrial arts.

Diego works hard in almost everything he does; he is an able math student, in the top track. Already he has received an honors score on the advanced-placement exam in Spanish. His Spanish teacher responded angrily when asked if, as a native speaker, Diego was advantaged on such exams, "Students who have English speaking parents aren't considered advantaged on English exams!" His Spanish teacher is his greatest advocate and support. In both his freshman and his sophomore year, Diego participated in mechanical arts and technical courses, with emphasis on mechanical and architectural drawing. He loved these courses, despite the fact that neither of his two teachers was able to use the computer software they had recently purchased, or the computers themselves, nor were they able to maintain orderly classes. Nonetheless, Diego felt at home in the midst of the pencils, drafting paper, and scale models.

Sean

Sean is five feet eleven inches tall. He is in his sophomore year at Lincoln, the same school that Alicia goes to. He hangs out in a quieter hall with a few friends. He has scoliosis, a curvature of the spine, which is not very apparent. In fact, he is attractive in a bony, tousled sort of way. He used to be on the wrestling team. He races motorcycles, lifts weights, and also writes poetry—a seeming anomaly. He loves taking girlfriends to plays at the local theater, which he can do because his sophomore English teacher gives him free tickets and gives ten extra points to students who bring back the receipts. He works after school at a local, modest country club, often from 4:30 P.M. to midnight. He does his homework during the advisory period and from 3:00 to 4:00 P.M. He is tired a lot but needs to work.

Sean went to Catholic elementary schools and would be going there still if his mother could afford it. She regrets she does not have the money to send him either to private schools or to the twice-weekly chiropractic visits recommended for his condition. Although he has not traveled far, never out of his state, he loves to visit his grandparents' hundred-acre farm: "I love running through the creeks, the woods. Me and my friends go camping there all the time on weekends. . . . I found the perfect site on a cliff for our tents, I mean a *big* dropoff, you can look over the river. And man, it's so beautiful."

Sean is less enthusiastic about the school than Alicia: "There are lots of fights here. Boys jumping guys from another race." He is nervous about it. He also does not like the lunchroom: "It's too crowded, less space than turkeys in a pen. You gotta walk stiff, like this, to get in there." His body stiff, chest forward like a figurehead on a ship's prow, eyes narrowed, lips drawn tight, Sean plows forward into an imaginary crowd. He got a five-day suspension for going off campus for lunch and felt very resentful, "The student that doesn't come to school—never comes—has horrible grades, isn't doing nothing for the school, they want to bring him back to school and treat him like a king, you know, trying to get him to come to school more often." He shakes his head at the injustice of it.

Still, he is positive for the most part. Biology is his favorite class: "Every day, we start with a film to calm us down and relax. He pushes us because for every five minutes left, he'll give us another ditto and say, 'Just do however much you can.' He makes good jokes like 'If you're in the woods and need to start a fire, just reach in your belly button and get some of that cotton and lay it down.'"

Sean is hopeful that he will get into the two-year electronics degree program run by a local corporation, "Right now is my chance. It's like the space shuttle when they go up, you know, they have a window that they can make it through and if they don't get it, then it's shut. The window's closed right now for me, but I'm working on opening it, and I just have to be able to open that window!" Sean would be the first in his family to go on to college.

Looking for Answers

We came to watch these six kids and their classmates to find out whether schools that are committed to improvement were more likely to enable and empower kids. We asked ourselves: Are kids in these schools making gains? If so, what and how? How are these changes manifest for kids?[4] When we observed change that was clearly beneficial, we asked ourselves: What changes made by the adults altered and enhanced the educational experiences of students?

To answer these questions, we observed and interviewed these students, a number of their contemporaries, their parents, and the adults in their schools from the fall of 1991 through the spring of 1994.[5] The methods we used combined the traditional—interviews, observations, examination of documents, shadowing kids—with the nontraditional. We built a partnership with each of these schools in exchange for the insights we expected to gain from them. To serve their purposes, we wrote lengthy reports to the schools after each visit to "play back" for them what we had learned. We hoped that such feedback might enable them to push forward faster, with greater awareness. We were not, by any means, unbiased: we hoped that these schools would exceed their own highest hopes, show us students who were better prepared, confident, and full of zest, and then teach us how they had rearranged themselves to produce such happy ends. We were advocates for the kids in their schools and by association for the efforts of the adults in the schools. What was most remarkable about this process was how open the schools were, how unafraid they were to show us how very difficult change is, how undefensive they grew to be when we pointed out that they may not have made the gains for which they had hoped. Further, they helped us understand when we oversimplified, missed critical information, or overstated an issue. In the long run, all involved felt more confident in what we discovered because of our reciprocal relationship.[6]

During the three years we observed these schools, our key question was: Can we see evidence of the connection between the changes adults are making to improve their schools and the students' educational experiences? We then spent an additional twelve months looking through the data to see what answers emerged. We knew that *positive evidence of student growth that can be causally connected to school reform efforts is the essential connection*—the one missing in much of the literature about school reform. It is this connection that will eventually sustain or eradicate current efforts and, potentially, the public school system as we know it. There are those who believe that public education is obsolete, too problematic, irretrievable. If reforming schools can show that some of the intractable problems that have plagued schools are solvable, if these schools can demonstrate the willingness and the intelligence to reshape their own practices to achieve better ends, then there is still hope for the system.

Given our data from a very small sample of schools, we believe that we saw evidence of this connection but that our insights will require further investigation to ensure that our hunches can be corroborated in statistically significant ways. We argue that to achieve this essential connection between reform efforts and student performance, schools must grapple with four embedded linkages, four stepping-stone connections to the major connection. We believe that these must be in place in schools in dynamic interaction to see effects for kids.

Before delineating the connections, we need to define briefly the key individual components. We then explain the essential connections.

- *Routines*—activities done with regularity to provide students practice and familiarity, hence increasing their security and self-confidence

- *Repertoire*—the range of techniques, skills, and approaches teachers use to stimulate their students

- *Caring*—a teacher's sincere concern for the welfare of students

- *Expectations*—the belief that all students can do high-quality academic work

- *Innovation*—any change made explicitly to improve student learning, including school structure, instruction, curriculum, and assessment

- *Rigor*—student performance that is precise and exact, is expected from all students, and meets and exceeds high standards

- *Small Scale*—small enough in size for students to receive adequate individual attention and for adults to grapple collaboratively with difficult issues

- *Civil Discourse*—respectful communication with a purpose of making decisions that are for the greater good

The four key connections are as follows:

- *Repertoire* and *Routine*
- *Caring* and *Expectations*
- *Innovation* and *Rigor*
- *Small Scale* and *Civil Discourse*

For instance, when routines were coupled with a teacher's broad repertoire, kids both honed the ability to stick to something in order to build skill and learned about the range of applications for a particular skill.

When caring and expectations were both present, special education students performed at much higher levels. Further, when students received more and better personal attention through advisory programs, this intervention enabled them to make wiser decisions about their course of study and the quality of their work.

When rigor was coupled with innovation, the kids engaged in new activities that were both fresh and challenging. For example, when schools devised graduation exhibitions that required mastery of important skills and concepts, students revealed that they had gained knowledge in a given field as well as the ability to integrate learning from diverse fields. (See Appendix A for a discussion of the exhibition as one of the Nine Common Principles.)

When the community of the school was small and the capacity of the participants to engage in civil discourse was increased, their ability to tackle tough issues more successfully also increased. Resolving these issues produced gains for students.

We do not claim that these are the only connections which have to be made to secure success. For example, teachers need to know their subject areas *and* they need to know how to teach. Leaders need to suggest new directions, *and* followers need to ask the very toughest of questions about the validity of these new directions. These connections are not completely new to school reform consideration; others have written about them before. Nor is it impossible to imagine other pairings within them—small scale and repertoire, civil discourse and innovation, for instance. We include these particular connections in this particular configuration because that is how we learned about them from students, teachers, parents, and administrators. These were the connections with which they were struggling. In some cases, faculty understood the dynamic interplay and illustrated for us how connecting both sides of the equation worked to kids' advantage. In some cases, faculty were struggling, and it was the absence of attention to one side or another that hampered their efforts to achieve their aims.

Describing the Connections

Each of the following chapters explores one set of these connections. Each attempts to define what we mean by the terms used in both sides of the equation and describes the strategies schools implemented in order to bring these terms to life. All of the chapters include teacher and administrator interpretations of each of the connections as well as student perceptions. They remind us of one of the greatest problems in tracking the effects of school reform efforts—that everything must first be sifted, sorted, discussed, and embodied in teacher actions before it reaches the kids.

We believe that the schools that are changing are having positive effects on their students but that the effects are unlikely to be substantial and lasting unless they purposefully join both sides of these essential connections in dynamic interplay. We learned that although each of the schools grappled with both sides of these equations in some ways, they tended to favor, or to pay more attention to, one side over the other. For instance, most of the schools emphasized caring more than higher expectations. The schools expended more energy on innovation than on rigor.

We believe that these connections can be explained to you most effectively the way we learned them—through student experiences. So we call on the six students described above and some of their friends to introduce to you what we learned from them. They represent the range of interests, drives, and complicated home situations that kids bring with them to school. We selected them out of the field of students with whom we worked because these six and their friends provide a balanced and fair representation of what we saw. We introduce you to Tommy through his mother because, initially, that was how we got to know him. Further, we learned from Tommy's mother and other parents how important it is to understand parents' hopes for their children, and how their perceptions of the school make their dreams feel either possible or impossible. Where appropriate, we introduce other students, friends, and classmates of these students, whose stories seemed particularly important to us. (For a list of all the students and their schools, see Table C.1 in Appendix C.)

Although these kids are real, we have taken license, allowing them also to represent some of the experiences of their classmates so that we might both protect their anonymity and provide readers with fewer personalities to come to know. All of the experiences, however, are real, as are the personality traits of the kids, their parents, their teachers, and administrators. Some of the kids have been positively affected by the efforts of their schools. Others have not. Though many of our fellow educators suggested that they would learn most from the positive examples, we believe we learned from both.

We also believe that the schools, even when things were going remarkably well, still had plenty of work left to do to reach all of the kids in their purview and all of their objectives in school reform. It is widely recognized that although reform is easy to talk about, it is very complicated to do. The argument we put forth here is no different. Even though the combination of these conditions may seem simple, even obvious, to put them in place in powerful combination while in the midst of the daily clamor of schools is anything but easy.

We profile our students again in Chapter Six. Where do they end up as seniors? Where are they going from here? How do they feel about their schooling? What kinds of skills did they gain? How do their parents feel? Their teachers? By examining where the kids end up against a backdrop of these interconnected sets of conditions, we think we are better able to answer our initial question: What is the connection between efforts to change schools and real change for kids? We hope to suggest some means by which all of us can turn our dreams of better, more compelling schools into a closer reality.

Chapter Two

Routines and Repertoire

How's School? The Kids Tell Us

We got a variety of responses and learned a lot when we made a simple inquiry.

Sally

"How's school?" we asked Sally Hempstead in the spring of her sophomore year. She was slouched over a table while talking, recounting new developments in her life.

> It's okay, I guess. I'm doing a little better than last year. Last year, I just like totally focused my life on my boyfriend. But now it's to the point where I know he's not going anywhere, so it's not like I have to worry anymore. Plus, I have to do all my homework before I can see him. So that gives me more incentive to do it. I get home by three, and he gets to my house around 7:30. So I have like four and a half hours to get it done. So it's good.
>
> I've ah . . . I've been feeling scared lately. . . . I'm scared about college and stuff. Because I feel like I can't really go anywhere. It's not like I can really go anywhere good anyways because I really don't have any money. So I'll be paying for it myself so that's limiting to begin with. But . . . I don't know. I'm just scared I'm going to be stuck in a crappy college that I don't even want to be at. You know? That's like no help. I'll probably have to go to a two-year college to get my grades up. And our guidance counselors. It's so hard to get

information. They confuse me, and I don't understand what they are saying. It's weird.

School is pretty much just the same old thing. I go to class and we do what we do almost every day. School is boring. It's just so boring.

But I like social studies a lot. The teacher is really good. Kids really have to push themselves in there, you know? Like do the work and the reading and come prepared. She really knows her stuff too. Like the other day, we were arguing about the election and the electoral vote. Pretty much we decided that the electoral vote was unfair, and then she switches positions and argues in favor of the electoral college. And she raises all the points that make it fair, that make the popular vote unfair by itself. It really pushes us to think harder. It's impressive how much she knows about history. She's a bit wacko. She just talks like ninety words a minute. She's always in a rush . . . rush, rush, rush! Sometimes, I do pretty well in there. Like I just got a ninety on the essay I wrote on the electoral college, but I failed the test on it that she gave earlier, so I have to take it over.

Another class I like, English. We have this humongous vocabulary list to learn. It's like one week you have list one. The next week you have to know list two and list one. And it goes up like that. So far we are up to almost a hundred words. It's good when I can just be organized. I write the words on index cards, and then I put the definition on the back, and my friends and I walk through the halls, and we fool around using the words and stuff. Like, you know, "Isn't today just *incongruous* with yesterday?" We just fool around and it's fun.

Feeling a little better about her ability to assess school quality, we asked her to be more specific about when and why school was just so boring.

Sally took Mr. Timar's consumer-law class. It was an elective class, and it generally drew from lower-track students—those who were uncertain about their college plans. Sally took it because someone told her it counted for a science credit. "I remember thinking, consumer law, a science credit? But I don't know. I can't understand the counselors though, so I just took it." She described how the class works:

Each week, we have to read a chapter in the book and do a chapter outline to hand in. Then there is vocabulary at the end of the chapter that we're supposed to know, and a set of questions on the case that is discussed in the chapter. We can expect a pop quiz sometime during the week on these two assignments, and sometimes we get one and sometimes we don't. Mr. Timar is gone a lot because he has other responsibilities, so we get quizzes from the subs. In addition, we have to find an article in a newspaper or in a magazine that deals with a legal issue discussed in the chapter. Then we have to summarize the article and hand it in. And we always have an extended research assignment for every six weeks or so. One was to research a federal agency. Another was to research one of the first ten articles of the Constitution. It's just such an easy class. He'll pass you no matter what. And it's so like out of the book. I don't do all the work because a lot of it is just like busy work. I like the current affairs articles, and some of the cases in the chapters are interesting. But sometimes it feels like he gives us the work to keep us busy rather than because it is important for us to know. Nobody does like everything. But it sucks because he doesn't care; you can just sit there with your bookbag all closed and everything and be lying down, and he won't say anything. It's not like he tries to be motivating you— like "Come on, come on, you've got to get this done." So it just leaves me feeling like, okay, whatever.

As it happened, Sally's observations seemed accurate:

Sally sits at a square of desks with three other girls. They are all friends and spend most of their time talking together. Mr. Timar does not press them in class but expects that they will get their work handed in on time. Some of them do and some of them do not. Sally says that she can still pull a B or at the very least a C without doing everything. They spend the first portion of the class talking about their personal lives as Mr. Timar hands back people's work. He stops by their table and asks them where they are on their federal agency research papers. They are vague. They are lethargic. He moves on to another table. After all papers are returned, he hands out the federal agency project assignment sheet:

1. Select a federal agency from the list provided.

2. Write to this agency requesting information. Submit your letter of request to me prior to sending it to the agency.

3. Research supplemental material from other sources.

4. Format: three to five typed pages. Sources included in the bibliography.

5. Content: agency background, purpose, how and why the agency came into being. Identify the current concern of this agency. Research this concern.

The grading criteria are as follows:

- Ten points: choice of topic and request for materials.
- Thirty points: introduction-background section. Should provide information as outlined on the research guide sheet.
- Fifty points: current event section. This section should be the major area of research and should explore one current concern of your particular agency.
- Ten points: bibliography.

Sheets handed out, students are to use class time to work on any of their ongoing assignments—the outlines, their current events, or their research projects. Sally and her friends reluctantly outline the chapter, which they can do without reading it by just following the subheadings. Interspersed in their search for answers is conversation about their boyfriends, what they did over the past weekend, what their plans are for the next weekend. Mr. Timar sits behind his desk correcting work they have handed in.

For a week, the pattern in the class was much the same. One day, they went to the library to get reference material for the federal agency papers. Sally told Mr. Timar she could not find any material on her agency. He went and got it for her—an intervention that she would never have asked for in English class because her teacher there would simply have told her she needed to look harder.

Mr. Timar talked with enthusiasm about the class. He felt that many of the points of law that they were studying had contemporary examples in daily newspapers and that the subject matter is particularly pertinent to these kids. Some of them had been arrested and were on probation for various infractions. He believed that the workload was appropriate, and the material could stretch the kids. He found it exciting when the kids saw the connection between how the government works and a particularly controversial issue. They were nice kids, just very hard to motivate. He thought that Sally, when she was interested, did creditable work, had passion and acuity. She was very moody but could also be delightful. He believed that being a teenager seemed harder these days.

Hakim

"How's school? What are you working on? Doing?" we asked Hakim from the Overland mini-school at Marshall High in the early winter.

"Well, I pretty much have it down now. I know what nights I have to do what so everything is pretty predictable. Some of my classes are really interesting and I like them. I feel like I'm learning in them. Some others seem just like we go through the motions day in and day out. Sometimes, I feel like a mouse on a treadmill. There are all these little hoops and we just keep running them and running them."

Tommy

"How's school?" we asked Tommy from Oak Hill.

"Doing dittos is ridiculous. One of my teachers actually told me to find fluff for a paper if I couldn't find enough substance! And we're doing science and math problems. Once I know how to do them, they aren't challenging. I think formulas are the death of active minds. I would prefer to know where the parts came from and understand how they relate, but some teachers say that you just need to know how to plug in the formulas. We call ourselves the numbers pluggers because we don't understand the equations, but we plug the formulas in and get the right answer. Geez."

❖

Melissa

A journal entry from a junior-level student at the beginning of the year shows how students begin right away to try to figure out the routines embedded in school. Melissa, another Oak Hill student, describes each of her classes in her journal:

> Advanced English: This is definitely a class that I think I am going to enjoy. We are going to spend a lot of time reading, and analyzing what we read. We have vocabulary, we had our first test on Friday. We had 50 words and while I knew some already, it was hard and I think I did well on it. Since school started, we've been talking about characters and themes in The Scarlet Letter. Then we read a short story by Hawthorne, "The Minister's Black Veil." We are using that and the book to discuss a theme that Hawthorne uses in his writing.
>
> Mr. Warren told us that he was going to rip apart our papers if he didn't like them and so we were all afraid, but he was not as bad as we thought. Most of us, maybe all of us, have to rewrite our papers, though. We have interesting discussions in class, and even though he will laugh at your opinion sometimes once you've given it, he at least encourages you to give it and seems interested in what you say. He gets very into the discussions and speaks dramatically so it makes you want to listen, maybe all teachers should take acting classes.
>
> American History: This class is going to be a lot of work. We have already done a couple of papers. Every week, we have to read a chapter in the book and then on Mondays we have quizzes over what we read. Then we write papers analyzing primary source docu-

ments. I think it will be pretty interesting though because she gets really into the information she's teaching about. She gets so into it that she starts tripping over things and bumping into her desk and pulling maps down, but at least it keeps our attention!

Ceramics II: I took this class because I really liked it a lot last year. There are only three people in Ceramics II so our class is scheduled for the same time as the Ceramics I class, but we will be doing different projects from them. Right now we are just helping the teacher get all the glazes organized—nothing thrilling.

Gym: We have a new gym teacher and she is A LOT stricter than the teacher she replaced. We used to get to vote on what we were going to play and the teacher didn't care if we didn't do laps or make up classes, but the new one does. Everybody is mad!

Pre Calculus: AAAAAAAHHHHHHHHHHHHHHHHHHH!!!!!!!!!! I already feel lost in this class sometimes. We are learning mathematical induction and everyone is confused. This year is also different from last year because we hand in our assignments every day, and then if we get problems wrong or don't finish them she hands them back as incompletes and we can fix them and get full credit. But we still begin the day by going over homework, then trying something new and doing that for homework.

German 4: This class does not have a textbook and it doesn't seem like the teacher has a set plan of things that she has to cover. Unfortunately, she doesn't have much control over the class even though she is really nice. I have a feeling we won't learn that much this year.

Chemistry: Wow, I am surprised. This class is simple. We did a lab where we had to find volume, mass, and density of different objects. I think we did a lab like this in 8th grade. After we did the lab we had to answer a million incredibly repetitive questions in the lab book. The questions just asked you to use the numbers in a couple of ways or fill them into tables. I understand that we have to review some, but it was so boring!!! Then we read half a chapter on potential and kinetic energy. We learned that in 9th grade. We had a 5 point quiz on the reading.

Right away, Melissa and the others worked to figure out what they needed to do in their various classes, what kind of feedback they were likely to get on their work, what kind of effort they would need to expend, and whether or how it might be received. They quickly tuned into the daily routines that emerged in each class. In Melissa's math class, each day their homework was handed back, and they reviewed any problems that students had been asked to work on. Then the teacher introduced the new material for the day—either an extension of a previously learned function or some new algorithm. They were assigned homework and were given a little time in class to begin practicing while the teacher circulated to work with them. Most classes had an internal routine very much like this—though the content, activities, and techniques varied from subject to subject.

How's School? The Teachers Tell Us

"How's school?" we asked a group of teachers sitting in a discussion group.

"Well, the kids are a little restless. Sometimes I feel like they just want to be entertained. And I don't always think school should be or can be fun. Learning to do things well requires a lot of hard work. Unless you know some basic chemistry, it's hard to talk about the role chemistry plays in our society. If I graduate a bunch of very happy people who haven't learned enough chemistry to be successful in a Chem 1 course in the college of their choice, then I haven't done my job," said Mr. Hodgkins.

A math teacher chimed in, "A lot of the work in math is just working problems, working problems. That's how kids learn to use the formulas. It's not very exciting, but it has to be done if they are going to get it. So that's what we work on, day in and day out. If somebody knows of a better way, I wish they'd tell me, because I hate the thought of getting to the end of my career and finding out there was a better way to do it!"

Routines

Every year in each school, there was an old tension between the students' mantra that school is boring and the teachers' irritation at the kids' lack of effort, connection to their work, and drive. Kids claimed that school was less stimulating than they would like. Teachers were irritated at student's attitudes or their lack of performance. Most commonly, teachers complained about their perception that in a media-rich world, kids just wanted to be entertained. To the teachers, that translated to nothing more than the kids' desire that the adults make school easier, that they dumb down the curriculum, make it more fun, more entertaining, less rigorous.

Schools are places where routines predominate. Many of the routines are helpful and provide a base for comfortable and efficient interaction between teachers and kids. There is the routine of coming to school each day. There is the routine of one class after another in what quickly becomes a predictable pattern that offers a sense of security and comfort. The breaks are helpful, and the movement is important both energetically and socially.

And there are the routines in each class. In math: review homework, watch a demonstration of a new problem, practice new problems. In English: read a book, work on vocabulary, have a discussion, write a paper. In science: read a chapter, work on vocabulary, answer the questions at the end of the chapter, do a lab, take a test. Like athletes, in each of their classes, students learn that practice is the way to push themselves toward a possible perfection. They practice playing music, drawing, building vocabulary, applying formulas, analyzing literature, discerning historical perspective, among other things. As students become steeped in the routines of their classes and the accompanying homework, they begin to hone their facility in using these skills and techniques independently, to know when they are appropriate, to distinguish a good performance from a bad. Without the practice, they would be limited to surface understanding and incomplete knowledge. Without the routines, they would not develop the skills they need to perform rigorous work. Within these routines, good students learn about the importance of drill and practice. Good teachers gain time to watch individual students, to uncover their particular learning problems and strengths. Students have the time to avail themselves of teacher expertise.

Routines can also have negative effects on student learning. As students moved through weeks, and then years, at these schools, there seemed to be a pattern when their energy and investment flagged, which had to do with the routines of school. Comments like the ones students gave earlier in this chapter indicated that some routines had a diminishing effect. Hakim noted that once he had the routines down, he felt like a mouse on a treadmill—locked into a routine that did not seem to be propelling him anywhere. Sally was bored when the routine was static and when there was little interaction between her and her teacher to prod her along. Tommy, adept at criticizing what he called the "baby stuff" that schools sometimes gave him, felt that the routines prevented them from delving into a topic deeply enough. He knew how to plug formulas in but did not really understand how they worked or how he could use them in any but a traditional math classroom setting. Students distinguished between the routine of practice to hone new skills and the routine procedures and activities that dulled their curiosity and inhibited their intellectual investment. Sergei, one of Tommy's closest friends, never complained about practicing music for a performance, but he did find the routine of studying math problematic. It did not allow him to see how he would use math on his own, independently. Repeated comments by students led us to the examination of the relationship of routines to a teacher's repertoire.

Part of what contributed to students' interest in and investment in schooling was the freshness of the approach that teachers chose. In classes where the routine was the same every day, teachers demonstrated fewer techniques for engaging with subject matter—they had a more limited repertoire. In classes where teachers varied their techniques, and the breadth of their repertoire was apparent, students frequently described their own enthusiasm, effort, and accomplishment as greater. The breadth of techniques that teachers had at their command needed to be used in thoughtful combination with routines appropriate to the discipline and to the students' abilities; thus, the connection between routines and repertoire seemed critical. Both were needed in order to foster student accomplishment. Students need the routine of practice in order to develop significant competence; at the same time, they need variation in order to sharpen their awareness, awaken renewed effort, and be exposed to new contexts in which learning takes place and skills might be used. In what follows, we explore a classroom that was stimulating for students but which also illustrates the problems of routine. A discussion and an examination of the complexities of building a repertoire follow, and the chapter concludes with a reflection on the implication of the connection between routines and repertoire.

Developing Routines

Mr. Warren, a history teacher, and Mr. Tydal, an English teacher, joined forces to teach a humanities class. Mr. Warren had been teaming for nearly seventeen years, eleven with Mr. Tydal, and felt that two teachers enrich the classroom experience. It was clear, though, that Mr. Warren's teaching style and his routine dominated in their partnership. His humanities course was conducted in very much the same way as his other classes. Students found this class very stimulating because of the lively discussions in which they were expected to participate. Mr. Warren's methods were quite different from other teachers', but students felt that they were pushed to greater levels of intellectual sophistication because they said, "You have to have good answers when you participate, and you have to have evidence."

Both students and parents reported that this class was extremely popular because of the integrated approach and because of Mr. Warren's engaging methods of pushing discussion. One student said, "For me, I like humanities because you talk about art, architecture, and literature. And you talk about a whole lot of things, and it's an exposure to something that you don't get exposed to unless your parents are writers or humanitarians. That is really the important part of learning to me, to get as much exposure as possible. I am an analytical person. I like to draw my own conclusions."

One of the class assignments was a field trip into the city, a follow-up to reading Ayn Rand's book *The Fountainhead*. On the field trip, they went to look at the Chrysler Building, the Stock Exchange, and a new luxury development called Battery Park City. The day after the field trip, as the students come in to class:

> Mr. Tydal hands out a copy of an article that suggests that Alan Greenspan, Chairman of the Federal Reserve, was significantly influenced by Ayn Rand's economic theories. Mr. Warren shows pictures of the buildings they saw and notes that he was pleased with the field trip. Justin, a student, referring to the new complex says, "The buildings seemed to be kind of traditional but modern at the same time."
>
> Mr. Warren asks, "Did they blend?"
>
> Tony responds, "They designed it to blend into the city."
>
> Alexis ponders, "They seemed isolated from the city. No, I guess I don't think they did blend."
>
> Sally arrives late. Mr. Warren asks Mr. Tydal to carry the conversation while he talks to Sally in the hall. He lets her know in no uncertain terms that coming late is disrespectful and an indication of her lack of investment in her own academic progress. Lateness is not appreciated. Mr. Tydal does not have to say a word to the class. They carry the discussion without missing a beat.
>
> Tony says, "I agree. The architect was a separatist, an elitist. It used to be low-income housing, but they moved all the poor people out. Now it is an ostentatious show of wealth."
>
> Tina disagrees, "Wait a minute! It shows how the city grows and changes and renews itself. Just because they have security guards and stuff . . . "
>
> Another girl disagrees with Tina, "The wealthy are trying to isolate themselves from others. I did not see a lot of people there."
>
> Mr. Warren says, "You mean minorities?"
>
> "Yes, he means people of color."
>
> Charles counters, "I did not see that the apartment prices were out

of line. They were $1,200 a month. Initially, apartments are much higher when they are new because builders are paying the buildings off."

The kids debate whether $1,200 is reasonable.

Jerry says, "Battery Park City has its own security force, its own streets, its own shops. It isn't designed to blend with the rest of the city. They created their own!"

Justin agrees, "Everybody should have the ability to live there; the city is built on blood money."

Mr. Warren counters, "What reward is there for hard work?"

The discussion heats up, moves fast, erupts into multiple voices, then returns to a whole-group discussion. Lots of ideas are thrown out, quickly, emotionally: Is this rent control? Who does rent control serve anyway? Things have to be available to everybody! I can't build a building unless I can pay for it! It's open to the public! Just because it's open to the public doesn't mean that everybody has access to it! Not everybody can afford to shop in those kinds of stores!

Mr. Tydal comments occasionally while Mr. Warren prevents any one student from dominating. They move students to a comparative example—a public high school for gifted students in the city. Back and forth, they debate whether public space and money should be used for the elite. During a split second lull, Mr. Warren waves the article. "Take a minute to read this, folks. The problems that Ayn Rand articulated in the forties still exist today. Read this quickly."

The students, however, jump to one of their favorite topics, the notion of first and second handers. In the novel, Ayn Rand suggests that there are two types of people in the world, those who create their own reality and those who plug into the reality around them. The students relate this to the elitism of the new Battery City development and to public schools for the elite. They have had a monthlong debate about whether first or second handers really exist in the world.

Mr. Warren eventually returns to the article: "This article is about Alan Greenspan, the head of the Federal Reserve, and about the detriments of inflation. It mentions that he was influenced in his thinking by the philosophy of Ayn Rand." He gives the students background on Ayn Rand's economic philosophy that emerged from the sociopolitical philosophy she had developed in the book.

The article outlines Mr. Greenspan's philosophy of zero-based inflation. Mr. Warren asks the kids to summarize what the article says and then what it means. They are confused, need time to think. He switches to his economics hat and guides them as they begin to make sense of it.

He asks the kids what inflation is and why it is detrimental. In between the students' responses, the teachers offer interesting information, ask more questions, such as, What does supply and demand have to do with inflation? They discuss a nearby town that has the fourth-largest supply of unused office space in the country.

Tony laments, "It makes me wonder even more why they want to fill the river in."

"What land is most valuable?" asks one of the teachers.

"Waterfront!" shout students in chorus.

Mr. Warren adds, "Right now we are at a record low on inflation. We are at 2.2 percent. The social security recipients will get the lowest increase since 1986–1987."

A student asks, "How does Greenspan control inflation?"

"Prime rate!" someone yells.

"That's right. He controls it through the federal reserve interest rates. The prime rate is what the federal reserve sets to control the cost of borrowing money. By raising the prime rate, he keeps inflation down," says Mr. Tydal.

More questions, examples, and exchanges of opinion fly out, as they relate the themes of The Fountainhead to current economic policy and to what they are learning in their economics class. Then the bell rings.

In this class, Mr. Warren and Mr. Tydal were attempting several things at once. They wanted to review a field trip and relate it to a piece of literature the class had read. They wanted to take one of the themes in the book—the rights of the elite versus the rights of those in the larger population—and relate it to contemporary economics. Another theme they wished to explore was architectural expression and purpose. The main character in The Fountainhead is an architect, who suggests that one of the central dilemmas in architecture is the tension between form and function. The teachers ended with a contemporary example of how philosophy affects economics. The pace of the class was quick, purposeful, carefully guided to allow students to explore ideas of interest to them as well as those the teachers thought it most important to stress.

In the classes in Mr. Warren's room, the routine of rapid examination of controversial issues was constant. Students loved his classes, partially because he taught subjects new to them—contemporary issues, economics, humanities. Because the content was new, they felt rejuvenated by the freshness of the topic, but also there were other reasons. In the course of the daily debates in his classes, he always managed to relate the issues to contemporary circumstances so that the relevance was obvious—as he did in this class with the Greenspan article—and he did not back away from controversy. The other reason they responded so well was that he was good at facilitating this kind of fast-paced discussion. No topic, no matter how controversial, seemed taboo; every student was asked to offer an opinion and, usually, he asked them for the evidence on which they based their opinions. They liked it, too, because he struck an honest deal with them: he always came to class prepared, interested, listened with great intensity, and was direct with them. As he did with Sally, he let kids know when their performance was unacceptable, or when he thought them ill prepared. They felt that he expected a great deal from them. When they delivered on their end, it was clear to them that he respected them, took the intellectual exchange seriously, and enjoyed their company.

Mr. Warren's classroom routine was to have students read important material that he had collected and sometimes material that they had collected first. He gave quizzes on their reading to ensure that they were prepared to discuss it, and then they were expected to analyze the topic. He would begin by asking open-ended questions. One person would respond. Mr. Warren would ask whether others agreed or disagreed and why. As the discussion moved, he was delighted not to intervene when students began to respond to one another, but he stayed right with them, intent. His role changed then to the facilitator, keeping the speaking orderly, making sure that one student did not dominate. With careful attention to timing, he would redirect the discussion in order to get the kids to explore another dimension of the topic. Students were aware of the pattern in his classes, and they believed that they improved in their ability to take a position and defend it because they got significant practice in it: they improved in the essential skill of being able to voice opinions backed by hard evidence. They learned not to interrupt one another and to debate with facts, not insults. They learned to tolerate differing opinions. Acquiring all of these skills, in addition to gaining important content on a wide range of historical and contemporary issues, was enormously stimulating. And they declared that it built intellectual confidence. Nonetheless, about midyear, each year, some students offered a common critique.

When Routines Become Problematic

Mr. Timar's class and Mr. Warren's class represent examples of two courses that were quite different and that elicited very different responses from students. Kids found Mr. Warren's class exceptionally stimulating because he had developed a routine that combined his subject area expertise with an intellectual approach—literary analysis or debate—that fostered students' growth. In this class, the students believed that the standards were rigorous, more rigorous than in other classes. They agreed that they had to work harder for good grades, that they had to think harder, and that to do really well, they had to be prepared.

Still, by midyear, when students were thoroughly familiar with the routine, they reflected that they had learned to "work the routine" so that they could do the least amount of work possible. They learned to read for critical issues, and skim the rest. They learned to share reading responsibility and to coach one another on the main points before class. Some of the students even complained, wishing that the class included more writing and more feedback on their writing as a break from the fast-paced discussions. Several wondered whether they got better at discussion or whether they really just got more aggressive, and they wished they had some means by which to measure their own progress in this regard.

Many of the classes in the five high schools were not as stimulating as Mr. Warren's and evidenced much less engaging routines. Take, for example, Mr. Timar's class. At no time in this class did kids noticeably push themselves. Mostly, they chatted. Though Mr.

Timar had prepared potentially interesting material for study, the students had only limited and sporadic interaction with him. Although he wandered the room occasionally to see what students were doing and answer questions, he did not communicate his own expertise or passion about his subject to the students. There was little intellectual exchange between him and the students. Although he did let them know what they had handed in and what was still missing, he did not push them to do more thorough work or to complete missing pieces or to think more deeply about the topic. He gave them their work and then left them alone and vice versa. The pace of the class was slow and the energy level low: we often saw a student sprawled across his or her desk, napping. Even though Sally and her friends liked Mr. Timar as a person, they did not like the class. It was boring.

Neither the material nor the workload was problematic, rather, it was the absence of any activity that might help the students learn about the significance of the work they did. They were not pushed to discuss the pertinence of their investigations. There was no meaningful exchange that made the information covered worthwhile, relevant, or important or that pushed them to more rigorous performance. As a result, students figured out the routine, expended minimal effort, and together, Mr. Timar and his students relinquished significant intellectual gains.

In all of the schools, classroom routines were familiar: read a chapter, answer the questions at the end, write an essay; review homework at the board, learn today's technique, begin working on homework; listen to a lecture, watch a demonstration, do the predesigned demonstration step by step, and fill out a report. Read a chapter, pick a project, write a report. Routines like these allowed students to hone skills, build confidence, feel more comfortable. What the students revealed, however, was that their learning curve was up at the beginning of the school year or the term as they worked to figure out the new routines but that by midterm or midyear, as their familiarity with the patterns and routines was firmly established, their interest and their engagement tended to wane in all but the most stimulating classes. Familiarity, it seemed in many cases, led to contemptuous and minimal student effort: "Repetitiveness, doing the same thing over and over and over gets really boring whether it's writing or reading book after book. Once you know what the teacher wants and can do that, you don't have to think. And sometimes all we have to do to get good grades is memorize without knowing anything about it!"

Teachers lamented, "If only we could figure out how to get them to work as hard on school stuff as they do on their social lives, their hair, their bodies, their jobs," and students lamented the sameness of their days and wailed that "school makes us zombies!"

The central tension for both teachers and students lay in finding the balance between routines and repertoire. It was the routines that helped students practice complicated skills so that they could eventually see the evidence of their own growing competence. At the same time, it was the introduction of a new technique or a fresh approach that lifted kids out of familiarity and the accompanying complacency and into renewed effort and interest.

Clearly, teachers in the less stimulating classes were not always simply lazy or unprofessional, although that seemed likely in some cases. Rather, the majority of teachers were trapped in a system of schooling that dulled their sense of teaching possibilities and restricted their best efforts to break traditional molds. The system all too frequently was one of too much isolation, not enough feedback, too many students, too much material to cover, too many tests that directed the curriculum, too little planning time, too little flexibility.

Before moving to the complexities attendant to building a teacher's repertoire, it is helpful to review a couple examples of the links between routines and repertoire.

Linking Routines to Repertoire

Kids made it clear when the routines of school were problematic for them. It was not practice that they found discouraging, rather it was what grew over time to be overwhelming sameness. The sameness of some routines made the kids feel dull, and, as if enveloped by a kind of numbing narcotic, they expended less energy, attended less closely, slipped toward minimal effort. The kids did not like this feeling. They preferred to feel stimulated, awakened, challenged, as if their time was well invested. Students described the kinds of activities that stimulated and engaged them, activities that increased the likelihood that they would do rigorous work as they got involved. Their descriptions underscore the value of a teacher's repertoire.

Sally described what was most stimulating to her: "I liked learning about fractals. That is anything that like repeats a math formula—it makes order out of chaos. Learning to plot these things on the computer helped me see the relationship between computers and mathematical formulas and art. While it was in math class, we were at computers and printing out stuff that looked like it should come from art!" This from Sally who hated math and felt so incompetent in it!

Sergei suggested a different experience: "I think it is so cool when we see that our teachers like what we've done. In music, we've been practicing this one piece for a long time, and we were playing it yesterday and our teacher put down his baton and danced across the room. He was just jivin'. That's the best feeling that I have in school—when we're really working on something and he really likes it. He appreciates our work."

Hakim had other ideas: "School is more interesting when we get to pick things that we're working on. It's different working for a grade and working on something for yourself. We work hard on things that are interesting to us. In fact, it brings out a whole new side of kids that adults aren't used to seeing!"

"Exhibitions are challenging," said Tommy, "because they are different than normal essays. They are more work, because to display something well, you have to have a fair understanding of it yourself. And a paper can be taken from an encyclopedia and you can rephrase everything. For an exhibition, you have to write it, then think about what you want to tell people, then you have to think about the questions they might ask."

"Yeah, but changing the names of essays to think pieces or exhibitions is not exactly what I'd call on the cutting edge of educational reform or fresh!" countered Hakim.

"Yeah, that's true. I like to go into more depth because then you have a greater understanding of it. Our social studies teacher is tied down by the state exam. She'd like to do more things, but it's hard. One day a couple of months ago, she did a Socratic seminar with us on medieval art. She showed us a couple of pictures and then asked questions about what the pictures revealed about life then. We had to back our answers up with evidence from the pictures. But now she has to play catch-up, so it's back to standard social studies."

Sean had his own ideas, "For me, school is best when we have to *do* things. I remember all the hands-on projects I've done this year, but I don't remember the tests I've taken. We did this experiment with beads in science to learn about permeability and water retention. We worked with it. We did a group project in science: I was a photographic journalist, sent to Kenya to take pictures of endangered animals. It was a three-week project. At the end of the three weeks, you were paid money. She had a store in the back of the room where we could buy stuff. It was a pain in the butt, but what I learned is that photojournalism is hard. There is a lot of preparation. A lot of things you have to be careful of. A lot of stuff to do. We had to use an atlas and had to say what clothes to bring, how we'd transfer money, where to find hotels, what airport you'd be landing at. We had to go to a travel agent. And all of that was just to get there. Then we had to figure out the angle and how to work."

One year, quiet Diego added, "Like Sean, I like hands-on stuff. Especially in my new English class. It's different from all of my other classes where I can expect the same thing every day. Whenever we go into English, anything can break out. One day we are reading something. The next day we are acting something. The next day we have something to research. We have to keep journals, and we do lots of different kinds of writing—like the assignment where we had to become a philosopher. It's a challenge. The teacher always has us doing something different."

What do these kids describe? They describe teachers who make learning interesting, lively, vibrant. They describe work that moves them from seat work to computers and that shows them connections between disciplines—art, philosophy, mathematics. Long practice rewarded by a change in the teacher's role from critic to appreciative audience. Work that allows students some role in selecting topic, method, format. Unfamiliar approaches. Doing things.

School is more interesting when students are caught a little off guard, when the steps, procedures, and roles are not totally familiar, thereby demanding greater concentration and awareness. This does not mean that everything has to be new all the time. Sergei's music example suggests the benefits of long, repetitive practice, when a musical piece comes together. What the kids do suggest is that breaks in the routine provided by new material, interactions, approaches, and techniques are helpful. Incentives are embedded in their work when students perceive that it takes them to new levels of sophistication—as Sean indicated when he became an international photographer, and when he practiced scientific observation by measuring water retention—or when they can see fresh purposefulness and usefulness in their efforts.

They also pointed out that new activities can quickly become routinized, if they spread too rapidly across the school without attention to the kinds of growth teachers want for students. "We have to get into groups in every class!" Sally and others wailed occasionally. Alicia mentioned that two different science teachers had asked students to teach chapters of the book. And the kids were savvy to changes in rhetoric but not action. Tommy and Hakim pointed out that to change the name of something without changing the substance of it is also problematic: calling a regular old essay an exhibition did not fool them.

Despite the occasional glitches that they mentioned, their enthusiasm rose as they described activities that pushed them beyond anesthetizing routines into different forms of participation. It was not that they were negating the power of practice or the necessity of working hard over and over again to master a particular skill. Rather, they were suggesting the essential connection between routines and their need for a broad repertoire of experiences. Routine and novelty or freshness were what mattered to these kids. It was the balance between routine and novelty that provided kids with both stability and stimulation.

Repertoire

Nearly all teachers described themselves as having, or at least building, a repertoire. But classroom observations suggested that this was not uniformly true. Most, in fact, had a relatively small number of techniques that they tended to use over and over again throughout the year.

The term repertoire is familiar in the arts. Diego's friends in Crossroads's strong drama program taught him about repertoire. Actors are expected to build experience in an established body of works and techniques that are proven, effective, and have lasting value. This is essential to their professional knowledge. This body of work and techniques varies depending on a particular actor's interests and intentions. A stage actor needs to have experience with Shakespeare, practice in fencing, and in different voice techniques. A film actor needs practice in camera work and in various theories of method acting. A repertory company prepares several plays that run throughout a season, offering theatergoers variety. From an actor's perspective, doing repertory means that they are able to build their own skills as they experiment with one persona in a comedy and another in a serious drama. Thus, actors build greater range and extend their own professional possibilities, avoiding narrow character stereotyping. At the same time, each individual actor in a repertory company is part of a whole effort to entertain, to induce thoughtfulness, to engage the local population.

Two objectives are important. The first is that the overall range of skills is significant: not novelty, or the strength of one skill over another, but scope and masterful variety. In addition, each actor functions in the midst of a group effort. It is the collective human effort that repertory companies hope will have an impact, rather than the standout performance of a single star.

Using the term for educational purposes, the meaning of repertoire shifts to accommodate the teacher-student context, but the development of a repertoire is a familiar concept in education circles as well as in theater. The education community has long believed in the importance of a teacher's broad command of a variety of skills and techniques. For years, education policymakers, philosophers, and teacher educators have been clear that teachers need to use more rather than fewer techniques with students.[1]

A good repertoire includes a variety of techniques, skills, and approaches in all dimensions of education—*curriculum, instruction,* and *assessment*—that teachers have at their fingertips to stimulate the growth of the children with whom they work. Repertoire is a multifaceted tool aimed at building the range of intellectual skills that a student can use to tackle a diversity of problems.

A good curricular repertoire includes a variety of material that is appropriate for different ages, cultural contexts, and particular circumstances. A teacher must also have a variety of ways of interacting with students—individual conferences, discussions, dialogic journals—to exchange thoughts and feedback on the student's work, whether it is a piece of literature the student is reading or a scientific experiment the student is conducting. The teacher's instructional repertoire includes intellectual approaches like literary criticism or Socratic dialogue or the scientific method. Some of these methods are based in a particular discipline; others cross disciplinary boundaries. Assessment techniques include the development of performance-based exams and scoring procedures for diverse activities—labs, essays, performances. To have a repertoire in one area only, say curriculum, is insufficient to the task of building student capacity. Teachers must have a repertoire in all three areas—instruction, curriculum, and assessment—because all three are interrelated dimensions of teaching that affect student learning.[2]

For teachers to make successful use of their own repertoire, they must function more like managing repertory theater directors or art school directors than individual actors or artists, because they are concerned with the capabilities of a number of students. Teachers must have a variety of techniques to be able to transfer or teach the use of these techniques to students, so the students can build their own intellectual capacities. Teachers also need a repertoire because it is important to their diagnostic skill—so that as they discern an individual student's learning patterns or problems, they can suggest different techniques or approaches that might stretch some kids or make more sense to others.

One of the most confusing aspects of building a repertoire is that it is possible for teachers to mistake simple variety for a powerful repertoire. Students, however, had no problem distinguishing between the two. Sean told us, "In some teacher's classes, it's real purposeful. We know what we are doing. In other classes, it's just a bunch of activities. We don't know how they relate or if they are meant to." Many teachers used a variety of approaches—a seminar one day, a project approach the next, journal keeping for a few days, and so forth. When these approaches were disconnected and lacked coherence, they did not necessarily build student capacity. To students, these teachers looked disorganized and random. Teachers who use the repertoire to their students' advantage know why they are using a particular technique at any given time. It is either to help push certain students or to give students practice with a particular intellectual tool. Thus, the repertoire is purposeful, coherent, connected to a larger plan for student learning. A critical component is the judgments that teachers make about what technique to use when to enhance student learning. "Like in electronics," said Sean. "First we learned about charges by making a bunch of them. Then we did airwaves. Then we worked on understanding transmitters. It's sort of one step at a time, but everything builds." Students are able to see the connection between techniques, approaches, and the curriculum and it makes sense to them.

Style differs from repertoire in that style deals with the distinctive manner in which a teacher uses a particular technique in the repertoire. For instance, Mr. Renzler, a well-loved but controversial English teacher from Oak Hill, had a dramatic style. As he engaged in literary criticism—the technique he used consistently—he used theatrical inflections, joked with students, and teased them. His style when encouraging students to become more adept at literary criticism made his classroom more entertaining, interesting. His individual style contributed to student engagement with him. Teachers can develop a particular style that enhances their work with students whether they use few techniques or a very broad repertoire.

Common Conceptions of a Repertoire

As suggested previously, most teachers describe themselves as having a repertoire of techniques for working with students. However, in many cases, their conceptions were narrower than the discussion above suggests. There were three distinct approaches to the development of a personal repertoire: content as the renewable resource, routine plus project, and a portfolio of approaches.

1.   *Content as the renewable resource.* Nearly all teachers honed a relatively limited set of techniques that they used with regularity and with confidence, and they used the course content as the variable to engage and renew student interest and effort. Mr. Renzler had a fine command of the process of literary analysis, an interesting approach to vocabulary development, a good critical approach to giving students understandable feedback on their papers, and an effective approach to generating meaningful essay topics, which all added up to demanding and provocative work. One math teacher devised a controversial approach, which students discussed at length. Students were to determine whether they would shoot for an A or a B. When they took a test, the ones who achieved their desired grade were conscripted to help students who had not earned

an A or a B. This teacher added the peer tutoring component to the regular daily routine, whereby he reviewed the homework, demonstrated a new algorithm, and then gave students time to practice this for homework. In these cases, even though classroom interactions involved few techniques, it was the *content*—a new author, a new set of mathematical computations—that provided the refreshment for students and teachers alike. Teachers saw the command of the discipline as central to both student growth and their own professional expertise.

2. *Routine plus project.* The second approach involved a set of preferred techniques like those mentioned above, with the addition of a yearly project that constituted a major diversion from the normal routine. For instance, in Mr. Warren's economics class, students moved out of their regular study of economics to track and trade stocks on the stock market. One of the teams at Lincoln had a county fair project that coincided yearly with the annual local spring fair. Teachers who took this approach believed that variety was important but also required a lot of work; their projects took more time, so only one seemed viable each year.

3. *A portfolio of approaches.* Still other teachers were working to build a broad set of techniques that varied from day to day, week to week, or in some cases from term to term, in keeping with our definition of a repertoire. In these teachers' classes, the patterns of their work with kids varied, maintaining a sense of freshness for both teachers and students. Within this category, teachers developed several approaches. Some teachers used a variety of approaches every day to keep kids on task. One French teacher, for example, who had been teaching for over twenty years, had an impressive repertoire in each class and a master plan for the full four years that she was likely to have the students.

> Twenty-seven students are crammed into the room. Speaking French, Ms. Bishop begins the class by introducing the day's activities. Students, working in pairs, then recite conversations in French. They move on to a new activity: all together, the students recite a poem that they have in their folders. The teacher moves around the room, listens to individu-

als, and corrects them quietly by giving the proper pronunciation. Transition: she signals the students to take turns reading the poem with feeling. Ms. Bishop flicks the lights to signal the end of that activity and sets a timer, which she also uses to signal transitions. Students review their notes for two minutes. Buzz. Then a quiz. Buzz. Two minutes to compare the quiz to their notes. Buzz. Activity with *les mots clef* (key words) on the blackboard. The students yell out which ones to erase. Buzz. The bell rings. Ms. Bishop stands at the door. Students rattle off some bit of the conversation to her in French as they leave.

Students described this class as fast paced, never dull, though they complained that they had to pay close attention. Every day, the kids knew they would do some drill on vocabulary. They knew they would be asked to conjugate verbs and attend to pronouns and articles. But they were kept on their toes by Ms. Bishop's ability to range through an extended repertoire of approaches. The activities, the content, and the assessments varied, and they built kids' skills and experiences. In addition to the constantly changing activities within a given day, Ms. Bishop had a four-year rotational curriculum of activities that revolved around a long-term relationship with a French school. Every other year, a small group of students went to France, and the alternate years, French students came to Oak Hill. So for two years in her rotation, class activities focused on visiting France, and for the remaining years, they focused on activities in the United States with the French visitors. This real connection provided a source of endless, varied activities—from fundraisers where students made hundreds of quarts of French onion soup to formal public presentations welcoming the French students to producing French plays for neighboring schools. Ms. Bishop had a long-term plan that took routines, skills, breadth of knowledge into account. In first-year French, students concentrated on gaining vocabulary and conversational capacity. In second-year French, they spent considerable time reading French literature and studying French history—a sore subject with the second-year students. ("We want to be able to speak French. Who cares about their history!") From focusing on conversation, and then historical and cultural awareness, students' work in French moved and built over the four years so that they gained both spoken and written competence as well as cultural sophistication.

Other teachers worked to learn a particular approach for the length of an entire term or extended unit. A ninth-grade English teacher, Ms. Santamaria, spent a number of years learning to teach writing-as-a-process. As a process, this approach has any number of techniques embedded in it. It requires that teachers help students develop the skills that professional writers use: brainstorming for ideas, drafting, getting critiques, revising, and finally, editing, polishing, and publishing. She then moved to team teaching with a social studies teacher to construct a curriculum that would enable students to understand the connections between literature and history. They had all of the arguments that teachers who team always have: Which discipline should lead the curriculum? Do we always have to follow a chronological sequence? What skills do we think are important to inculcate in students? Which are particular to English? Which to social studies? Which cross disciplinary boundaries?

Ms. Santamaria's classroom approach was varied, and, at the same time, she valued routine in that she maintained a *writers workshop* one or two days a week. Writers workshop is a common approach to teaching writing using the writing process. In this teacher's workshop, students worked on written projects of their choice—a film, a poem, a short story. Then they moved to reading literature or reading or watching some type of contemporary media coverage (films, newspapers, television news specials, and so forth) of world issues that corresponded with themes in history. She and her teammate used a variety of techniques to help students understand what they were reading, including the reader response log (a kind of a journal in which students keep a written record of their responses to a novel, a poem, or a story) and the Socratic seminar. The Socratic seminar is a technique designed to engage students in close textual reading and to provide them with experience in building an argument that extends beyond personal opinion to authorized opinion—one that is corroborated by evidence from the text.

The teacher's role is to ask a framing question and then to facilitate student discussion by directing them into the text and requiring that they provide evidence for their assertions from the text.

These teachers also built a series of mini-exhibitions into their curriculum during the year.[3] These mini-exhibitions were performance-based assessments: presentations, public debates, and written reports designed to help students build the skills they'd need for a final exhibition nearer to graduation. With each successive assessment, these two teachers concentrated on helping students focus on a particular aspect of performances and presentations— from diction and speaking voice to supplementary materials like film clips, overheads, or computer-generated materials.

In the midst of this, Ms. Santamaria was helping students build meaningful portfolios. Portfolios are another educational assessment technique. Just as an artist collects a sample of his or her work to demonstrate depth and breadth of knowledge, so students collect samples of their work to demonstrate the range and depth of their accomplishments. The fact that this teacher had students selecting their own pieces for their portfolios attests to the fact that she was working to help them build judgment about their own work. She was notably self-reflective about the process: "I tried to build a system where there is a fair amount of choice for kids, so that they can work on things of interest, try new things, move to their own strengths. And while I can point to a number of kids and their portfolios where I think that is happening, I can point to other kids where I really think they are just going through the motions." She was the most sophisticated at honest self-analysis, and she would work at a particular technique until she felt that she understood the strengths and the weaknesses of it and had developed at least some corrective strategies that strengthened the approach for her students. Then she would move on to a new technique that she perceived to be lacking in the total experience she was trying to build for kids.

We wondered why she was so particularly analytical. It turned out that earlier in her career, as she was learning to teach writing-as-a-process, she had participated in a study that directed its participants toward reflective practice. At the same time, she was an early member of the Coalition's National Faculty—a large cohort of teachers who received extensive training in reflective and analytical activities in order to foster change in their schools. Her own reflectiveness spread to the other faculty as she worked with them on various projects.

Over the course of several years, she had worked on three new techniques—Socratic seminars, portfolios, and self-assessment activities for students. For instance, she and her team partner—the two of them taught all the ninth-grade English and social studies classes and were working on reshaping them into a unified humanities course—took a Socratic seminar class together after school. Then they tried seminars out, one teacher at a time, the other one functioning as an observer and coach.

On one occasion, Mr. Garland, Ms. Santamaria's teammate, had conducted a Socratic seminar with their combined ninth-grade English and social studies class. The kids had read a short story about a young South African boy who goes to a wedding. The story revealed cultural differences, and ethics—a meaty tale. Mr. Garland had not conducted many seminars, so the two of them set an hour aside to debrief, so he could get a sense of what went well and what he might do differently. Ms. Santamaria asked him a series of questions: "What did you think? Did you feel like it was out of control? Did you think asking each of the kids to comment at the end, that final go-around, was productive? What was going through your mind about the questions we planned to use ahead of time? I wonder if some of the questions you asked needed more lead time, more quiet time, before kids answered."

His understanding of the session expanded enormously as the two of them reflected on what had happened. At the end of their session, they agreed that she would conduct a seminar the next day with a different class, and they agreed to a few changes in the original questions. In addition, they planned to set another hour aside, so this time he could guide her as she tried to understand this new technique better.

As Ms. Santamaria grew to know the techniques better, and she used them with more competence, the routine in her class seemed more varied and less predictable to students. Each week, the students spent a couple of days writing in various genres of their choice. Then they would either read or watch some material, or they would research third-world issues. Each week, the kids spent some time examining and studying their own learning. They scrutinized what they had learned and evaluated their own progress so that they could build their own sense of what constituted quality work. Ms. Santamaria was keenly aware that the approaches she took in the classroom gave her students skills they could use in other classes, in other avenues of interest.

Her students were very respectful of her, primarily because they said that she treated them as if they were capable of important responsibility and spoke to them and listened to them as if they were adults. When students who were graduating related what they had gained in high school, they invariably mentioned some of the techniques they had encountered in Ms. Santamaria's ninth-grade course.

Building a Repertoire: The Complexities

Many of the teachers understood that they needed to build a broader repertoire of techniques, curricula, and approaches in order to get to heightened student performance. Though there has been widespread support for professional development over the years, many of these same teachers were aware that too few of the techniques they had learned about in courses taken at the district office or at the local university actually made it into their daily, weekly, monthly teaching routine.

Building a repertoire of fresh approaches meant that the teachers began by experimenting with innovations. (In Chapter Four, an innovation is defined as any technique with which the teacher has not previously worked. What is an innovation to one teacher may be old hat to another.) As we point out in Chapter Four, the connection between innovation and rigor is central to the successful development of a repertoire. Without innovation, it is hard for teachers to expand their repertoire and to challenge students with fresh experiences. If there is no rigor, then the repertoire has served no useful purpose. Without fail, nearly all the teachers who tried new techniques encountered difficulties, no matter how masterful they were at techniques with which they already were familiar. The following three classroom descriptions illustrate the complexity of building a repertoire. All three teachers had considerable expertise with other techniques.

Initial Steps. Mr. Landon, a well-respected, hardworking teacher, was enthusiastic about his work. He wanted to vary his instructional strategies by adding Socratic seminars, described earlier in this chapter, to his repertoire. He had taken the district-level training on them and had tried several seminars previously. His class had been studying the Trail of Tears in an American studies class. They had done some background reading on President Jackson's policy of moving all Native Americans in the East out beyond the Mississippi. The teacher asked questions to make sure everyone in the class understood their background reading, and he filled in missing details. Now he wanted them to explicate a poem.

> Mr. Landon asks his students to make a circle with their desks for the Socratic seminar—a very large circle. He reviews the ground rules. "Please say 'pass' if you don't have an opinion or don't care to answer a question. There are no endings or right answers in a Socratic seminar. They aren't about closure. We will just stop when it's time to do some group processing." He asks them to take a few minutes to read a fourteen-line poem, "If We Must Die," by Claude McKay.

> If we must die, let it not be like hogs
> Hunted and penned in an inglorious spot,
> While round us bark the mad and hungry dogs,
> Making their mock at our accursed lot.
> If we must die, O let us nobly die,   5
> So that our precious blood may not be shed

In vain; then even the monsters we defy
Shall be constrained to honor us though dead!
O kinsmen! we must meet the common foe!
Though far outnumbered let us show us brave,   10
And for their thousand blows deal one deathblow!
What though before us lies the open grave?
Like men we'll face the murderous, cowardly pack,
Pressed to the wall, dying, but fighting back!⁴

Mr. Landon asks the following questions during the course of the thirty-minute seminar:

- Who's the "we" in this poem in line 1?
- Look at line 10. What does that mean?
- Can you think of times when that has happened in our history?
- What do the first two lines refer to?
- Who are the monsters?
- Tyisha, would you explain lines 8 and 9?
- Tristen, what are your thoughts? Any other comments?
- Can someone explain line 12?
- Sean, what do you see in line 11?
- Sherita, do you agree with what he said?
- Okay, let's look at the first two lines.
- What happened in the Trail of Tears that we read last period? How would the Native Americans have responded to these two lines?

When they finish, there is a debriefing. Everyone comments on how they think the session has gone: "pretty good," "interesting," "good," "better than the last one," "it helped me to understand." There are some critical comments too: "We needed more speakers." "Some people didn't participate." "I got lost." Mr. Landon thanks them and announces that he is organizing a once-a-month Socratic seminar group among the teachers to share ideas about this technique.

The Socratic seminar was largely a series of questions that had specific answers, which Mr. Landon asked the students in rapid succession. The kids were very quiet and attentive while the other kids answered each question. Mr. Landon did not comment on their ideas. He sometimes repeated what a student said without giving any indication of whether he personally agreed or disagreed. He tried to call on students who were quiet and gave others an opportunity to speak by asking, "Does anyone want to add to that?" There were no follow-up questions or probes that asked students to explain in more detail. Once Mr. Landon got a response, he turned to another part of the poem and asked questions to move students through the fourteen lines.

Mr. Landon was a lot like Mrs. Oublier, a teacher involved in California's effort to shift mathematics practices from rote learning to learning for greater understanding.[5] Teaching for understanding means that teachers design activities so that kids can grapple with new concepts, skills, and knowledge, and eventually the students will be asked to demonstrate how to use these concepts, skills, and knowledge. Despite her participation in significant professional development, Mrs. Oublier translated much of what she had learned away from a student-centered approach back to her previous teacher-centered approach. What Mr. Landon did with this class was similar. He moved just a little distance from his own most comfortable teacher-centered discussion technique: he moved kids into a circle, he provided a specific text, he reminded students that participation was expected, and he called on a variety of students. Still, Mr. Landon did not appear to have a central overarching question to guide the discussion. The questions he asked were designed to elicit specific answers and were typical of teacher-led discussions, which provide evidence that students have read the text. He had not yet moved to more broad-based questions, which require students to go beyond their own opinions to text-supported opinions.

The debriefing he did with the students was designed to check their perceptions about how it had gone, to check their comfort level. Although several students made important comments that revealed their growing understanding of Socratic seminars, the questions he asked were not designed for substantive critique of the method, nor did the discussion result in the growth of their mutual understanding (students *and* teacher) of the purpose or the conduct of Socratic seminars. As a novice, his understanding of the technique was rudimentary. He seemed aware of this because he organized a discussion group of teachers to share ideas about Socratic seminars.

Balancing Content and Process. Ms. Mosback, a social studies teacher, was trying to teach about treaties by involving the kids in consensus decision making. She had not tried this before but believed that kids might better understand the difficulty of treaty making through this approach. She understood both that treaties are forged through lengthy negotiations and that consensus is required to bring about ratification. She thought this would be an interesting angle, one that she had not tried thus far. She was a conscientious teacher, had a very good relationship with most of her students, and was working hard with another teacher to integrate English and social studies. Her central interest was engaging kids so that they would dig deeply into their learning. This was Tommy's tenth-grade social studies class. They had reviewed the Treaty of Versailles and the purposes and qualities of a good treaty prior to launching into the following conversation:

Ms. Mosback:"How would you define a treaty? An agreement?"

A student answers,"An agreement between two or more parties over rules and regulations."

Ms. Mosback looks at the rest of the class."Does everyone agree with that? Any additions?"

Tommy:"Isn't it mostly a peace treaty, saying we will not fight?"

"Does this group agree?" Ms. Mosback points to a group of students. They nod."Does this group agree?" More nods."Good. What is the ultimate objective of a peace treaty?"

A chorus:"Peace."

A student chimes in:"But the Germans weren't too happy about the Treaty of Versailles."

Ms. Mosback:"Let's not worry about the Versailles Treaty. What is the objective of a perfect peace treaty?"

Student:"Each side would get what it wants?"

"Is the Triple Alliance like a treaty?"

Ms. Mosback: "It's an alliance."

"A good treaty will be a compromise. Everyone would get what he wants."

She asks, "Should a treaty punish people?"

"You need punishment so a nation won't get out of line."

She responds, "Should a treaty be fair to all?"

Tommy: "Forget the past. Start with a clean slate."

"Punishment should be given!"

One student yells at another, "Don't write on my desk!"

"If a treaty is to prevent war, and you're talking about punishment, can a treaty ever make all sides happy?" asks Ms. Mosback.

"Everyone wants something different."

Ms. Mosback attempts to get the group to come to some agreement: "We have some disagreement here as to whether it should be the victor, the vanquished, or a neutral observer who sets the terms of the treaty. Let's get some consensus."

"The people who were fighting should put in what they want. Why should neutrals be involved?"

Ms. Mosback asks again, "What were the difficulties involved in the Treaty of Versailles?"

"There were lots of nations involved."

"To punish the Germans."

"Austria, Hungary, France . . ."

"Italy."

Ms. Mosback passes out a handout, "The Peace Settlements," and asks the kids to read the bottom portion on the provisions of the treaty. The provisions included restrictions that Germany must accept, the requirement that Germany accept complete responsibility for the war, and the establishment of the League of Nations. She asks, "Is this a good treaty or a bad treaty according to the criteria you set? Make sure your group agrees on your position."

The kids shush one another. For ten minutes, they talk in groups. A student asks, "Why does Germany have to accept the guilt?"

Ms. Mosback asks each group to focus on reparations and accepting guilt and write down what they feel about that. Each group is called on to report in turn whether this is a good treaty or a bad treaty. Tommy responds for his group that a good treaty is fair to most, both sides compromise equally, and work to prevent future wars.

Ms. Mosback asks students for their attention: "Who started the war?"

A student says that the treaty is problematic because it was not drawn up in a neutral place.

The group one reporter says, "Germany was not responsible for beginning the war."

A second student says, "I did it differently than my group."

A third says, "It's your fault for going to war!"

Another responds, "That's because you're German."

Another says, "You can't be forced to accept guilt!"

Ms. Mosback: "I want to get all groups in."

Group three reports: "Germany got too much guilt. They have to rebuild. The German colonies got taken away by the victors."

By the time group five makes its report, the recorder notes that it has all been said before. Each group indicates that the treaty was not a very good one.

Out of time, the class departs as Ms. Mosback calls out: "So the consensus is that this is a bad treaty?"

The class kept a lively pace that students enjoyed. Tommy said that Ms. Mosback uses such a variety of techniques that he is always on his feet. Here, she tried something for the first time. By the end of the class, Ms. Mosback's focus shifted from the content—student understanding of the Treaty of Versailles—to the technique of reaching consensus—as that was the innovation she was trying, though she did not teach much about consensus. Ms. Mosback's next lesson moved on to the Holocaust, even though many students did not appear to have a thorough understanding of the conclusions to be drawn from the First World War before moving on to the Second World War. Given the limited amount of time Ms. Mosback had for reflection and the press of the next unit, one that she and her teammate had worked the hardest on all year, it seemed unlikely that she would spend much time thinking about how the consensus technique had worked. The students had been engaged, after all, and like many treaty negotiations, they moved toward agreement as the deadline drew near.

Ms. Mosback's approach illustrates a common occurrence that happens when experienced teachers try new things—her focus shifted to the activity or the technique and away from what kids were learning.[6] In this shift, clarity about what she wanted students to know and to be able to do diminished, both in terms of content (the Treaty of Versailles) and in terms of the process she had hoped they would learn about (treaty building). In addition, when trying something for the first time, Ms. Mosback, as many teachers do, miscalculated the time needed to finish the lesson more thoroughly. Nearly everything takes longer than teachers first imagine.

Insufficient Background. In English class, Ms. Tommich, a young, energetic teacher, was doing a unit on short stories. She was interested in pushing herself, was very committed to building a repertoire, and was constantly searching for and trying new techniques. Over the years, she matured as a teacher, eventually working into a comfortable, positive relationship with students. Whenever possible, she tried to build good relationships with other teachers and her administrators so that she could get feedback on her work.

Tommy was in this class, and he and Ms. Tommich alternately struggled and made progress, struggled and made progress. He vacillated from being mouthy, difficult, despondent, irritated. She vacillated between wanting to help him and wanting to scream.

In response to students' requests that they have more choice in their reading, Ms. Tommich designed a new unit on short stories. She selected fifteen stories, and multiple copies were placed in folders in the back of the room. The stories included "A Night in June," "The Eighty-Yard Run," "Enero," "First Confession," and "Hills like White Elephants." Students were to read six of the stories and write responses. The kids could choose several formats in which to respond: (1) mapping out events in the character's life; (2) masks, making a reflection of the character's concerns and questions, possibly using a paper bag, oaktag, plaster of Paris, or papier-mâché; and (3) writing a letter from the character telling the story from a different perspective. And there were others. Four of the entries were to be selected by students for revisions and for inclusion in the portfolio for this unit.

Because everyone was working independently, she circulated through the class, using a new assessment technique—an anecdotal record. This was a technique she recently had heard about in a course she was taking. It was designed for elementary teachers to keep track of students' individual learning progress. With this approach, teachers attempt to record what kids are doing during a particular learning experience. The anecdotal record becomes the source of data that teachers use to inform children and their parents about how the kids are learning, where they are having problems, and what alternative activities they might employ. Again, this is Ms. Tommich's first attempt. One of her anecdotal records looks like this:

> *Tommy*—March 6: starts "Too Early Spring." March 9: Health Assembly, starts graph and turns in. March 10: starts "First Confession." March 11: works on writing for "First Confession," a letter. March 12: reading "Pair of Silk Stockings." March 13: writing his response, talks with others a fair amount. March 17: works on mask with TJ last night, reads "My Sister's Marriage." March 20: absent. March 23: fusses in the hall with Tammy, finishes SS, will write.

She intended to use these records to conference with students to help them understand their own learning process. However, the difficulties she encountered were substantial. First, she had too many students and limited time to take notes, so the record really only named the activity in which students were engaged for the day rather than describing their learning process. Second, she found that to be thorough, she had to devote most of her time to the record, so it limited her ability to interact with kids. Third, she had never really seen an example of an anecdotal record in a high school class, and none of her colleagues were familiar with them either. She ran out of time to use the technique with her students but gave them a copy of the record. Tommy said, "It was like she was keeping track of what we were doing for discipline reasons." Still, she was pleased to have tried something new and put it aside for further reflection. She would need to think about how she might try it again, but she and Ms. Mosback were now launching into the Holocaust unit, and it was time to focus on that.

In this case, Ms. Tommich simply did not have enough exposure to the technique, which was designed for a very different working context—elementary schools where teachers work with a
smaller number of students all day—nor had she had the time to
think seriously about how the technique might best be transformed
to work in a high school setting. Nor did she have colleagues
around who could give her enough critical feedback to enable her to
try it to its fullest. The technique itself has great potential to inform
students and to assist them in their growth, but her working context
had not changed substantially enough to plant it in fertile ground.

❖

The examples of teachers attempting a variety of innovations as
they struggle to build a bigger repertoire illustrate how difficult it is
to add new techniques and strategies to one's repertoire. The dilemmas differ from one teacher to the next. Mr. Landon stepped only
an inch away from his usual teacher-centered approach. Ms. Mosback, excited about a new technique, shifted her attention away
from the kids' learning to the technique itself, "So do we have consensus? Was it a good treaty or a bad one?" Ms. Tommich adapted
an elementary technique with marvelous potential but had little
local expertise to help her translate the uses of anecdotal records to
the secondary context.

Part of what made these activities exciting to both teachers and
students was that they were fresh and new. All of the problems were
correctable, so the challenge was to encourage teachers to continue
to build their repertoire and to help them learn about necessary internal routines that would bring the innovations from simple variety to greater rigor.

Implications of Connecting Routines to Repertoire

To get kids to more rigorous levels of accomplishment, teachers
must balance the routines of schooling with a professional repertoire that allows them to respond to the differing needs of their students and to provide students with fresh experiences. It seems that

schools have, over the last century, worked hard on building routines, some very positive, some less so. More attention needs to be focused on building different kinds of experiences that lead to expanded teacher repertoire. To develop a repertoire that engages students in experiences that are rigorous and fresh demands a great deal from teachers.

Collectively, these schools were working very hard to institute any number of innovations, but their focus was more on structural changes than on changes inside the classroom—the all-important interactions between students and teachers. Consequently, they paid less attention to teacher repertoire than they did to schedules, governance, or other new projects. Although it is admittedly hard to know exactly where to begin or what to do first, it is clear that teacher learning is a critical link in the connection between student achievement and successful school reform. Mr. Garland reflected on the complexity of what he, Mr. Warren, Ms. Mosback, Ms. Tommich, and many other colleagues were struggling with:

> Until you see, say, a Socratic seminar—though it doesn't matter what kind of technique or activity, it could be any of them—in action, how do you know what you might do? Where are we supposed to get ideas from? Then if you haven't seen it and you try it, how do you know what you're doing? Even if you have seen it, it's still hard to know. For a lot of people, what do they have to draw on? How can you enact change if you don't see change or know what change is? And that's the most difficult, frustrating part. Until you see some stuff and talk about it and try it and talk about it more, how can you get good at this stuff? You can't close down school for a day. We're lucky in my school. The English and social studies teachers at ninth and tenth grade work well together including the special ed teachers. This is hard, it's just really hard. Just as hard as it is for the kids to learn challenging new stuff.

To build a repertoire requires that teachers constantly cultivate new techniques and approaches. If school faculty have not made such teacher learning a priority, the likelihood that teachers will get heightened rigor from their students is almost nil. The litany of impossible conditions remains, mentioned already in this book—too many kids, not enough planning time, not enough adult contact time, not enough feedback, and so on.

To get results, it seems most important to think about building four conditions—all of which are designed to foster teacher learning. They are:

1. *Time.* Teachers need time to learn about all the dimensions of teaching—curriculum, instruction, and assessment—as part of their daily responsibility and over the lifetime of their career. Nearly every report on problematic conditions in schooling acknowledges that teachers need time as part of their professional day to learn more about their work. The current structure of schooling does not allow for this, nor do many in local communities see it as integral to the development of children's capabilities. Although all reformers acknowledge the need for teachers to expand their repertoire, few faculty or central office staff or state departments have yet created adequate conditions for adult learning in their schools. Until this is a regularity, teacher development will be haphazard, reliant on the good will and professional drive of individual teachers rather than a professional requirement for the entire teaching force.

2. *Collegiality.* Teachers need the opportunity and the expectation that they will work together to build the repertoire of skills that their students need. Still, despite the fact that we have understood the importance of collegiality for a number of years, most schools maintain a strong culture of individuality and isolation. It must be made explicit that collegial work will focus not just on school structures but also on helping individuals learn about teaching techniques and practices. In these five schools, when teachers built a common agenda for their development and talked together about what worked and what did not, their own skills developed much more quickly and to a deeper level of understanding than did the skills of teachers working in a less collegial culture.

3. *Analytical capacity.* Further, teachers need to build their analytical capacity. Donald Schön and his colleagues have made

major contributions to our understanding that teachers need to be reflective practitioners, that to think about their work is critical to their grasp of what constitutes effective teaching and productive learning.[7] We agree that teachers need to be much more reflective but would suggest that some of the reflective activity needs to be more critically analytical. To gain analytical skill, teachers need to practice watching their own teaching and that of others. They need to ask themselves why they are attempting new techniques, and they need to look for substantial questions embedded in new approaches. They need to ascertain what problem it is that they are attempting to solve for their students. Then they need to examine whether the changes they are attempting are getting what they hoped for from students by both asking students directly and reflecting on students' work. To be more critically analytical, teachers need to develop the skills of giving and receiving regular feedback on their work in classrooms.

4. *Expertise*. Teachers need a readily available support system of experts who are knowledgeable about a particular technique. It is difficult for teachers to develop a sophisticated understanding of a new technique or strategy that is quite different from their own well-established pattern. It is difficult for them to see the potential and the difference between their early interpretations and the full promise of the technique. A common practice is to suggest that a teacher who has been out to a workshop function as the resident expert for the school. Unfortunately, sophisticated understanding takes a great deal more time and effort. As teachers use a technique, they need to interact with experts so that they can determine whether their personal interpretations—translated to new subject areas, new age groups, to an existing learning culture—are accurate.

So far, the reform movement has only paid lip service to establishing teacher learning as a regularity in schools. More time is spent telling people that they need to change than helping them create realistic circumstances in which they might actually build a powerful and sustaining repertoire. The school reform movement needs to emphasize less about innovation and more about helping teachers build a thoughtful, useful repertoire. Ms. O'Leary's science class shows her in the midst of building such a repertoire, but with the support of her colleagues and administrators. Their assistance helps her with the routines so that her work builds appropriately for kids. This final classroom example shows what is possible for a teacher who is in the process of expanding her repertoire.

A ninth-grade earth-science teacher under pressure from her principal to do something new in her classroom, Ms. O'Leary worked over the summer to develop a new approach to teaching the relationship between the moon and the tides. Her objective was to make the scientific concept of interrelationships more engaging and to ensure that more kids actually understood the concept at the end of the unit. She had taught it out of the book for years, given kids the fill-in-the-blanks lab, but she was not satisfied that kids really understood the central relationships. As she recalled:

I can tell you what's been painful, pushing me off the beaten track. I had tremendous success rate on the state exam. My average was an 86 percent pass rate. I thought for years that I was really doing things right. I didn't want to change. But the principal came in to watch my class, and she was looking for active students. I was teaching the way I usually taught. Students were working on the lab in the book about the relationship between the moon and tides. I only helped them if they got stuck. I wanted them to get it or figure it out themselves. I thought I was an engaging teacher. I don't give volumes of notes, because I thought they were doing hands-on things and that they were involved. And the principal said, "You're not trying anything new. You're teaching right out of the book. What else might you do to help these kids out?"

Well, I was shocked. All my insecurities came out. I felt like I was in a land where I didn't know the landscape. I felt threatened. What should I be doing? It was horrible. I laid out my options. I could refuse to comply or I could try. I felt angry while I was being nudged because I thought she was telling me I wasn't any good. I didn't really hear what she was saying. So I went to my colleagues in the science department, and they talked it through with me. And then I started trying to figure out how I might do it differently. So we decided that I would try to get the kids to function as scientists. Instead of doing the book lab, we'd learn about the interconnectedness of nature by conducting a month of observations regarding the moon and the tide and see if the kids could uncover the relations through their observations. Seems pretty simple now, but I was terrified then. The other teachers in the science department made themselves available to watch and help. So we just did it.

I was flying by the seat of my pants when the kids started coming in and talking science to me. I was shocked. They became more curious about what was going on: "Ms. O'Leary, our figures are different from last night. Why would our measurements be different?" or "Ms. O, the moon is hidden behind the house for the last couple of days. How do I indicate that on my map?" It didn't matter whether they were the smart kids or the less bright kids, they all enjoyed doing it. They were using terms like analysis, angles of declination, ascension, tide markers, compasses. They enjoyed it. But we lost time. So then I had to figure out how to rearrange the rest of the year's curriculum to accommodate the time this had taken.

For each of the three years we were in the school, she continued to hone and refine this unit. By the third year, she was off creating another large unit. Because Ms. O'Leary taught earth science to all the ninth-grade students, she ended up with large class sizes. The science department agreed that someone would come into her class to help her should she need it. As a result, her colleagues were in and out of her room, and available to listen to her, to look at the directions she had given the kids, to correct the graphs and the data-gathering techniques the kids were engaged in. In addition, they gave her feedback about how they perceived it was going and made suggestions. And she had the support of the principal, who was willing to spend time with her while she worked through this unit.

Ms. O'Leary found it enormously stimulating but also felt herself right in the midst of a maelstrom—the dilemma of coverage versus deeper understanding. Units like this took more time. To do them meant that she would have to reduce the curriculum that was set by the state. She was not yet confident enough that kids would be able to compete with kids from other schools on the state's standardized achievement tests. Still, with the help of her colleagues and the administration, and kids' enthusiasm, she persisted.

Every year, students and parents mentioned this activity. Tommy's mother said, "My son had to keep a journal, and they had to keep some kind of data and draw some conclusions from the data. It was very engaging. Every night for a month, he was out there whenever the moon was supposed to be up, and at eight o'clock he measured the river. He graphed how high the moon was, how high the tide was, and graphed the difference. It was great. The most important thing for me is to see evidence that my child loves to learn."

Given a good nudge to change and the support of her colleagues, Ms. O'Leary found the new approach stimulating and productive for her students. Over the course of three years, she worked to break her own routines and to establish new ones by building her repertoire. First, she would determine a new approach. Then she worked to put sensible routines into the midst of these new techniques. Then they would all look at the kids' work to see what else needed to be done. With the help of her colleagues and her principal, she was able to change the routines for her work somewhat as well. She got collaborative support, plenty of feedback, and time to redesign assignments. As a teacher, she felt herself expand: "I am more confident. I am more curious. And I think that's what the kids got too. They gained self-confidence and self-reliance. They gained good attack skills that will serve them in any class. What we're hoping for is a whole school that is in dialogue about whether we could teach things another way, a better way. That'll be exciting for everybody!"

Chapter Three

Caring and Expectations

The second morning bell has rung at Lincoln High. Ms. Murray begins her math class by reviewing the previous day's work on algebraic equations. She goes through a problem with her students, asking questions, coaxing, providing clues. Then they move to the main task of the day. On an overhead transparency, she draws a table with additive inverses and absolute values. Continuing to question and prompt, Ms. Murray completes one entry to the table, showing how the job should be done.

She begins to divide the class into groups of five students each. During the transition, students are attentive, quiet, and virtually all of them seem to be following. Only Alicia is not with the rest. She has her head down on her desk. At one point as Ms. Murray goes around the room, she gives Alicia's back a pat, saying sympathetically, "I guess you're having a hard morning." Alicia's grandfather had died during the school's spring break, and Ms. Murray knows how hard this is on Alicia.

Rather than telling students to get themselves into groups, Ms. Murray passes out colorful cards with geometric shapes: "Triangles over here, please; circles in the far corner." Then, writing on the overhead, she jots the collaborative skills they will be emphasizing along with the math concepts. There is a master list on the back bulletin board, and for every group activity, Ms. Murray and the class select several. Today, they pick three skills—no put downs, with Ms. Murray adding a comment about not calling one another names; checking (they are to read one another's papers); and listening. She writes these on the overhead as she speaks. Then they pick some roles, also listed on the back board—recorder, observer, and seeker. (Ms. Murray had added the seeker role five months earlier, because when students had trouble getting along, knowing they would have the chance to summon her seemed to prevent disruptions.)

Once the skills and roles are established, she asks the students to move their chairs into groups, reminding everyone to sit close together in a circle. "I'm going to count to ten, and I want you to be in groups by the time I reach ten." She starts the count, and everyone bunches their chairs together, an impressive feat, as some have to move across the room. No one begs off, claiming math phobia. (Earlier in the year, Ms. Murray had made it clear that she absolutely refused to believe that girls or minorities lacked the necessary intellectual tools to learn algebra.) At the count of ten, all four groups are working on the additive inverses.

Ms. Murray walks around the room, answering questions, usually by asking questions in return. She coaxes one student to give an answer, then asks the student who had asked the original question if that helped. She clearly expects complete statements in the conversations: "Yeah, what? Tell me more. Talk in sentences." What she does not expect is vulgarity. When one boy whispers "Damn," she whispers back, "That's not appropriate in this room," then perches herself on the edge of a table. Very pregnant, she quips, "You'll pick me up if I fall?"

The pace of the class remains brisk. Students are always doing something—answering, writing, asking questions, solving problems. She often refers to work completed earlier in the spring, reminding them how everything is building, fitting together.

One group includes a boy who imperiously directs the others. "Okay! Is everyone ready? Okay! We have to do this time line!" Ms. Murray knows he is in group therapy, has great difficulty making and keeping friends. The kids often roll their eyes at one another whenever he is overbearing. Today, he is directive in a quiet way. No one in his group seems annoyed or gets rude about it.

Alicia's head is still down on her desk. Yet she holds a pencil upright in her hand. Ms. Murray comes over to give her another pat, and she asks the group to be patient. They pass their papers to her throughout the hour, sometimes pushing them right under her nose and arm. From time to time, the top of her pencil moves; she is, in fact, trying to check the papers.

Ms. Murray's class was shaped by her friendly relationships with students, but her notion of caring emphasized mutual obligations: "Just being a nice guy, making life easy, giving them a way out, that's not what's best for our kids." She wanted students to be responsible, not just in their daily behavior, such as punctuality, but in mastering first-year algebra skills that are necessary to do well later in second-year algebra, or in going to the school library to read newspapers for current affairs reports if the family did not subscribe to a paper (as many at Lincoln did not). She regretted that some teachers let students avoid responsibility for their laziness: teachers who curved grades when students did poorly on a test, allowed truants quick ways to make up six weeks of missed assignments, and lowered standards in after-school and summer remedial courses all bothered her. "Caring has to go both ways. Set strong goals and expect them to live up to those goals as you encourage and nurture them." To Ms. Murray, every student was capable of learning algebra. She believed that her task was to convince them and then hold them responsible.

Ms. Murray's effectiveness derived in large measure from the strong goals she set for herself. She pushed herself to experiment and innovate. From a districtwide algebra collaborative, she picked up methods for using calculators and writing group tests that also gauge individuals' contributions. On her own, she began to include more practical applications in every class—fees for electricians, angles of ski slopes, and average heights of females from birth to age twenty. She welcomed the new statewide math requirements because they "get kids to look just a little beyond what is asked in the question." In a family of thirty, what are the odds that two members will have the same birthday? She liked that question because the students had to restate the problem in their own words, solve the problem with correct calculations, explain in clear prose how they solved it, and offer predictions or generalizations about differences and similarities for determining the odds for a family of forty rather than thirty.

Neither Ms. Murray's caring nor her high expectations came effortlessly, and fatigue was a concern to her. As a well-regarded teacher in a well-known school, she was swamped with requests. "Every day someone comes to my door to ask, 'Couldn't you do this? You'd be the best person.'" The offers of out-of-school projects were not the incentive for her that others imagined them to be, because she felt obliged to prepare careful plans for her substitutes when she was away from her classes—amounting to double the work for her. Even without special projects, her work weeks were draining. Helping so many students from broken or dysfunctional families took its toll. In 1991, she admitted that "I can't play mother to the students of Lincoln all my life." In 1992, she requested and took a transfer to Madison, an upper-middle-class high school across town, the school where she had graduated in the early 1970s.

Unfortunately, the transfer disappointed her. The indifference and hostility to students at Madison fell short of her own standards for both caring and expectations. In math department meetings, instead of discussing the curriculum, teachers would ridicule kids: "This one is dumb; that one is stupid." Ms. Murray felt the faculty could not accept the fact that even in higher socioeconomic strata, adolescents and families have changed since the 1960s. "They were judgmental on students and their family lives for being different— which is something students cannot help—and they wanted to hold on to all the things they thought the school had once been." Because students were not respected, they in turn lacked respect for the teachers. The game was, "You're out to get us, so we're going to get you." Ms. Murray had more markers stolen from her overhead projector at Madison than at Lincoln.

After one year, she came back to Lincoln. She resolved to say no more often: "I can't make school the only thing; I may have to let other people down a bit in order to have a more balanced life." She believed she could do that and still honor what she saw as Lincoln's best side: "The majority of the faculty have the students' concerns in front. Most of us expect a lot of them. I think kids want that. I know they need it. They may rebel in the beginning, but they truly appreciate it." Their appreciation for Ms. Murray was evident over the past five years. The senior class twice named her their "most influential teacher."

The benefit to students of Ms. Murray's conscientious struggle to find the right balance between caring and high expectations is exemplified by Alicia. Alicia's attitudes toward math, her skills, and her understanding of the discipline in general grew much stronger during her year in Ms. Murray's class. Alicia began her sophomore year sure that it was good enough to know the right answer in math class without needing to explain it. She had never liked math, felt uncomfortable in it, and lacked confidence in her ability. After the first month of school, she was proud that she had learned how to add and subtract negative numbers. She drew pictures of balloons to illustrate how she had learned to do so: "See, these are air puffs and these are sandbags. You put your balloon on positive three, then take two air puffs away so the balloon sinks." She showed how five plus negative nine should be figured. "Have to put in nine of these old sandbags so the five sinks down to negative four." When asked to subtract negative nine from five, she fidgeted and said, "That makes me so mad. It doesn't make sense to me." When asked why anyone studies negative numbers, Alicia shook her head: "I don't know. I know what it is but I don't know why." She could repeat procedures. She knew by heart all the rules for group work, and she remembered the number line laid across the floor of the classroom, what Ms. Murray called the "algebra walk"—but deeper understandings eluded her.

By the spring, Ms. Murray had worked closely enough with Alicia so that she was beginning to understand the logic and the utility of math. Alicia claimed she did not care what her grade was as long as she understood the work, revealing a breakthrough in her feelings about math. She opened her notebook to show off her quizzes, homework, and class work. "I pay attention. Have to." Last year in ninth-grade math, she could daydream and talk in class: "That was a blast. But this is better." What helped her understand was going beneath the formulas to grasp why and how they apply: "I had been used to memorizing rules. That's the way I was taught in middle school. I fought Ms. Murray until she made me see that it's not good learning by the rules because you don't know what you are doing. All you know is a half plus a half is the answer. That's all. You don't know how you got it. You don't know why you got it." Now she knew.

Caring and Expectations: What Are They?

In Ms. Murray's class, it was impossible to separate her high expectations and her caring. By putting both into dynamic interplay, she conveyed standards that were expected for the students' dispositions, habits, and temperament. The academic work ethic she sought entailed values, beliefs, and commitments—connecting both head and heart. Traits like persistence and cooperation marked intellectual as well as interpersonal aspects of her classroom.

Caring was important to these youngsters; they said that they responded better to adults who were concerned for their welfare. Caring teachers appeared more interested in youth and treated them more respectfully. Young people suggested that they worked harder for teachers who cared about them than those that seemed indifferent or cared only about their subject matter.

At the same time, it was critically important for young people to feel pushed, to feel that their teachers believed in their capabilities—sometimes more than the kids did themselves. They responded when their teachers were clear that students could do difficult work but that it would simply take effort and time. Students resented teachers who implied that some work might be too difficult for them; they felt patronized, and it affected their self-esteem. They cited many examples where teachers had told them that they would not be capable of difficult work because they were not honors or advanced-placement caliber or because they were girls or because they had not shown much talent in a particular subject.

Prominent scholars who have written about caring suggest that high expectations are part of caring—that teachers cannot be caring without expecting a good deal from their students.[1] In the study schools, most educators agreed that both caring and high expectations were critical; however, the fusion of the two was more unusual than one would expect, given the general agreement about their importance. Even when sustained efforts were made to link caring and expectations, teachers generally emphasized one over the other. In most of the schools, it was more common to find teachers who emphasized caring than high expectations.

For Alicia, caring meant her teachers' hard work and availability for extra help. For her friends, the same word meant helpfulness, patience, a sense of humor, willingness to listen, and concern. In another school, the emphasis was on fairness, and in a third site, respect was the most frequent synonym. The wide range of students' definitions and descriptions of caring is striking. Yet the scope of the notion of caring is further compounded by social and economic woes outside school that educators cannot and do not ignore.

Teen pregnancies, troubled families, greater poverty have made schools ever more aware of important needs for students. Schools were increasing their services in order to provide badly needed care for their students. Several of the five schools opened day-care centers, health care clinics, and dental clinics and provided group therapy sessions to meet the nonacademic needs of students. Emotional pain, physical ailments, financial hardships, and other difficulties rarely go unnoticed for long, especially if the distress is acute. At one school, the youth services center could only help the neediest, but its clientele included a third of the school, and its annual budget of $90,000 equaled half of the school's discretionary spending. Care extended beyond the walls of the school. As one administrator put it, "We provide a lot of emergency assistance—food, eyeglasses, clothing, tons of clothing. In fact, if a child here needs shoes or a jacket, we'll take them shopping." The many provisions for adolescent "wellness" multiply the instances of caring for students.

Other studies have reported equally vast notions of caring. Chaskin and Rauner concluded that "caring concerns relationship and commitment, mutuality and reciprocity, participation, and continuity, concern for and acceptance of the other."[2] In that article, a slew of definitions came also from students. Adolescents mentioned dozens of examples of caring: helping with schoolwork, treating students as individuals, showing respect, demonstrating tolerance, explaining, checking for understanding, encouraging, and providing fun activities were the most common illustrations of teaching practices that students thought demonstrated care in class.[3] Additional dimensions emerge in other research, in which caring extended beyond teacher-student relations to the entire school as a caring community. In these cases, notions of shared purpose, democratic decision making, and a sense of belonging widen the meaning of caring.[4]

In contrast to these broad definitions of caring, the definitions of high expectations focus more narrowly on teachers' beliefs about student capacity for learning. The conviction that all students can reach at least a rung or two higher than they themselves think they can climb is the heart of it. Teachers with high expectations in the five schools refused to believe that some students could not, needed not, or would not do serious academic work.

In the five schools, teachers with high expectations consistently differed from colleagues with lower expectations in two crucial ways: they held an undiminished faith in the potential of their students, and they persisted when a class seemed unable or unwilling to work hard.

However, it was not uncommon to find teachers like Mr. Dee, who had low expectations and who was overwhelmed by the baggage the students brought with them. A math teacher, Mr. Dee admitted that "dealing with fourteen-year-olds all day wears me out." In this particular year, he had 120 ninth graders, with only ten or twelve he considered attentive and motivated. One period was "wall to wall special ed kids. That's tough. I lecture and walk the aisles. All ninth graders, with massive problems. Drug use, wrecked homes, bad love life, pregnant girls, girls wondering if they are pregnant, breaking up with boyfriends, sitting here crying and whining. I'm trying to teach math but it's like talking to a brick wall." In his view, kids today are so distracted, indifferent, or ornery that teachers face a thankless, even hopeless, task of working with unmotivated students who do not value education.

Mr. Dee joined three other teachers to form a team, but he considered the major problem—unmotivated students—to be beyond group solutions. Students "come in here in turmoil, not because I did anything wrong. They're so upset they kick the wall or pick a fight." He estimated that 15 percent of his students had been in drug rehabilitation, and at least 50 percent needed professional therapy. Mr. Dee wanted to work with kids who wanted to work. He had taught adults in night school: "They do their part. They've had their fill of $4.00 an hour jobs and are looking for a better life." Those were the students he sought, students who already had a work ethic: "I can't take somebody that doesn't have any desire and change that." Mr. Dee acknowledged some successes with his team. They had established discipline rules that they all enforced consistently. That helped, as did the agreement for everyone to slow down so the special education students were not totally lost. Teaching study skills and giving points every day for participation encouraged more students to try. But no team could give him what he craved: "Better kids, on grade level, who are academically motivated." He decided to retire.

Mr. McCarthy's sophomores had as many emotional complications as Mr. Dee's freshmen, but he reacted quite differently to their woes. Sean described some classmates in third-period English: "Ozela has herpes. Harriet weighs about 350 pounds. LaTosha's stepfather is in jail for murder. BethAnn is manic and went to a hospital four times this year. Jim is hyper and jumps out of his chair. George works until midnight so he usually sleeps in his. Sharon sucks her thumb and when she starts, Michael does too."

On his own initiative, Mr. McCarthy searched, with more optimism than Mr. Dee, for new ways to teach. He took graduate courses, paid his way to summer conferences, and raised money to qualify for matching grants to bring guest speakers into his class. Every year, he took the class to see several plays and concerts in the city. Scheduling those trips became easier after all sophomore teachers joined teams. His three teammates rearranged the day's work to make time for the outings. Like Mr. Dee, Mr. McCarthy knew that some efforts would fail, but unlike Mr. Dee, he persisted, determined: "The traditional methods I once used do not work. I am trying to find another way to capture the kids' interest in reading, without threatening them. I want to encourage them to like it enough so they won't run away from reading. I think if we keep writing, their reading skills will improve. I wish I could get better results faster. I haven't found the way, but I'll keep looking."

In short, high expectations are about push and a belief in capacity, whereas caring is about everything from good manners to social work. So why was it that more schools focused on caring than on high expectations?

One common answer stems from a particular notion of how kids learn. Caring is supposedly so crucial that it has to precede academic challenge. When one administrator said, "They have to know you care before they care how much you know," her logic connected academic challenge with caring but assumed that caring was the first step, the prerequisite of academic performance. Until students feel comfortable with one another and with the teachers, not much will be learned. That same administrator said, "Here's something that folks who want to hit the academics from day one don't understand: you have to get that student feeling good about himself first before you can even start teaching."

Many teachers enter the field because they care about children. When they see the problems confronting today's children, they are often overwhelmed. The immediate urge is to hug children, show them that someone loves them, that they are not really alone. With books like *There Are No Children Here* and *Amazing Grace*, which describe the deplorable conditions that so many children face today, it is not surprising that teachers feel that the need to care is predominant.

But that therapeutic perspective on learning and teaching is not universally held. Many teachers think academic achievements are the building blocks of self-esteem. Trust can follow, not merely precede, hard work. It is the absence of high expectations, not their presence, that signals a lapse in genuine caring. A colleague wrote, "Caring is certainly an essential part of what we can give. But however much we care for them as people, we must also give them our love of learning, our commitment to standards, and our passionate resolve to know the truth about things."[5] Diego remembered how his English teacher made the same point, less abstractly, on the first day of class: "I won't insult you by drawing smiley faces on C papers or writing, 'Very good! Very good!' if it's not."

A second answer comes from the strong pressures on high schools to *do* something. There is enormous publicity about schools being impersonal, about kids wasting time, dropping out, skipping classes. Parents, school board members, special-interest groups, and state officials want fast action, immediate results. So high schools respond by creating new programs rather than by altering attitudes, which is a slower, more subtle, less glitzy approach to school improvement. Changing structures are visible, can be described, and put in place. It is easier and faster to put in a new program than it is to try to change the dispositions and habits of the faculty. When programs take precedence over attitudes, high expectations get less attention than caring.

To explore why this happens, this chapter examines three places where caring and expectations were designed to intersect. Advisories and inclusive classrooms for special education students were two strategies on which all of our schools were working. The third example is in the regular classroom.

Advisories

All five schools wanted all students to have a designated adult to know them well and coach them through their academic careers. By matching small groups of students with a teacher in a regularly scheduled period (shorter than a regular class and meeting less often), schools could provide teens with a time and place to discuss personal and academic concerns, handle paperwork, and link home to school, with the advisor as the point of contact. The familiar homeroom of older American high schools usually lasted fewer minutes, deferred to public address announcements, and offered little or no serious interaction between adults and students. Advisories, in theory, should do more. Advisors were to know their advisees well, keep track of their work in school, learn about them so as to support them in their progress. Advisories pair each student with an adult who might have ten to fifteen advisees. The advisor's role is other than teacher or coach, and the hope is that advisors will gain more knowledge of the home and school lives of their advisees. Done well, advisories offer every student an advocate, reducing the chance that a young person might go through four years of high school without the type of close individual attention that children need.

Most certified guidance specialists—counselors—want to be available to students, but their workweeks usually include a heavy load of administrative tasks. Scheduling, college and career placement, special education team meetings, liaison with community services, giving and gathering state tests, record keeping, and the flare of small and large crises keep guidance staff on the run, acting more like assistant principals than counselors. To make matters worse, in a typical high school, most counselors are responsible for three to four hundred students, far too many to deal with in any meaningful way.

That is not to say that advisories redefine the teacher as a professional counselor, therapist, or even parent. The goal is not to usurp the proper place of either social service providers or adults at home. The appropriate diagnostic work is intellectual more than psychiatric. As Deborah Meier, founding principal of Central Park East Secondary School, put it: "It's hard enough for us to know kids as teachers, much less becoming their 'social workers' and 'psychologists.' A good teacher will become a mentor, ally, and model, but we need to see that as the outgrowth of coaching them to use their minds well. Any illusion that we can become their parents—amateur or professional—is not only too exhausting a thought for many teachers to accept but also counterproductive, threatening to their real guardians and families. It's a trap that burns us out without bringing us allies."[6]

Meier's perspective on advisories—coaching students to use their minds well—links high expectations with caring and serves as the ideal. When advisories worked in this way, students were pushed, prodded, cajoled, or encouraged to tackle more difficult projects or subject matter. When advisories worked well, students felt that their academic interests were more central to the school's concerns. We watched advisors who barely had enough time as they checked to see where each student was in his or her classes, gave suggestions to those needing some direction, prodding those who were lagging behind.

"Sergei, where are you with the novel for English class? You're supposed to be done."

"Madelaine, your math teacher mentioned that your homework is late. What is this? I thought you'd formed a good study group?"

"Tommy, how's your mom doing in her course work in the city? It sounded fascinating to me. Tell her hello."

"Okay, folks, we agreed to do your community service project as a group, and we decided that we'd do a nature trail in the woods outside the elementary school for the students. We have several tasks that need doing: a group needs to go to the elementary school to interview teachers and students to find out what would be helpful; we need to contact the Forest Service again to find out where they are; and we need to set two or three Saturday dates to get started."

Unfortunately, advisory periods seemed particularly difficult for many advisors. As high school teachers, they were trained as subject area specialists and felt uncomfortable functioning in a more general role. They were uncertain about how to use the allocated time, and they frequently asked for more formal training because they did not have an image of what they should be doing.

Lincoln High's advisory, called Teacher Guided Assistance (TGA), consisted of a daily break between second and third periods, and teachers could allot the half hour TGA as they saw fit. Some students got passes so they could seek out another teacher, but many students used the time to catch up, do some homework, rest, or talk. There was no shared, schoolwide goal for TGA. It became an independent study break, during which teachers were available to help students in smaller, more informal groups than the crowded, impersonal study hall period of bygone years at Lincoln.

In contrast to Lincoln, Crossroads wanted to plan its advisory period, and the counselors took responsibility for it, but the planning was rushed. Each counselor worked with one-third of the faculty, but teachers still felt they had little tangible material or training. Everyone got a small packet with suggested activities, without an indication as to whether the packet carried administrative and district endorsement or merely reflected the unpaid summer work of several well-intentioned staff. Furthermore, when first initiated, the advisories were scheduled for Friday only, a day with a schedule so different from other days that many students took that timing as a sign that advisory was not terribly important. Their sporadic attendance bore out that view. Often the parking lot was jammed at the start of advisory, with one-third to one-half of the school cutting.

Mr. Donnette's relaxed and informal session was representative of the kind of laissez-faire approach with which some teachers treated the advisory:

> Mr. Donnette talks with a senior about nominating her for outstanding senior. "I know I can nominate you. You have done so much."
>
> "Oh, I'd really be happy! I've tried so hard here. You know everything I've done? I could get you a list, should I do that?" Mr. Donnette nods as he walks to the side of the room. Nine students are in their seats, and Mr. Donnette starts a video about dancers from a Spanish class who appear on local television. There is no explanation for why this is shown. During a commercial, he reminds students what they need to bring in for their portfolios. He reviews a list written on the board—pictures, best works, autobiography, résumé, video, work experience, awards and honors. Students stare at the board, and two write down notes as Mr. Donnette talks. No one asks questions. Two more students enter the room.
>
> Back to the video. The host interviews the Spanish teacher in Spanish, and Mr. Donnette mentions that one of the boys interviewed is in this advisory (but not today). Most of the kids are watching. Two girls write in their notebooks, and one girl kneels next to a boy's desk, chatting and laughing. The video continues, the girls keep writing, and the boy and girl talk on.
>
> Video over, Mr. Donnette ducks into his office adjoining the room, comes out and resumes his review of the portfolio. He encourages students to work hard on them. No mention of the video.

He says, "We also have to take nominations for Teacher of the Year. You have to nominate on more than saying the teacher is cool. We need two freshmen and a junior to be on the committee picking the winner." One girl volunteers. "During spring break, there are possibilities for community service," Mr. Donnette continues. Two girls offer to work to build a greenhouse. He encourages two junior boys to join but they are not interested.

Next, he talks about "Zero Tolerance," a school paper that spells out unacceptable behaviors and the consequences for infractions. When he gets to the one on fighting, he stresses that a student's parents have to attend classes for a whole day on the student's return from suspension. "We as teachers can't be responsible for everything. We think parents should assume more responsibility."

The class bursts out laughing. "It's too extreme!" "How could they do this?" "Most parents have to work; they can't make our parents give up good money to come to school!"

Although not all of the advisories were like this and although many students were well served, most teachers agreed with Mr. Donnette, who felt it had been unfair to create the advisories when the purpose was not clearly understood by all

This lesson had been learned at Oak Hill, where student government issues were the initial focus of their "seminars," their version of advisories. The seminars began in 1989, with six faculty volunteers for the entire freshman class agreeing to meet once a week for thirty minutes for four years. The principal brought in a local consultant for training sessions. Initial anxiety was obvious: "No way I'm doing that psychological bullshit." "I'm not going to be their shrink."

The principal kept at them, brought in more consultants, and urged them to keep talking among themselves. They grew more comfortable, realizing they were not expected to become psychologists. Each year, more teachers volunteered to take a seminar, and during the summer those involved resolved important details— working to include a clause in the contract recognizing seminar as an extra preparation, talking with students to decide that the seminars should mix students from all four years, and broadening the focus beyond student government. By 1993, the faculty decided that everyone should serve as an advisor rather than relying on volunteers.

Even with that agreement, there were still a variety of views of what seminars should do. Careful planning had not guaranteed that advisors would link caring and academic expectations, because the advisors retained markedly different notions of what to do. For example, a social studies teacher, fascinated by moral development during adolescence, borrowed materials from friends in Maryland: he wanted vigorous discussions about ethical issues. Other teachers considered that approach too confrontational, likely to stir up friction and hard feelings. They preferred a more relaxed seminar, a time to let students know what was going on in the school.

Oak Hill students agreed that the quality of advisories was dependent on the advisor and that individual's concept of advisory. Given that there were stark differences, students recommended that there be more organization to convey a clear purpose. Tommy wondered, "Why are we here and what's the point?" No one wanted so much structure that seminar would become a traditional class, with texts, lectures, overheads or assignments, but the looseness of it disappointed them. Teachers did not want to turn seminars into another class, another preparation, yet many felt lost outside their own academic field and yearned for activities to fill the time rather than focus on the central point of a good advisory—getting to know students as thinkers.

That was the biggest challenge in each school—keeping the focus on how kids learn. Advisories were instituted to support students' academic progress, and using the time in advisory to learn more about how each student learned—where they were strong and where they were weak—was the area of greatest need. Often, faculty confused their advisory role as similar to that of aunts and uncles—caring about students' personal lives, sports, and home lives—rather than focusing on their academic work. For instance, for a girl whose father was on chemotherapy, the caring that followed had nothing to do with academics: the time of a school party was changed so she could attend. One superintendent expressed the central concern, "People can tell you what's happening in Johnny's life, but I doubt if they know why he can't get this math concept or why he screwed up in French last month." It was that kind of diagnostic skill that teachers needed to work on in advisory to guide students' academic progress better.

Special Education

All of the schools were redesigning the ways in which they provided services to special needs students. The current trend was to move to *inclusion*, which meant reinterpreting Public Law 94-142's requirement that schools provide special needs students with the least restrictive environment. The hope was that by expecting more for these students, by placing them in regular education courses as much as possible but taking care with their progress by providing intensive support, the students would achieve more. Interestingly enough, though changes in special education services were mandated by law, all of our schools counted their work in inclusion as part of their internal redesign, something they did not do with other state and federal mandates.

Tony—tall, lanky, and fifteen—had been in a separate resource room class for eight of his first ten years in the Oak Hill schools. He had trouble reading and struggled with numbers. He felt he was slower than everybody else and not as bright. Starting his sophomore year, he was nervous at the prospect of taking regular classes with everyone else, worried he would fall behind or be embarrassed in front of the other kids. Despite his fears, he flourished. He took regular classes most of the day, with two periods set aside for resource room assistance. His special education teachers went to class with him and the other special education students, who had previously worked together alone in the resource room. Though the regular education teachers felt challenged by this new arrangement, the special education teachers planned with them to make adjustments in assignments and to anticipate problems. This group of specialists was relentless in its determination to make this work.

Because Tony was pushed to new approaches by his teachers and his parents, he passed all of his courses and earned a regular diploma. By the time he was a senior, the school had instituted a new graduation requirement—a senior project that involved substantial research, an internship, and a final presentation in front of a panel of evaluators made up of parents, community members, teachers, and fellow students. Students did not attend class the last month of school and went to internships one day a week during the last three months of school.

Tony was expected to undertake this, and he approached the independent study with relish. Interested in weather since childhood, Tony chose meteorology for his senior project. He devoted Wednesdays and all of May to his research, preparing for a presentation.

He astounded everyone by accurately predicting the weekend's weather, a skill he had learned at a local forecasting station where he had held an internship. He stood for questions with poise, the kind that comes from passionate interest and hard work. He exuded an unmistakable and infectious enthusiasm. He concluded by assuring the panel that if his forecast erred, he had four years of schooling ahead—he had just been accepted at a local university to continue his study of meteorology. Neither Tony nor his parents had initially thought that he would make it to college; their delight—and his—was enormous.

Breakthrough moments like Tony's richly rewarded the staff for their investment in working collaboratively toward higher expectations and caring. When not isolated in separate classes, special education kids often come through for both regular and special education teachers. Caring and high expectations yielded great gains for Tony and most special education students. Why did the coupling seem more powerful, more effective, here than in the advisories? The attitudes of the faculty were first and foremost. The fact that the special education teachers felt this to be a powerful and important transition and were there to help the regular education teachers made an enormous difference.

The dedication of most special educators is unmistakable. Even with the blessing of relatively low student-teacher ratios, they must (and want to) work hard to get to know their students as individuals. Instead of seeing students in groups as advisors do in seminars, the special education staff spend most of their days working one-to-one. Structures are thus tailor-made to fit the individual students. For instance, modifying classroom assignments to match a student's Individual Educational Plan (IEP), which is required by law, calls for ingenuity and energy. In one instance, a teacher knew that a learning-disabled boy liked to play guitar, so she copied parts of the first chapter of a book on advanced scale improvisation. He struggled with written texts, but this was very similar to reading schematic diagrams of electrical wiring, which was the assignment in his principles of technology class. At other times, the caring is less about curriculum than about encouragement and basic information:

Ms. Fried moves to one of the boys with his head down on his desk. She says, "What are you doing?"

"I'm studying."

"No, you're not. How are you going to make up what you've missed?"

"I didn't think I had to pass all my classes because I play basketball. They'll average my grades."

Ms. Fried continues to talk with him about the fact that, of course, he has to do the work in every class. She asks, "Do you know what eligibility means?" She talks quietly, firmly. He begins to seem concerned. She persists: "Joe, if you are serious about passing, you can begin today on some of the work you've missed." Rousing himself to slow action, Joe asks where he should start.

In contrast to the regular education environment, the self-contained special education classrooms often stood apart as separate programs, which labeled and discredited the kids there. Tony's mother recalled the stigma for her son when he had to go to "that little room upstairs with five others. You're just marked. It followed him all the way through. A marked person."

Sally, also from Oak Hill, agreed, "They used to be hidden. They didn't even eat in the lunchroom. I'd only see them when they'd use the bathrooms. We called the guys REBOs—retarded boys." With inclusion, not only are they seen, but many students do not even know who is a special education kid and who is not.

As students were included, so were the teachers—their isolation ended as well. Regular education teachers teach a wider range of students and coordinate instruction with the special education staff. Much of the success of inclusion in the five schools hinged on good relations between the special education staff and the regular education teachers. Each needed to feel the other was doing legitimate and conscientious work.

In some schools, doubts and misgivings were shared. The regular education faculty on one staff complained regularly that the special education faculty would not engage with them, that they set their own hours, that they did not share responsibility for grading papers and preparing lessons, that they assumed positions more like aides than full-time faculty. Not surprisingly, special education staff at times felt as if they were treated as clerks or aides because the regular education teachers were unwilling to change their central role or the curriculum in the classroom. Whenever collaboration based on mutual respect took hold, the odds of successful outreach to students increased.

Oak Hill linked special educators and classroom teachers without giving extra status to either group. Ms. North and Ms. Capraro explained why inclusion was working: "We developed our own model. The special ed staff go to math, science, and English. We do see a few students in the resource room, for projects or assignments they might need help with. Others we work with in their regular classrooms."

> As Ms. North's students disappear down the hall, she takes advantage of her planning period to run downstairs to catch Ms. Capraro, who is providing in-class help to some of her special education students. Ms. Capraro is at her desk reviewing the week's assignments with several students. Behind her on the blackboard is a list of all the work that students have due in various classes. The short story assignment for Ms. North's sophomore English class is right at the top. The list reminds students of their deadlines and of the assignment requirements.

Ms. North has brought the assignment sheets for the upcoming Holocaust unit and goes over the requirements with Ms. Capraro. Several books on the list are appropriate for kids who have trouble reading. Ms. Capraro reviews the information, asks several questions, and says that she is looking forward to doing some of the reading and watching some of the movies. The two teachers work easily together and chat about students, until several students remind Ms. Capraro that she has to go to math class with them.

Ms. North acknowledged the difficulty they had faced initially: "Teachers are responding in various ways. Some are very frustrated that their program slowed now that they have to work at a different pace. And special ed kids sometimes have a slew of personal upheavals to contend with. They can't seem to separate school from family life, so some teachers became their mothers, social workers, guidance counselors, friends . . . and teachers." Fortunately, inclusion was phased in over three years, beginning initially with teachers who volunteered to have special education faculty work with them. The faculty understood that eventually it would include everyone. Teachers hoped for more training and in its absence worried about dumbing down their curriculum, but the constant advice and support of the special education teachers gave them the sense that inclusion would mean extra help and individual attention, not relegating the slowest kids to second-class work or retracking within a supposedly untracked class.

The diplomatic outreach to the regular education teachers required persistent, tactful caring from the special education staff, but it ultimately enhanced the ability of teachers to extend both caring and high expectations to their students.

The Regular Classroom

Because the bulk of the school day is not devoted to special education services or advisories, the place where caring most often links with academic challenge is the regular classroom. The Ms. Murrays of the world carry the burden for coupling caring and expectations. But they do not carry the burden alone. Students also have responsibility to respond to teachers' combined efforts to expect much and to care.

Students in the five schools had little quarrel with the caring extended to them; it was the high expectations that they often ignored, resisted, or misunderstood. Many students began high school with the notion that learning means sitting still, working alone, memorizing, and recalling facts. That is a pervasive view of education, which millions of freshmen hold even if they have done some group work or finished a few comprehensive projects before entering high school. They think: teaching is telling, learning is listening, knowledge is in the textbook, the desks are in neat rows. They want learning to be fun, yet feel that it cannot be real learning if it is very much fun. That, they think, is middle school stuff.

When high expectations go beyond the familiar you-know-it-or-you-don't format of objective tests, many students think that is unfair. After their state revamped its annual testing to include a dozen essays (open-ended response questions) along with 148 multiple-choice items (which counted for less than the essays), the teachers at Lincoln used sample essay questions in their classes before the exams, coaching kids to write detailed answers. Lincoln paid $7,000 of its own so all students, not just the seniors, could take the tests. Practice and familiarity would build motivation and competence, the staff hoped.

Although most kids took the week-long, ten-hour test seriously, the novelty of the open-ended questions surprised many students. The unfamiliar topics in the questions puzzled some kids accustomed to test items closely matching what they had covered in class. Questions about the orbits of two planets and the number of blocks in a pyramid startled one bright junior girl, "That's stuff I'd never seen. How am I supposed to do good when I've never had it?" A senior felt disadvantaged on an item about New York City in the nineteenth century because he had taken social studies a full year earlier, as a junior. One girl froze when she saw a math problem about a robot. "Oh my gosh, what's that?" she thought. For those problems, the students tended to see material that reformers call real life and authentic problems as remote, strange, and unfair puzzles. To the students, these new open-ended questions sometimes seemed as contrived as the old multiple-choice, true-false exams that reformers deplore as artificial.

Some parents helped their children shape new notions of what a school should do. Several loved a science project at Lincoln that required building a container to protect an egg to be dropped from thirty feet. Even the mom whose best pillow was ripped apart to make a better cushion appreciated the project because her daughter got so excited. Sean's mother was thrilled when Sean one day announced in the car that he could calculate in his head the height of the trees along the roadside. "When I went here," she recalled, "the classes were like, copy the answers from the book. Now, they let them use their minds, their imagination. He doesn't just sit there, bored."

But many students said their parents had less adventuresome notions of schooling. Alicia's mother wasted no words: "Show up and shut up. Do the work and follow directions." Often parents' goals were expressed as the *absence* of mischief: stay out of trouble, don't cut class, no phone calls home from unhappy teachers, rather than the *presence* of particular habits of mind or intellectual curiosity. The point, as these parents saw it, was to reduce, not heighten, complexity and uncertainty.

Another major reason why many students shrug aside high expectations is the lack of incentives to work harder. When the rewards and payoffs are inconsequential, student effort lags. The open-ended state tests at Lincoln are a case in point. Ms. Norton, one of the proctors overseeing the test, said, "They took them in April. Had no impact on their grades. By then, they knew they'd graduate, they had their credits, many had been accepted to college, had their scholarships, so why bother?" She urged students to write something, to at least try the open-ended questions, but many "just gave a lick and a promise."

Some took back their booklets at her request and wrote one sentence in each blank space but grumped, "I did 130 multiple-choice questions, so what's the big deal?" As one senior said, "I got tired of filling in circles. It didn't mean nothing to my grades. I just went tch, tch, tch, tch [making pencil checks rapidly]."

Many teachers hope that problems drawn from everyday life will be a sufficient incentive for students to work hard. Sometimes the real-world example prompts genuine effort but still comes across as schoolwork because it is not sufficiently connected to students' interests and experiences. Mr. Gordon had his science class check the thermal resistance of a plate. As he explained it, "I said, okay, you're going to add to your basement, and you need to know the resistance of the materials you'll use. They hear that, but what they think is, 'Man, that's ten years away. I'm in tenth grade and it's time to play.' They do the lab and earn the points, but I'm not sure they take it out of here. When they leave, they're thinking about basketball or hanging out with their friends. It's like school stays in the classroom."

Though Mr. Gordon tried to find a practical hook for his students, it was still too distant a concern. When the incentives were more tangible, more immediate, students were more likely to accept high expectations. Within its Public Safety program, Lincoln students preferred the law enforcement area, in large part because there were paid internships with the city's police department. As part of the internship, students rode with officers for eight hours a week and wore uniforms, which, one boy said, "catches a lot of attention and respect" from other students. Juniors and seniors could also earn credits through a local community college's courses. The program not only "feels like a real job," as one kid put it, but the building was cleaner than the main campus, the bells not as jarring, and there was less smoke in the bathrooms. As there are rewards for good work, so too are there consequences for poor work or bad behavior: "We know if we mess up, we're out. Most of us want to stay back here." The incentives were unmistakable, and the work expected—a departure from fact-finding in textbooks—made good sense.

Mr. Thornton's class illustrates the effective pairing of caring and high expectations:

Being very precise, Mr. Thornton explains, "When you go back and get your power amplifier, double-check the IC [integrated circuit] orientation. Be sure pin one is where it's supposed to be. Make sure you don't have any of the capacitors backwards, or we'll have a premature Fourth of July. And take an ohm meter to verify that you don't have a zero ohm condition, a short. Now once you get the power amplifiers that work, I don't want to have them smoking! So be sure you double-check your work when you set it up.

"Some of the tables in the back have been pushed together. Please move them apart. And be careful with the table with the ferric chloride solution. I don't want that spilled on the floor! If you need a soldering kit, take one of these, but bring it back."

When Mr. Thornton finishes his instructions, the kids get their projects and gather at their tables. Sean is at the ferric chloride solution, etching his plate. As he works, he explains how he covers the circuit board, a slab of plastic, with a thin copper layer on top: "I'll cover what I want to keep with an acetate stencil and put the board into the ferric chloride. The solution eats away all the copper that's not covered by acetate, leaving paths for the current to flow to different parts. Once I have that, I'll drill holes through to solder on electrical components like ICs, capacitors, and resistors."

When asked what part of the project he is working on, Sean explains, "The SAD [serial analog device] 1024. It runs the power through this, and then it goes through the buffer. And this hooks up to the power amplifier. You can take a Walkman and plug it in, and it'll boost up to about twenty-five watts."

Sean was a student who clearly had benefited from the real-world approach taken by Mr. Thornton. Sean had his own business cards. He and two friends installed car stereos, and they bought the components for their customers as well as installing them. His current project at home was taking apart the back seat of his own car to rig up new speakers. When he played the system, the seat would rise several feet to unleash stereo powerful enough to rattle windows a block away.

He not only had an incentive to apply what he knew, he also saw the payoff for going beyond memorization of isolated facts to see relationships: "The SAD part of the project won't work without the buffer. The buffer can't work without the SAD. The power amplifier can work by itself, but it won't be as good or sound right." And looking ahead, a significant incentive was the offer from a local two-year electronics program to grant up to thirty credit hours—$3,750 of the $18,000 tuition—to Lincoln graduates as skilled in electronics as Sean.

He regretted the one time he had risked all this by bringing a pornographic Christmas card to class, passing it around, and leaving it on Mr. Thornton's desk, wrongly thinking his teacher's caring and friendliness guaranteed shared hilarity over a racy picture of Santa Claus on top of Prancer. When Mr. Thornton said he would not return the card, Sean took the pencils off Mr. Thornton's desk and said they would not be returned until he got his card back, at which point he was sent off to the assistant principal's office. Sean wrote an apology the next day and returned the pencils. The card went in the trash.

Mr. Thornton compared his students to unmined ore, an upbeat image that reaffirmed the worth of what they brought with them to his class. He built on their interests, particularly in music and cars. He talked with pride of his students: "Sean and those guys know what a power amplifier is, and they know what mixers are. When we talked about filters, they plotted the responses on one of these dB [decibel] meters I brought in. Then they'd say, 'Wow, I saw the same figure when I was out shopping for a speaker cabinet! It was right there on the label inside the speaker.'"

His emphasis on doing enhanced rather than diminished academic subjects. He took pains to point out the mathematics needed for problem solving in electronics: "Sitting here, they go through an integrated circuit spec and performance manual and read voltage and megahertz and tell me how much time delay they get, or they can look at a speaker box and check out the wattage. They use algebra in their heads when they do that. I tell them, 'This speaker will dump out forty-five volts peak, and you have a hundred-watt speaker rated for peak. What's the peak current you can throw through that speaker?' With problems like that, they actually like the math."

Some students wondered if they could rise to his expectations. A project that involved designing a dragster on the computer and then building it scared some of his classes. Tyesha would shake her head and mutter, "I'll never be able to build this thing, never, never." Mr. Thornton had the students work in pairs, rotating through eight separate workstations. First, they watched two introductory videotapes, the one for the instructor as well as the student tape, because only the former explained the principles underlying the magnet levitation track. Later, each pair made its own short videotape to explain to classmates the tasks at their workstation. After the computer-assisted design work, the students built the miniature cars and tested them on a track inside the classroom. Bill, a blind student, made his with the help of his adult aide and his student partner, who taped sections of the car so Bill would know where to cut, carve, and paint. And Tyesha finished her car. "When she did, she was so proud," Mr. Thornton recalled, "we needed a shoehorn to get her head through the door."

Beyond Structures

As we looked up and down the halls of these schools, we realized that we had learned about the real connection between caring and expectations from the teachers and the students who congregated daily to work together. As the faculty attempted to link caring and high expectations, we became convinced about the gains for kids when an intentional connection between the two took hold. Alicia no longer disparaged herself as "math retarded" after a year with Ms. Murray. Sean developed a passion for electronics as his self-confidence grew. At Tony's exhibition, there was not a dry eye in the house when he finished his sterling presentation on weather forecasting. And there had been an eerie moment of silence after he left the room when his parents and teachers understood that his potential would likely have been severely limited if the school had not expected much from him and cared for him while expecting it.

Still, despite such successes, there were the teachers who cared enormously but whose expectations were too low. Too often, these teachers did not interact with students in important ways, nor did they require rigorous work, and they accepted minimal effort from students. In some cases, their expectations reflected old beliefs. In other cases, it was because they were trying new strategies in which they had invested too much confidence and not enough critical assessment. Then there were the teachers who prided themselves on having very high expectations and, in doing so, served only the top students—those who generally had the greatest access to advantages. These were the teachers who had grown up in an era of tracking, who had come to believe that the best teachers taught only the best kids. To them, this different approach—today's teaching—seemed too limiting, too ignoble.

To see benefits for students, the connection between caring and expectations requires more than new structures. Structures, like advisories, do not ensure in and of themselves that students will be both better cared for and more pushed to achieve. Our schools seemed to invest heavily in structures, but without regular assessment and adjustment of those programs, it was difficult to realize the full benefit of their potential. The link required that each structure be attended to with tough-minded thoughtfulness and serious, self-critical inquiry: Is the program getting what we want? What more needs to be done? How might we tweak this to get better results for our students? Teachers' beliefs about their students, how the students learn, and what the students' capacities are affect student accomplishment. No structure, such as an advisory program, is, in itself, powerful enough to overcome teachers' deep-held beliefs. It is all too easy to subvert the best-planned structures to reflect one's old habits, old beliefs. To move forward, schools like these will have to examine their beliefs in order to serve all their students well.

Chapter Four

Rigor and Innovation

Sergei, from Oak Hill, lived with his mother, as his father had passed away when he was quite young. He and his mother both believed that the school should be more engaging, more pertinent to the rest of his life and that it should expect a lot of him; they were both supportive of the changes and impatient that more should happen faster. He had, after all, only four years to give. Though he struggled in some aspects of school—math, science—he did well in others—music, English. Outside of school, he was a fantastic sailor, a sought-after race crew member. In this arena, he was confident, buoyant, energized. He was a tall string bean with long, dark hair and a thin, thoughtful face, fair with sharp angles and green eyes.

During the course of his high school years, as he grew taller and thinner, cut his hair, grew it again, decided to be a poet, gave that up, dated, stopped dating, hated school, then did not hate school, and became an excellent trumpeter, a number of changes took place in his school that affected him. The schedule changed so that he had longer class periods: "The new schedule is quite a radical departure from what we're used to. Some days, we have regular forty-minute classes. Other days, we have four classes that are an hour and twenty minutes. The days when we have double periods are tiring. The longer time really extends your attention span, and it is possible to lose your concentration. I really am enjoying the opportunities opening up in dance band. We play more music and really practice, not just run through two songs, which is about all you can do in forty minutes. Even though it is hard to play the trumpet for an hour, it makes me try harder and builds my strength."

By his junior year, the honors classes had opened to any students who wanted to take them, whereas previously, teachers selected the honors students. He had long wanted to try honors and felt more challenged in this class and pushed hard to get the most from it. In addition, the school added a community service component. He worked on a project related to solving the environmental issues facing the river on which he spent so much time in the summer.

When he was a junior, the school instituted a new graduation requirement, an independent project with a public presentation and defense. The faculty wanted to cure "senioritis," the dreaded lethargy and arrogance that overtakes most seniors after they have received their college acceptance letters. And they wanted to see how the kids would do in some kind of culminating activity requiring them to show what kind of skills and knowledge base they had built while in school. By his junior year, as he watched the seniors get ready for the new requirement, Sergei had already begun thinking about what he might do for his senior project: "I already have an idea of what I would like my project to be. My plan is to work in a yacht designer's office and learn some of the basics in design. Then after getting a feeling for that type of designing, I would like to design a thirty- to forty-foot boat on paper, then make a four- or five-foot scale model of it that actually floats. This is in the field I am interested in—sailboat racing, boat building."

His was the second class to experience this requirement, and the faculty had made significant changes in the structure of the final research project or internship to ensure that it was a rigorous culminating experience. They decided to start the kids earlier in thinking about their projects and so set up a series of planning meetings between kids and their mentors. They added a journal requirement so that there would be a record of the process, reduced the number of half days the kids would be excused from school, and increased the full-time release days so that kids would have adequate time to work on their projects or internships. With a parent committee, the staff developed a kind of training program for community members, students, and parents who would be scoring the exhibitions. On request from the first class, they added a returning graduate to the panel of judges for each student, and they added a junior student so that younger kids would know what to expect.

By October of his senior year, Sergei was discussing his project with the program coordinator, a full-time faculty member: "It seems ambitious to build a scale model and the sails and everything, but I'm eager to immerse myself in something that interests me and that has some practical use."

By November, he felt differently about the schedule but not about his senior project: "This schedule is getting to me. It is great to have longer classes in some subjects but not in others. I have tedious classes—economics, math, and physics—which seem to drag on forever and leave me wanting to sleep for twenty-four hours! I am still working on setting up my apprenticeship. I am meeting with my advisor and the program coordinator. It seems a long way off, but I am really excited about it."

By December, he was the victim of senior jitters: "I am very nervous about how next year will turn out, whether I will be accepted to the college of my choice, or if I will be really disappointed. Obligations at school—tests, quizzes, papers—seem to be piling up uncontrollably, just contributing to my uncomfortable feeling. I don't like it."

By the end of January and the end of the first semester, he experienced a new technique in math, his most problematic subject. Some of the faculty were beginning to think about how to build stepping-stone activities that would prepare kids for the senior exhibitions. The math faculty had been talking for a couple of years about how they might make math more interesting and engaging as they developed techniques that helped kids get abstract concepts down thoroughly. According to Sergei, "We have been doing some interesting work in math. We had to present an exhibition to the class. We were paired in groups and given a math problem to solve. We had two class periods to work on it, but it took other free time. We had to write out the steps we took to solve the problem and draw a graph of the solution on transparencies so that the rest of the class could see them. This was a good exercise because we really needed to know the material in order to answer the questions the teacher and the other students had." Sergei generally struggled with math, and this was a breakthrough for him.

By March, he had encountered some difficulties in organizing his final project but made necessary adjustments: "I have a fairly certain plan for my internship. I could not find a naval architect who would be able to help me as often as I will probably need. So I am going to work on a five- or six-foot boat at my house. I'll visit people who offered to help me for a day at a time. I think this will work out because I'll be able to be at home, have flexible hours. I know a local sail maker, who I am going to call, and I'm sure he'll help. For the final exhibition, I want to sail it around the park down by the river by remote control."

Finally, the time for his internship arrived. He had the last month of school free, worked mostly at home, and worked with occasional advice from a couple of local boat builders and several people at a local hobby shop. He learned from these mentors that he needed to do a smaller-scale model before doing the final scale model as that would provide the measurements needed and would show any problems. Sure enough, when he tackled this unanticipated step, the first smaller-scale model was too wide across the beam, which hampered the boat from turning as quickly as he had hoped. For racing, it would have been absolutely inappropriate.

On the day of his exhibition, he brought in his drawings and several transparencies to show the mathematical calculations, his first miniature model done in balsa wood, and the final five-foot model done in teak. The latter was draped for an official unveiling. The larger model had a mast but no sails and was in the midst of what he described as the interminable sanding process; but even in this unfinished state, it was beautiful, sleek, smooth. He was easy, full of his own new brand of lanky confidence, as his mother, the panel of judges, and a few friends and teachers assembled. He had gotten into the college of his choice and would be going into naval architecture. That helped.

During his exhibition, he talked about why he had wanted to do this task in particular, explaining that it had required him to take a number of skills learned in school and use them in a personal career interest. The model was to be of a racing boat, of a relatively new design. First, he showed drawings he had made using skills he had learned in technical drawing. Then he shared segments of his journal so that the audience could sense the movement of the work in progress. He explained, "The equations I am learning are fairly self-explanatory except for Froude's number. This number is the theoretical maximum speed of a boat without any helpful influence from the waves or surf. I have drawn up a side view of a *Trip 40*, a racing boat launched in 1990. There are only two hundred built so far. It has a really quick frame. That's what I want to build as a scaled-down model. I will elaborate and make final drawings."

He showed his smaller model and discussed what he had learned about the problems his larger boat would have had executing the kinds of turns it needed to make. Then he unveiled his final model. He was sheepish in noting that he had overestimated how much he could get done working more than full-time on this project. Still, though much remained to be done, he was genuinely proud of his accomplishment, and the audience was visibly impressed. The boat looked quick and big but elegant.

At the completion of his presentation, he stood for questions. His math teacher suggested to him that he had, in the past, struggled with math. How had he found working with equations in this circumstance? Sergei laughed in agreement at the accurate description of his math classroom performance but was serious when he answered: "Math in the abstract didn't mean anything to me. It was very frustrating to spend so much time on something that I never used in my regular life. Doing this, it was fun and I didn't struggle. It made sense to me. It was helpful. The unknowns were not unknowns. They were real problems."

A member of the review panel from the community asked him if he could explain in more detail why the width of the boat influenced its speed. First, he showed how the deck plan on the smaller boat had been wider and how he had modified it on the bigger boat.

He talked about the ever changing shape of America's Cup boats in recent years. The trim of the boat can cut winning seconds off the final time, and he cited several examples. He then showed his own calculations from the smaller model, illustrating the error he had made and the corrections.

Questions fly: "What did you learn about yourself as a learner? What did you learn about sailing that you didn't know?"

"How are boat models similar or different from other models?"

"Could you have used technology to help you with this, and if so, what kind and why didn't you use it?"

"Is this boat for a short race or a long race, and how might we tell from the design?"

"How did the school help you? What remains to be done, and do you plan to finish it?"

"What kind of sails are you most interested in and why?"

He answers each question with precision, demonstrating a legitimate depth of knowledge. Someone finally asks him to articulate the benefit of doing this. Sergei grins, as he says, "Well, I learned a lot about precision. I've had to sand and sand and sand. That's really important. In order for the boat to be seaworthy, it will take fifty coats of aerogloss white paint. You really have to be very precise. And I learned a lot about wood and its treatments."

Sergei becomes serious as he tells the assembled group, "I learned that I can teach myself things, that I can figure out who to ask when I get in a jam. I'm not a natural at school, though I am very interested in learning. In doing this, I learned to set my own schedule, to pursue my own questions. All along, I used stuff I learned in school. It helped me to see the value of a lot of stuff we did, which was good. And I developed something that I can take with me."

His sense of pride and accomplishment seem to build, as he tells those assembled, "I went to visit the college I am going to next year, which has a naval architecture school in it. I took my model. The head of the department was pretty impressed. He looked over the model with me, and we talked for a long time about the design. He said I'll be ahead of the others in my class with this kind of experience. This was tough to do, don't get me wrong. It took a lot more hours than I thought. But I got a lot of help, and everybody just assumed that I would turn out something that would be really good and I did."

Before Sergei left the room, his mother thanked the school officials for giving her son this opportunity. Then the two of them left so that the judges could rate his performance. Tommy, who had yet to do his own final exhibition, gasped, "I loved the raw facts. He had a ton of raw facts. And I loved the math he put into it. He *hates* math!"

A parent and community member said, "That was masterful . . . the breadth of knowledge . . . the confidence really came through."

The returning senior said, "The hours he put in are really obvious."

Another parent, head of a technical educational facility, commented, "He cared passionately about what he was doing. He made a lot of connections—between his reading, his research, and doing the model. He used mathematics and a number of the sciences and his tech ed experience. And we couldn't stump him with our questions. Not a bit."

Mr. Warren, his economics teacher, who had been a skeptic about the quality of the presentations the previous year and, as a result, about the whole senior project effort, said, "If he taught himself, he is a phenomenal teacher. The fact that he could go to a book and find what he needed to know is our ideal. What we granted was time, and the depth to which he extended himself was uplifting."

His mentor, who was not on the evaluation team but who was allowed to comment, said, "I have known him I don't know how long. Since he was nine maybe. I got him some yachting books, but he went way beyond what I got for him. My job was easy. We had some very legitimate disagreements, but he gave 155 percent. He built relationships with the people who could help him, even though nobody was willing to take him on full-time. He made it work. He's a very self-motivated young man." And the group set about the task of rating his performance.

Sergei got very good marks on his final project. He and his mom went home feeling on top of the world and believing that high school had been valuable to him, slowly building his skill, his knowledge base, and his confidence.

Tommy went home feeling pressured by the quality of his friend's preparation and overall effort, a list running in his head of the things he had to get ready before he was scheduled. Mr. Warren said to another of his skeptical friends, "I wish I could get kids to work that hard in economics. If the presentations this year match Sergei's, then this new requirement is worth it."

Sergei's work on his final project and the faculty's work to strengthen these new requirements from one year to the next illustrate one of the critical connections that reforming schools must make if they are to reinforce the relationship between their efforts to make school better and student accomplishment. The purpose of reform has always been to move students to higher levels of achievement. The current push is to get students to achieve at levels never demanded before—world class standards. In addition, we now want higher achievement for *all* kids, not just the best, or the brightest, or those who are socially advantaged.

Neither rigor nor innovation is new to schools. Many schools throughout the country have been demanding rigor and getting it for years—from *some* of their students. What is different now is that the goal is to get more from all students, rather than just those for whom school is the easiest. It is also true that schools have been innovating regularly—a new curriculum for the gifted kids, new texts to teach writing, new computer labs, and so forth. At times, schools have seemed to be enamored with change for its own sake. However, it is no longer enough just to change: it is necessary to change in order to achieve a higher degree of accomplishment. The changes made must manifest results in students' work. Thus, the connection between the two—rigor and innovation—has become much more important.

To get all students to higher levels of achievement, it is necessary to change long-held patterns and structures. When this begins to happen, school faculty find themselves grappling with rigor and innovation—both individually and in connection with each other. Innovations are the changes that they make in order to get more from their students. The concern for rigor asserts itself as schools begin to examine the changes they have made to see if they are indeed pushing kids to new levels of accomplishment. It is impossible to push all students to higher levels of achievement without changing some practices. It is equally impossible to achieve greater accomplishment without examining and refining the changes made with an eye toward heightened rigor.

As we watched Sergei, we saw how the Oak Hill faculty implemented a new graduation requirement—an innovation. However, the innovation, by itself, simply was not enough. Because they wanted to ensure that Sergei's and other students' work was rigorous, they established means by which to examine exhibitions—the assignment, the directions, the activities that the teachers conducted along the way that might ensure appropriate support—and made changes so that each year they moved a little closer to their goal. They put their concerns for innovation and rigor into dynamic interplay.

The following discussion defines rigor and innovation briefly and then illustrates three confounding dilemmas that challenged the five schools as they worked to put both in place at once.

Rigor: What Is It?

Students had their own definitions of rigor. Sean described rigorous learning experiences this way: "It's attempting to do something you've never done before, something that pushes you beyond yourself, beyond what you did last time. It's something that forces you to reach; it's something that doesn't come easily to you, like reading Faulkner, who has stylistic complexities that you have to reach for. It forces you to think, to draw on what you know but also on your own creativity."

Alicia took a different tack by talking about understanding and what it means to use information and skills gained, "If a teacher came up to you and said, 'Tell me everything that happened' that would be easy. If they said, 'Tell me everything that happened and why it happened,' then you have a challenge. You have to look at it differently, you have to go into more depth. You have to think on it more."

Rigorous work requires demonstrations of deep understanding. As Alicia put it, "You should be able to analyze stuff and draw conclusions based on what you read and what you see and be able to go somewhere with it, not just spit it back." Students echoed the definitions of teaching for understanding that are currently promoted by researchers and cognitive scientists. "In Coalition schools, we're supposed to learn to use our minds well," said Alicia. "The teachers and the principal want us to work harder, think harder about stuff."

Despite their clarifications, rigor is a tough word to define. In its original sense, rigor meant inflexibility, severity. Over the years, it has come to mean precision and exactness.[1] When determining what it was that, when coupled with innovation, pushed these schools' reform efforts into the realm of important gains for kids, we chose the word rigor because it has embedded in it attention to quality—precision, depth of understanding—and attention to disciplined learning—practice, rehearsal, correctness. Rigor means that teachers require more precise and exacting work from students, work that demonstrates thoughtfulness, attention to detail, planning, revision, and solid effort. Rigorous work goes beyond mere effort to reflect high-quality performance such as Sergei demonstrated in his exhibition. Rigorous work meets and exceeds high standards.

The distinction between rigor and high expectations is an important one, as much of the preceding chapter was concerned with expectations. Although rigor and high expectations are related facets of the quest for more intellectually competent students, these two attributes are different in important respects. High expectations are part of individual teachers' and whole schools' belief systems about student capacity and about how learning takes place. "I believe that Sergei can do a good independent project," said his teachers. Believing in kids oftentimes precedes actual accomplishment.

"I believe that kids, black or white, Jewish or Catholic, Irish or Iranian, are interested in and can tackle significant local dilemmas before they leave high school—setting up recycling efforts, working with city councils on local problems, building nature trails for schools, unraveling complicated local court cases—that sort of thing." This is another example of a teacher's belief that kids can achieve to a high level of competence. For years, schools have held differential expectations for students. The expectation was that honors-track kids could truly achieve but that other students, usually those from low socioeconomic circumstances and students of color, could not do serious academic work. In the study schools, every mission statement included the belief that all kids can, will, and must learn to use their minds well, indicating a new set of expectations for students.

That the Oak Hill faculty agreed that Sergei would do a top-quality exhibition before he left for college illustrated their expectations for him. That they designed and carried out the exhibitions illustrated their commitment to rigor—action beyond expectations. The faculty worked to assure rigor—top-quality work—as they put appropriate support structures and activities in place to help kids meet their expectations.

Rigor is built on high expectations, but it concerns itself with the means of bringing those expectations to life in the kids. The Oak Hill faculty were attending to rigor when they reviewed the first year of student exhibitions and made adjustments to the ways in which they supported the kids. A Coalition colleague calls these kinds of activities "tuning mechanisms," as in fine-tuning.[2] It is the fine-tuning of an innovation that increases the possibility of rigor and heightened student accomplishment. Faculty at Oak Hill were attending to rigor when the math teacher added a practice exhibition into her math curriculum six months before the kids would have to do their independent performance. Rigor is establishing a demanding task and then examining a sample of a student's work to ensure that the activity reaches the level of quality the teacher seeks.

It is also important to clarify the relationship between rigor and standards. When a faculty builds a rigorous requirement for students, they need to set the standards—the level of accomplishment they deem acceptable—to evaluate whether the kids reach the level of accomplishment that the faculty wants. The standard is equal to the crossbar in pole-vaulting. The bar reminds everyone of the agreed-upon level of accomplishment that students must reach. Rigor is the work, the practice, the steps that kids must go through in order to vault well beyond that crossbar. To achieve rigor, teachers have to make the standard explicit to everyone, students in particular. To get to that standard, faculty have to make what it is that students need to do explicit. In addition, they have to keep examining both student work and the steps that they, the faculty, have put in place to support kids in their work, so as to evaluate whether they are getting the rigorous quality they want.

Our observations of these schools have led us to conclude that in its own right, rigorous work should manifest three characteristics:

1. It moves students to accomplishments beyond current levels of achievement.

2. It requires concern for quality as well as effort.

3. It combines the need for content-based information and the intellectual skill it takes to explore this information.

In short, rigorous work helps teachers help students meet the expectations that good teachers have for them.

Innovation: What Is It?

Innovation defined broadly includes any change that is made with the hope that it will improve student learning. Such changes can address school or classroom structure, instruction, curriculum, or assessment. However, innovations, like rigor, are complicated. An innovation for one teacher may not be for another who has been using that particular technique for years. An innovation can affect an individual teacher, groups of individuals, or the whole school. An innovation often involves changes in all of the above aspects of schooling simultaneously. Further, all innovations have implementation considerations.[3]

At the same time, it is true that there are few real innovations in education; many of them are practices that have good historical precedents but have faded from current practice for a variety of reasons. The Socratic seminar, freshly common in the five schools, is a good example. These are seminars, run on the principles of education that Socrates and his students espoused: Teachers should foster curiosity, precision, and authorized opinion by organizing class sessions around some kind of text. In modern terms, texts would include a newspaper clipping, a book, a science experiment, a piece of art. Then the technique involves asking a series of provocative questions that lead students to thorough exploration of the topic without reducing it to simple right or wrong answers. Even though this was an innovation in these schools, the technique has been around for over two thousand years.

Because the five schools had been at the work of reform for some time, and because they were part of a network through which approaches and techniques were shared, many of the same innovations were in place across the schools (see Appendix C). All of them instituted some new form of governance. They all had advisory programs. They rearranged schedules to ensure longer blocks of time. They were interested in teaming and integration of curriculum. Many were in the midst of designing more performance-based graduation requirements.

Impediments to Connecting Innovation and Rigor

As all these structural changes were taking place, individual teachers or teams were attempting to promote more active student engagement in the classroom. The challenge for every faculty member was to ensure, as the students pointed out, that innovations moved beyond a new gimmick to a new practice that resulted in more rigorous performance. Three important and difficult impediments to connecting rigor and innovation became clear:

1. The schools looked to innovations as the means to get to heightened rigor.

2. Shared understandings about both rigor and innovation were the exception rather than the rule.

3. When schools selected innovations, they tended to adopt solutions from the contemporary pool of reform strategies rather than starting first with serious internal analysis.

Believing That Innovation Will Lead to Rigor

As indicated in previous chapters, the schools tended to lean toward one end of the connection dyad rather than considering both in dynamic interplay. A majority of our school faculties thought more about successful innovation than about the establishment of more rigorous standards of student accomplishment as the means by which they would improve public schooling. This was their primary focus, and more often than not, it was not linked to discussions about rigor.

Conversely, state departments, legislators, and presidential candidates concerned themselves with setting standards. They seemed to believe that if they established the ends, then schools would meet them, whereas the five schools were asking questions about innovations as a means by which to improve student performance: What should we do? How should we do it? Who is for it and who is against it? How might we get the rest of the faculty or the parents to buy in? How might we get these new ideas and strategies in place, and what form should they take?

There was an implied assumption that tradition—in the form of old practices and structures—was the bugaboo. To be sure, the focus on innovation caused a good deal of dissension among the ranks, as many teachers held some traditional practices dear—the favorite lecture, the best prescriptive lab, the yearly vocabulary contest. Still, when we asked them what they were doing to improve their schools and student accomplishment, they rattled off any number of innovative projects under way in their schools and almost never mentioned standard-setting activities.

Why did they focus more on innovation than on rigor? Two explanations seem plausible. The first is that school faculty perceive that for the last forty years, someone else has been setting the standards for rigorous accomplishment, that it is not a task that belongs to teachers. Theirs is to teach; others will determine to what end and how measured. For years, state departments of education, more recently governors and legislators, and colleges and professional organizations have looked to those in particular disciplines to supply standards. The National Council of Teachers of Mathematics and the National Council of Teachers of English, for example, have set the standards that students must meet in their fields. These are articulated to teachers in the form of state-mandated curricula, state-administered assessments, and norm-referenced standardized tests. Teachers and principals in the five schools were accustomed to the fact that standard-setting took place externally and that they were invited in as participants in token numbers only, as representatives of a so-called "educational workforce constituency." Whether teachers agreed with the external controls or not, those in schools concentrated on the *means* to get to rigor—the innovations (as they saw it).

However, that does not mean that the schools were uninterested in standards. Some of the schools did try to influence the standards they were asked to meet. One of the schools made a significant effort to challenge state testing standards and to engage faculty in a discussion of standards with representatives from the state department of education. Oak Hill all but eliminated the state exam by substituting its own teacher-generated exams that they considered to be more challenging and that would allow teachers to have a clearer understanding of students' grasp of the material. State department officials approved these exams. Lincoln objected to the state's plans to test twelfth graders. This resulted in a modification of the state's plans, both in the content of the test and in the administration of the exam for the whole state. Another school watched while the state defined new standards; then the school contributed staff who led efforts to develop the new authentic as-sessments that would be used to meet the standard. The other two schools watched what the state was doing but saw it as remote from their own work in reform. The schools were aware of what was going on, and they understood that they were provided opportunities to cooperate with the state's efforts. But for the most part, standard-setting was something they reacted to or accepted rather than initi-ated internally.

School communities were not uninterested in the debate about standards, the setting of them, or the need for them. There was fre-quent debate about standards. It was common to hear teachers express their belief that outsiders either underestimated or over-estimated student capacity. A number of educators ridiculed externally set standards as too remote, idealized, impossible to im-plement. Still, there were many teachers who believed that it was well and good that others determined what rigorous performance might mean. Most of the teachers believed that standardized tests were the preference of parents and community members at large. They had been conditioned to believe that these tests offered eas-ily understood information on how kids were doing in comparison to others around the country and in doing so, they provided the in-formation that parents, counselors, and universities cared about. Standardized tests determine program placement and college ad-missions, and it had been that way for so long, that although many teachers complained about the mismatch between the tests and their curriculum, many did not question the authority of the tests. A science teacher explained, "The test keeps us honest. We cover a little bit of everything, which has a positive side to it. We don't have too much depth in any one place, which may be the lesser of two evils. It is a hindrance to substantial experimentation though, because the test means that we have 180 days of curriculum to cover—jam-packed."

"I agree," said a colleague in a math department. "These tests set a standard that kids can use as a comparison with thousands of other kids. It works for public relations. The scores mean something. It is widely accepted in our state, and the test does cover the things you need to know if you want to go on in mathematics." They were satisfied that others took responsibility for determining final standards and that these scores were used in a variety of ways for accountability. Teacher responsibility was to determine what rigorous work meant in their daily interactions with kids and to determine the standards that achieved an A or an F so that they were responsible for determining rigor and quality only in the short-term, for daily work, and individual course work, but not for the overall performance of a child.

The second explanation for the focus on innovation is historical precedent. More experienced school faculty talked frequently about the innovations they had been through. Mr. Warren, for instance, started team teaching, joining two disciplines of study, during the sixties. They joked in the faculty room about the various changes that had come and gone. They would banter about which change came when and how they had responded.

Looking for and implementing a new innovation suggested momentum, that schools were staying current, that they were changing right along with the times. The fact that innovations were so common in their lives had contradictory effects. Many were interested in change and felt that it was a means by which they kept up, but nearly everyone was cynical because the constant changes seemed to have so little overall effect over time.

In retrospect, it may well be that many innovations did not come to fruition because adequate attention was not paid to rigor. In the study schools, when a school or a teacher neglected to link rigor to innovation, the innovation itself seemed to lack merit.

Alicia's usual bubble turned to grumbles as she considered whether several innovations that her teachers had organized were really eliciting valuable, rigorous work:

My teachers work really hard to come up with interesting projects
for us, and they all teach together because we have them for five

periods, and we have our own end of the hall. In the afternoon, it's like, we all go out to play a game or a sport together, teachers and kids, and that's PE [physical education]. Sometimes we play baseball, or we play volleyball, or sometimes people do different things. It's a better way to do it. And our math teacher tries to figure out where the math we need to know fits into the projects we're doing so that sometimes we even forget it's math.

Sometimes, though, it doesn't work so well. This year, one of my teachers was teaching us about art history. He says we're doing work just like real art historians. We look at slides of famous paintings and then mostly he talks about them. Sometimes somebody makes a comment. Anyway, I can't figure out why we're doing this, and it gets boring looking at one slide after another. I haven't asked too many questions because I don't want to interrupt him. I guess the pictures have to do with what we're studying in English and social studies, but how isn't clear to me.

In a senior humanities class, her observations proved accurate:

The teacher prefaces the examination of a number of modern art slides with these comments:"We are not going to test on these, but I wanted you to see them. What is the value of these?"

One student ventures, "So that we will know real art?"

The teacher refers students to a handout he has given them on different periods in modern art:"Don't take it out now, but the material on it will be on the test. Keep that in mind as we look at these slides. Be thinking of which art and artist you prefer. If you were buying, which would you purchase?"

Out go the lights, and he clicks through the slides:"Matisse. This is called *The Red Studio*. It's definitely red! Do you recall the late nineteenth-century artist? Keep in mind Van Gogh; we are jumping from him to this.

"Chagall. Look where we have come. Would we have guessed this? What's that in the background?

"Duchamps. One day I had this slide backwards and I didn't even know it.

"Gris. What do you think this one is called? It's called *Breakfast.*"

A student calls out,"It looks more like lunch!"

"Kandinsky. He died a poor man.

"Léger. What do you think? Could you do this? Maybe on the final we should try it. My wife isn't too crazy about modern art. She bought some oil colors, but she can't do too much yet."

Alicia offered more insight about how some of the teacher innovations affect her:

And another class has been bothering me. Last year, we had to teach a chapter in our science book to the other kids in the class. It was fun because we prepared it and then we taught it. Our teacher was there, and she asked us questions if we left anything out important, and she would make sure we understood the most important stuff. This year he doesn't say a thing. It's almost like we really don't have a teacher, like he feels like he doesn't have to work, and I can tell you that the kids are getting really hostile about this. It doesn't seem like it's helping us at all.

Often, teachers suggested that they were innovating to improve student performance, but closer scrutiny revealed that the innovation was fraught with problems, as in the humanities teacher's case. Surely, Alicia's teacher had limited exposure to the real work of art historians. He may have confused art historians with the professors who taught the art history course he took in college. The technique he put forward to students seemed reminiscent of a college-survey, art-history class in that he had students looking at slides of art by famous artists, often those responsible for having introduced a new form. His accompanying comments made it appear that, unlike a good college lecturer, he knew little about the paintings or the artists. The way he conducted the class asked little of students intellectually. This suggests that the teacher was not attentive enough to the quality of learning gained by his students.

The implications of the fact that schools see innovations as the means by which to improve schooling are threefold. First, it sets the schools up to be charged with making change for its own sake. Second, if innovation is the means by which to improve, schools can continue to innovate forever but without measurable accomplishments for students. This appeared to be an underlying assumption in the minds of some staff in all of the schools. Third, if staff do not know the ends for which they are aiming and always concentrate on the means, they tend to avoid determining whether the innovation is working.

Little Shared Understanding of Rigor and Innovation

The second impediment was that schools spent little time generating shared definitions of rigor or innovation, nor did they talk much about the rationale for either. Students discerned that teachers had different views about rigorous work:

"My chemistry teacher says that if he doesn't introduce us to all the terms and processes we need to know, we won't do well in college chemistry. He says that if we don't know everything we're supposed to know, that we will be weeded out of premed or other competitive fields. So we really cover the stuff. Sometimes we wonder what is more important—to cover the stuff or to get it," said Diego.

"In my school, different teachers define it in different ways. My health teacher says that to get good grades in her class, we have to come to class on time with everything we need—no forgetting a book, or she'll send us to detention," sighed Sally, as if this were excessively demanding. "But other teachers, like Mr. Renzler, want you to come to class having done the reading and all the homework, ready to think hard about it. He wants us to write interesting papers that show that we've really thought about what it all means. He has specific processes, too. First, we read the book or whatever, then we analyze it, then we talk about what it means, and then we write about it. That's pretty much it."

"That's not what we do in my class. My English teacher says that if we know the parts of speech and how to diagram sentences, we'll be much less likely to make mistakes. We spent nearly a whole year doing that."

"Yeah, my math teachers all seem to think that in order to get math what you have to do is watch him demonstrate a formula, then we practice it and do homework on it and then correct it and repeat that process until we've covered enough formulas to take a test."

Tommy thought his current math teacher had another idea about rigor: "In my math class, we just get one ditto after the next. My math teacher doesn't like the textbook, so he works up his own work sheets, and he gives us a million of them every day. If we get through all of them, we can pretty much get a good grade."

Sean concurred, "More often than not, I am more challenged by workload than by the quality of the ideas. Most of my classes would be challenging if they weren't so mundane. I get home late and spend more time thinking about prioritizing the load than thinking or doing things that require creativity."

"In our advisory, two of our teachers were talking about the fact that schools used to be good before kids were mouthy, or wore hats in class and were allowed to show their belly buttons at school. They said that they thought grades would go up and schools would be better places if the rules were just stricter and if there were consequences for parents if their kids skipped school. One of them said that we should force parents to spend a day at school with their kid when a rule is broken. We told them 'No way! Parents don't have time to come and hang out in school!'" Hakim seemed amazed at how out of it some teachers were.

Tommy shared what he believed was a good example of rigor (which was also innovative) from his science class: "In ninth grade, we did this moon-tracking activity. It was the first time I can remember in school doing something that wasn't in the textbook, that was real, like we were real scientists or something. We had to keep data sheets, measure the time and the angle of the moonrise every day for a month. It drove my mom nuts because sometimes we'd be eating dinner, and I'd look at my watch and race out the door! We had to measure the river near us to see how it was affected by the moon. I spent a lot of time outside while I was doing that, and I went down to the river more than I have in my whole life, I think. Then we had to do the calculations, that was another step, and we had to chart our findings. The test was to analyze your findings and tell what they meant about the relationship of the tides and the moon. It was hard, and you had to know what you were talking about or you didn't get credit for it. I don't know. I felt that I did something real, and I could see the benefit of it. It was wild. Then we went back to the textbook to study the stratosphere and stuff. I wished we could have studied it in the same way, but I guess that would be pretty impossible since it's so high up and invisible and everything."

Students suggested that, in essence, individual teachers generated their own understanding about rigor, and it was different from one teacher to the next. The range of definitions suggested that rigor consists of

- Curriculum coverage
- Better behavior
- Work sheet skill and drill
- Subject-specific process
- Serious student engagement

Without a common definition of rigor, most teachers in a school were moving toward different targets. Kids were accustomed to figuring out what it meant in each class, each term, every time they shifted to a new teacher.

Similarly, the kids clued into the various attitudes, beliefs, and definitions that teachers held about innovations. Oftentimes, because teachers had so little time to talk to one another, or because they were uncomfortable raising their views with other adults, they talked to their students.

Sergei shared an observation that other students frequently corroborated: "My history teacher must have just come home from another workshop. We can always tell because she immediately gets us busy trying something new. This time, we're trying a new kind of discussion technique she called Socratic seminar. She must have learned about it at one of the meetings she is always going to. She thinks we really have to try a lot of new approaches in order to find one that works for us because all of us learn differently."

In contrast, Tommy said, "In our school, teachers don't agree about whether we need to do new things or not. One teacher says he doesn't bother because whatever change they want him to do will be gone as soon as we get a new principal or a new governor. He says he's seen all kinds of them come and go. Then I have another teacher who says that he is only doing this one activity because he's supposed to, but he's not sure that it's going to help us any. He says all this 'get into groups' stuff is for kindergarten and doesn't belong in high schools. He says he is not going to baby us because somebody has to help us get into college."

"My team of teachers is always trying something new," said Alicia. "They like experimenting, so they build new activities all the time. I've been with them a long time, and they hardly ever approach something the same way twice. Mostly, they build big projects like Summer Fair Days, where we designed a county fair, cooked food, set up stalls, calculated the expenses and the income, figured out what we'd spend the proceeds on. It was a lot of fun and not hard at all."

"My teacher says he is already doing everything that the Coalition says he should be doing and that he has been for a long time. He says there is nothing new in education anyway. That doesn't seem right to me because they are always learning new things in other fields, so it seems to me like they should be learning new things about education," said Diego.

Tommy thought his English and social studies teachers worked hard to change but found it difficult: "My English teacher works with my social studies teacher. They are always trying something new, but they are always talking to each other trying to figure out how to do it right or better. They say they are learning about teaching all the time, just like we are learning about English and social studies all the time. They must like it, because they sure work at it."

Diego and Hakim made similar observations about the English-social studies teams in their school.

The range of attitudes and beliefs about innovation demonstrated that teachers did not share a common understanding about the need for innovation or about the benefits of it. If the students' perceptions were accurate, and classroom observations suggested that they were, teachers' beliefs about innovations ranged across the following:

- Temporary and impermanent
- Likely to decrease rigor
- Always better than what they had been doing before
- Old hat
- Necessary but hard to get right
- Like new fashions—ever changing

Why teachers do not build shared understandings is important to understand. Few of these schools had scheduled substantial and regular common planning time for the faculty to grapple with schoolwide issues in order to build common understandings and definitions. Although several of the schools had common planning time for teams of teachers interested in building a shared curriculum, faculty meetings were the only forum in which they could tackle substantial issues, and the length of time—anywhere from forty-five minutes to an hour and a half—was inadequate. Issues like rigor and innovation raised enormously emotional responses based on teachers' beliefs about who can and cannot learn. Without adequate time, the opportunity to have substantial discussions that did more than raise people's ire was rare. Without adequate time, teachers left these meetings feeling that there were really just two camps—those for and those against. This oversimplified the issues by leading teachers to believe that the real issue was a Hamlet-like quandary: To change or not to change? In reality, the considerations involved were always more complicated.

Another problem, the age-old autonomous culture that pervades most of the schools, is a long-standing tradition.[4] Even though more and more teachers were looking for ways to collaborate by joining teams that either shared common groups of kids or that wanted to integrate curriculum, the majority of teachers still worked alone. (The Overland Charter, a mini-school at Marshall, was an exception in this regard. The teachers in this school identified with their fellow charter members as their primary colleagues, rather than with the teachers in their departments.) Although discipline-centered departments were common, shared professional cultures within departments were uncommon. Individual concerns overshadowed collective goals.[5] Most teachers held sole responsibility for setting the standards that existed in their own classrooms. To talk with others about what constituted a good math activity or a good solution to a problem was unfamiliar, ever the province of individual discretion. Seldom did teachers teach the same curriculum as their colleagues. Seldom did they compare tests. Even more seldom did they ask one another's opinion about the quality of a student's work.[6] Nor did they talk to one another about what constitutes quality teaching. When they did do these things, however, the gains were striking.

Most faculty resisted the notion that they should come to shared understandings about what constituted rigorous work. This seemed inconsistent because part of the faculty in each school railed among friends about whether the innovations the school was implementing were resulting in the hoped-for gains in student performance. Those attempting new innovations complained in equal measure against those who were skeptical about the need for change. To entertain discussions about mutually shared definitions of rigor might have clarified matters for both groups, but instead, the suggestion led both groups to suspicions that the principal or the change-advocate group in the school had a subversive agenda, a one right way, an orthodoxy that some teachers did not believe existed. (In Chapter Five, this tension is discussed more fully.) As a whole, teachers generally subscribed to the notion that differences between teachers were part of students' training about the world. "Seldom, in any job, do all the bosses want the same thing or value just one standard of work," they would say to one another, in agreement that common standards were not a necessary component of high-quality schooling.

These norms of individual responsibility for determining rigor and standards were incredibly strong. At the same time, individual teachers selected the innovations of their choice and were hesitant about asking others what they thought, what they might recommend. Many believed that teaching was simply too complex, that advocating a certain approach was overly simplistic and dangerous in that it could suggest a single right way to do things. One thirty-year veteran expressed it this way: "There is no bottom line in this teaching business as far as I can tell, and I've been at it a long time. Teaching is an extraordinarily complicated business. An awful lot of things work for different people. We all have memories of extremely exciting teachers. And intellectual engagements that were incredibly meaningful. And I'm not sure that I find it terribly easy to find the common denominator between all of those things. Frankly, I just find that it's more mysterious than that."

The implications of not having common understandings about rigor and innovation were far-reaching. First, faculty did not have a common goal or standard—no crossbar in the pole vault. It meant that faculty had little means to gauge whether the innovations they were implementing elicited collectively agreed-upon rigorous work. It seemed both contradictory and confounding that they chose to work on innovations to improve schools and that these innovations were also the subject of a good deal of controversy in each of the schools precisely because there was no mutual, ongoing effort to develop a shared understanding of rigorous performance.

It also meant that understanding about what constituted rigorous work was a moving target for students. Students confirmed year after year that there was little common agreement about what rigor is and how it is demonstrated. "I don't know," said Diego. "It's pretty much up to the teacher. They tell us what they expect, and we either do it or we don't. One teacher can be really hard, expecting typewritten papers and good, rigorous work, while another just gives work sheets, and if you do them, you get credit." Each semester, as students moved to new classes, they had to learn about new criteria for grading, new standards of rigor. Each teacher set these individually and the variation even within disciplines required students' serious attention. Although good students pay attention to these differences, indifferent students tend to ignore them and then suffer the consequences.

Finally, that there is no common definition of either rigor or innovation *within* schools makes it difficult to determine what it is *among* schools. Had we surveyed a broad sample of schools, all of the schools in this study would have been described as highly innovative. Frequently, their descriptions of the innovations in place were more romantic than the reality. At the same time, without any common definitions, all of us are less certain about which strategies promote gains for students in diverse settings.

Building shared understandings is extremely difficult. Shared understandings are dependent on time and school size, and unfortunately, the larger the group, the harder it is to provide adequate time to discuss complicated issues thoroughly.

Lack of Sufficient Internal Analysis

When the schools selected innovations, they tended to adopt solutions from the contemporary pool of reform strategies rather than starting first with serious internal analysis.

To determine which innovation they would choose to work on, faculty visited other schools, brought ideas back from conferences, listened to suggestions from principals, ascertained current trends from journals and magazines, or took workshops that suggested particular innovations. Though all of these were good sources of inspiration, none was sufficient by itself. Seldom did faculty engage in an examination of their own practices to determine what needed to be changed. The lack of prior examination or the failure to make such an examination returned as an impediment again and again when faculty found the innovation more difficult or more disruptive than they originally had imagined. Without adequate internal rationale for change, it was easy to condemn the effort as poorly conceived or naive or too problematic when the wider implications of the change became apparent.

For instance, joining forces by teaming teachers of different disciplines to teach a common group of kids or to redesign courses that included more than one subject (like humanities) is an innovation that some teachers in all of the schools chose as a means to improve practice. In no case did teachers indicate that they spent significant time determining the need for teaming within the existing system or thinking through the implications for other dimensions of the institution. Rather, they felt it a good idea, one that others in educational reform were valuing and so tried it themselves. They were not clear about why they would be engaged in teaming. Teachers believed that teaming would reduce the isolation in which they worked, help them understand their students better as they could see the kids from the perspective of other teachers, and perhaps build better curricular connections for students. But they had not engaged in scrutiny of their own teaching circumstances to determine the larger implications of moving to teams.

Simply creating several teams did not necessarily mean that teachers actually worked together. As one teacher pointed out:

> We tell everyone that English and social studies are teamed. I would love to do some team teaching . . . between English and social studies, if you really figured that one out and went for it. I think that's interesting. I think that the pedagogy would fall in place in some sense as you tried to think about making this as engaging as you possibly could. But that's the real trouble. You see, you get to the junior and senior year, and there are four of us in the humanities. The two English teachers have essentially said they'll have no part of it because it can't be done and it's not worthwhile and this whole thing is nonsense and they didn't buy into it, and so why should they have to do it. And we have no time, so our team is not really a team.

Sometimes teams who did work together concentrated on sharing information about kids but did not go so far as to share strategies for curriculum, pedagogy, and assessment. In this case, even though kids benefited from teachers' shared information about them, the kids did not necessarily have different educational experiences in their classes.

Even when teams did work well, other complexities arose. Teams of teachers developed into new, but separate, units within the school and as such began to function as political units within the larger school. They negotiated for collaborative planning time, slices of the budget, and new conditions for selecting resources, further complicating and stretching ever insufficient resources. In addition, they often divided the school. Because teams of teachers could easily be identified with change, they were often perceived as the change groupies in the school. Those not on teams often believed that the change advocates were critical of their long-held practices. It was also apparent that when the change advocates were not perceived to be the strongest teachers in the organization, teaming was panned as a strategy for lazy or weak teachers. "Them that can't, team," suggested the critics. Another complication of teaming occurred when those uninterested in working collaboratively called for scrutiny of the new practices, claiming that at the very least, no harm should be done to the kids. The inconsistent part of this was that neither they nor their colleagues under attack hardly ever suggested that all approaches, including the more traditional, be examined. This further illustrates how seldom faculties engaged in collective reflective practice.

Adopting new trends without establishing the conditions that warrant improvement within the local context jeopardized the change effort. The innovation was too open to interpretation, too loosely defined, not centrally located in the school's agenda. When school faculty clearly understood the need for an innovation (not as suggested by research or by neighboring school districts but in terms of their own specific context), clarity of purpose was greater as was commitment to solving implementation problems. Any innovation is more likely to be rigorous if it solves a problem that is defined in the local context; understanding the problem thoroughly helps people define the parameters of the innovation and helps them shape the means by which they will assess its success.

Alicia, Sean, and other students pointed out repeatedly that innovations themselves provided no guarantee that increased student skill and competence would result. The fact is that the faculty adopted the innovations without a clearly defined problem context, which suggests that they were adopting mechanisms for change without attending sufficiently to the underlying beliefs and attitudes that are so central to deep-seated change.

Again, there were implications. Without a thorough rationale based in the needs of their particular student population, the faculty leaned more toward defensive support of changes made than to thoughtful critical analysis. For example, in all of the schools, teachers who were teaming defended their strategy in the face of the questions from faculty who were more reticent. Seldom, however, did they examine the nature of their teaming relationships or attempt to track the effects of their teaming on student performance. Too often, faculty used the language of sales: "We need to sell teaming to the rest of the school." Selling suggests promotion, not self-criticism or analysis. In the interest of getting other teachers involved, the change group too often left their innovations unchecked. Although sales obviously plays an important part in American life, its appropriateness as a metaphor for school change is questionable.

A further difficulty was that innovations in some cases became teachers' most persistent practice. Because change is highly valued in those who advocate for school reform, a number of teachers developed the habit of innovating all the time. In classrooms each year, fall and spring, teachers tried something new. Though these teachers were highly enthusiastic about whatever it was they were trying, students like Alicia pointed out that there were always bugs in every lesson, bugs that could have been ironed out if the teachers had tried it again. Yet, these teachers were more interested in trying new things than in refining them.

Consider the following example about a physics teacher's experiment with innovation. This particular teacher was not a regular innovator, but his experience shows how important it is that teachers refine innovative practices by trying them again and again.

Mr. Dobbs kept a journal for two years. Early on, he had decided that he needed to do something to reflect his beliefs about change in the classroom. Previously, he had served on a number of committees and had been very active in supporting structural changes but had not done much in regard to his own teaching. As a science teacher, he may well have believed that his classroom was more hands-on and engaging than most, although the regular classroom routine was that students watched him demonstrate a set of steps that produced a predefined reaction during labs. (Admittedly, kids found labs a welcome break from seat work, but they were more excited by work that actually required them to behave like scientists than following the steps to a scientist's predetermined ends.) Slowly, as he sat on more committees and learned more about change, it occurred to him that reform might mean more in his own classroom. Like many teachers, his own understanding about possibilities in teaching was limited by his own experiences as a student and as a teacher who saw few others teach.

Mr. Dobbs had heard about an innovative approach from a science curriculum that is receiving some play in reforming schools. He and a colleague in tech ed decided that they would teach the concepts of kinetic energy and momentum by having the students build models. In both classrooms, prior work had been done to define these concepts and demonstrate them. The activity was designed to allow students to grasp the interplay between the two concepts and to gain firsthand experience about how the principles of kinetic energy and momentum play out.

The following journal entries chronicle Mr. Dobbs's experience with the new approach. Afterwards, Tony, a special education student (discussed in Chapter Two), reflects on the activity as do the principal and Tony's mother. Their perspectives add interesting insights about the nature of innovations. Their perspectives also illustrate the impact that innovations ultimately can have on kids, as seen through the eyes of an administrator, a parent, and a kid.

From a Physics Teacher's Journal

Two weeks ago, Sam Weiss and I decided to try having my applied physics class and one of his technology classes do a project that I encountered from the Star Schools' curriculum. The goal was to design any apparatus out of paper, white glue, and masking tape, which would allow a marble to roll down it. The marble could not get stuck and stop before reaching the table level. The object was to design the apparatus which would take the longest time for the marble to reach the end. I introduced the project. I created random groups of four students each. I gave them the bulk of the first day to plan and brainstorm. We used class time for eight days to construct the things. I intended to use only four days, but they were nowhere near done. The deadline was today. We were going to have the great roll-off.

I have to comment here. It is obvious that our present educational program is not preparing students to tackle a problem like this. I was inspired to try this as an "ill-defined problem" like we heard about at a conference I attended. Well, my class just floundered. I was trying real hard not to make suggestions on how to do the project. After two days it was obvious that they had no idea what they were doing. Nobody assumed leadership. Some worked hard at rolling paper (for supports, they told me). Others watched their teammates roll paper. I tried to get them to draw me a picture of what they were going to construct. No idea. But they kept rolling paper.

In the middle of this the principal was doing his obligatory observations. Well, in my enthusiasm, I told him about the project and suggested that he might want to see it. He did. He came in and saw students rolling paper. Then, today, he came in for the exhibition. What a disaster.

One group from my class and two from Mr. Weiss's met the requirement of keeping the marble rolling. So I tried to salvage the catastrophe by saying that anyone whose project failed had to redo it and that it had to beat the longest time of the day, which was twenty-two seconds. It sounded reasonable to me. Then one of the students blew up. Said he was *not* going to do it. It was unfair. He was going to cut class and did. I don't know how the principal took it but it was the worst class that I have ever had. Boy, if I was not convinced that we need to do something different in science than we have been doing, I would retreat to the security of what I know that I do well, whether it was working for students or not.

So what have I learned? The students used up four years of masking tape in two weeks. Next time, limit the materials. With unlimited materials, they could waste as much as they wanted. Next time they will have to be forced to plan. I would require that they submit an acceptable plan—drawing before starting to build. I would make them assign roles and responsibilities to all members of the group. I would also make the actual building of the apparatus an all-day, in-house field trip. Trying to do it in forty-minute blocks of time is wasteful. You lose momentum and have to reignite the initial excitement over the project every day.

Eight days later:

I set the date for the project roll-off for two weeks from today. I spent today processing what I saw happening with the project. One student was a big help. He had the only project that worked before the vacation. Over the vacation he built a bigger and better project for extra credit. He volunteered that in class. It makes the project seem workable to those who still have to do it. The kid who walked out earlier even showed up for class today, so maybe he'll do the project. Meanwhile we return to the study of heat. There are a lot of relatively straightforward experiments in this topic. The applied physics class usually enjoys this section.

Two weeks later:

We had the roll-off today. Projects came in. All but three students have now successfully completed the project. What a difference in attitude. They felt good about the whole thing. I videotaped it. Some of the projects showed good work. I am glad I was hard-nosed about making them persevere.

A Parent's Perspective

Our son, Brian, had to do this thing for Mr. Dobbs. He spent so much time on it. He had to create a maze only using paper and tape and a marble. It was supposed to run for twenty-two seconds. He tried and tried. It was supposed to be with a group, but he felt that his group wasn't doing anything so he decided to do it himself. It was interesting to see him approach it. He was doing it on a table in the basement. He was determined to get it, but the most he could get up to was thirteen seconds. Then his father got into it, and I went by and gave advice and then his brother came home and had a few recommendations. "Cutting the paper, your angles are too sharp. Put more in." "Add another piece here." "Reduce the slant." We thought, if it runs thirteen seconds this way, well, what if you turn it around and let it roll back up. He said he couldn't do that. Really it was all of us brainstorming and all of us using our minds well. Finally, he said it would just have to do. Twenty-two seconds is a long time when you're using paper and masking tape and a marble. We found that out!

Tony's Perspective

We made this weird contraption, kind of like a giant curve that went all around. It was an applied physics problem to learn about kinetic motion and momentum. It didn't work the first time we made it because it would only go to a certain point and then stop. So we redesigned it to zigzag toward the bottom. We made pillars to support the run by rolling big tubes of paper and wrapping them in tape to make them more sturdy. We taped these pillars to a piece of board. It was about a foot and a half tall. We rolled paper tubes and attached them together for the ball to roll through. At first, I didn't like physics because it wasn't about mechanics and motors, but now it is more interesting.

The Principal's Perspective

A lot of the teachers are experiencing some discomfort when they try new things that offer kids the opportunities to be constructivists—you know, construct their own knowledge. They are working on giving them more real problems to solve, like Mr. Dobbs and Mr. Weiss did in their physics experiment. Mr. Dobbs was upset on the day the kids were to present their projects because the projects didn't work as well as he would have liked. From my perspective, it was just a matter of building stronger structures, prompts, and benchmarks that will enable the kids to improve their performance. I was glad he kept at it. Some teachers just stop there and blame the kids. The next time he does it, he'll have more of these kinds of guides for students from teachers that lead to higher performance.

One of the problems here was that Mr. Dobbs backed clear away from intervening with the kids, a common response when teachers try something new. When teachers like Mr. Dobbs were trying to understand what it meant to get students to do the work, to take responsibility for experimenting themselves, there was confusion about how much support teachers should give. In much of his previous work, he had shown students what to do through demonstrations and by asking them to follow the exact steps he had taken in order to get predictable results. The objectives of this lesson were quite different: students should generate their own hypotheses and test them out. Discovering how he might be helpful to them without showing them what to do was problematic in that he did not know how much help was enough or too much. As a novice with this technique, he believed that no help was the only way. Had Mr. Dobbs and his colleague spent some time looking at the way they usually teach to be more cogent about the actual problem they were trying to solve, they may well have anticipated that allowing kids to generate their own hypotheses means that the teachers would have to help the kids be more analytical while they are working. They might have anticipated that as teachers, they needed to move from student group to student group to challenge the kids' approaches early on and to ask the kinds of questions that might have sent kids in more productive directions.

Fortunately for Mr. Dobbs, he got thoughtful and productive feedback from the principal—that he simply needed a few more benchmarks. This was useful and helped clarify his role for him. Had Mr. Dobbs not gotten the positive feedback from the principal, the likelihood was, by his own admission, that he would never have tried this innovation again. It simply seemed to him that it was too chaotic and left him feeling too insecure about what the students were gaining. When teachers only try innovations once, they do not have the opportunity to reassess and to strengthen the learning activity; in essence, they eliminate the link between rigor and innovation. Innovation without thoughtful analysis gives the illusion of serious participation in school reform but short-circuits the potential for student accomplishment and significant teacher growth.

Relationship Between Rigor and Innovation

All of the schools were committed to increasing student competence and described themselves as well on the way. As proof of their commitment, they referred to the numbers of innovations on which they were working. Students like Sean, Alicia, and others were able to point out when an innovation reaped gains and when it did not. The fact that most of the discussion of standards took place outside of the schools gave the schools little guidance for evaluating the quality of their own work. At the same time, as a rule of thumb, most of the teachers avoided discussions of rigor internally in the face of long-term autonomous practices. Although individual teachers developed their own standards, they were often without the kind of collective yardstick that would have helped them better understand whether the innovations that they were trying were resulting in more rigorous work for students. These were the common practices and conditions in schools that prevented students, teachers, and parents from linking rigor to innovation and innovation to rigor. It was the link between the two, however, that established the gains for students and that provided important data to support the work of school reform.

Faculty in reforming schools need to examine their plans and projects to ascertain what local problems they are addressing, and they must determine what it is they believe kids can and should achieve. By doing this, the schools in the study gave themselves the means to assess the quality of their reform efforts. Once they had these practices in place—investigation and shared understandings about what constitutes rigorous performance—they had the means to improve student accomplishment. Each year, they examined whether the changes they had made brought about greater or fewer gains and looked toward additional innovations as appropriate.

It seems imperative that school faculty be involved in generating common standards of rigorous work, so they might articulate and meet common goals. Otherwise, they will be unable to guide students in any consistent manner. When teachers were engaged in these kinds of discussions, what was most critical was not that they reached absolute agreement but that they reached a deeper level of understanding about possible variations and common views. If this crucial activity is ignored or ceded to some more distant body that undertakes it in the abstract—without familiarity with children's work and without an understanding of the differences among children, communities, school resources, capabilities and constraints, and state contexts—it is unlikely that we will ever have standards that propel students to higher levels of achievement. As we saw in Sergei's case, when faculty agree on a rigorous, new innovative task and then argue about whether students are meeting it or not, they have the data to examine and regulate their own performance in relationship to the standard. It is the purview of organizations external to schools to provide schools with information, with recommendations, with processes to grapple with, set, and then achieve higher standards. But unless the school faculty themselves are centrally involved in both the means and the ends of the standards discussion, what they do with kids will always be remote from the recommendations made by others.

Further, when teachers in our schools were working on common definitions of rigor, and they engaged their students so that young people began to develop more sophisticated understandings about the characteristics of good work and the kind of effort it requires, they were more likely to help students reach a more sophisticated understanding of the relationship between rigor and innovation, between quality work and effort. In Sergei's case, he was required to serve on the panel of judges for students in the class ahead of him. This helped him gauge the requirements and the effort that would be required of him.

Interestingly, in the schools where student performance was less rigorous, kids suggested that effort counted for rigorous work. In the higher-achieving schools, students were clear that, in the end, it was the rigor invested in the work—which showed up as quality— that counted. Effort, though important, was not what finally won top grades.

That many faculty in each school saw innovation as a key factor in achieving better results from students is very important. It is true that almost all educators need a wider range of techniques to grapple with the limitless variety of student interests and needs. No good teacher can effectively push students without considering new alternatives, new possibilities. Innovations, however, like rigor, are slippery. Innovations, in and of themselves, provide no guarantee; likewise, employing constant innovation disallows building ever more rigorous practices. Faculty need to ask themselves whether the innovations on which they are working are resulting in more rigorous performance from students. If not, why not? If so, what gains?

How might these be explained and shown to parents and community members?

Students and their parents complained or wondered frequently about the "guinea pig syndrome." They worried that teachers' innovative practices were rendering students as objects of experimentation in science labs. As a result, they were concerned that the quality of education was diminished. Our observations in these five schools, based on responses from teachers, kids, and their parents, was that although many of the innovations were not perfect the first time through and would be strengthened for subsequent cohorts of students, students were none the worse for having had new experiences, and in many cases they were actually better off. Brian, the student in Mr. Dobbs's physics class, is a case in point. Had Mr. Dobbs done his traditional lesson on kinetic energy and momentum, Brian would have maintained his belief that physics was not about machines and not interesting. Instead, he gained a good grasp of kinetic energy and momentum, created his own group at home with his family when he felt his school group to be ineffectual, and remembered this assignment and the concepts embedded in it for the remainder of his high school career. Though there were exceptions to this observation, our general belief was that to be a guinea pig was beneficial more often than not.

Whenever innovation was tied to rigor, kids like Sean described their experience as more comprehensive, tougher, more challenging: "Our teachers all year long worked us up to this final assignment where we had to adopt a country, and we had to write in first person. We had to write and rewrite until we really gave a sense that we lived in the country and knew it well. Until we could convince other people. It was hard and it took a long time, but what we ended up with was a lot better than what we started with." They were more enthusiastic when the work they did in school was fresh, new, and out of the ordinary.

At Marshall, the team of teachers in the Overland mini-school argued long and hard about their final exhibition. The science and math teachers argued that the final assessment should reveal

accomplishment in more than just the humanities. They maintained that for several years, the teachers had generated largely
humanities-oriented final tasks. Finally, after lengthy discussion,
agreement was reached, and they redesigned the tasks so that students' work reflected more of their study in science. The new tasks
were exciting to both humanities teachers and the science staff, so
much so that they agreed to alternate the primary orientation of
their tasks every year.

At Oak Hill, the ninth- and tenth-grade teachers determined
that there should be an exhibition at the end of the first two years
of high school, it should reflect the gains students had made in
knowledge over the two-year period, and it would be scored by all
four teachers. In the first year, with the best of intentions but because of the constraints of time, the tenth-grade teachers were
largely responsible for designing a task that they believed reflected
the larger curriculum. They invited teachers from throughout the
school to come and watch. Soon, there were rumblings from two
quarters: the ninth-grade teachers were not satisfied that the task
took the previous year's work into account. Other faculty who attended saw some exhibitions that they thought were meritorious
but others they were troubled by. For instance, one teacher wrote,
"I saw some presentations that were pretty good, but for the most
part, the work only reflected English and social studies. I am confused. Do these teachers mean to communicate to kids that they
will only have major work in these two fields? Should the science
and math department be doing something too?" Another teacher
commented, "The presentation I watched was poorly prepared and
poorly executed. It by no means convinced me that the participating students were capable of moving on to junior-senior work. What
do we do about this?" And as the originating teachers had set up no
process for feedback, this teacher felt unable to express his concerns
about rigor. Once the four teachers got wind of the concerns, they
created a review process whereby interested teachers could watch
videos of presentations and make suggestions about rigor. In addition, they put together a formal committee of teachers, parents, and

students to make suggestions about how they might get to more rigorous work.

In another faculty discussion at Oak Hill, faculty had a very direct confrontation, in which staff who were supportive of innovations were challenged by those who were not. In the face of this challenge, those who were not trying anything new were also asked to examine their practices so that everyone in the school would be involved in an analysis of their practices that would allow them to get more rigorous work from their students. The point, made and taken, helped the faculty move beyond oversimplifying the controversy in their schools as a debate among those who were willing and those who were resistant. Their common objective was to examine their work in light of their aims for students.

Lincoln High School took much longer to move the entire faculty toward teaming than other schools may have tolerated. The faculty committee who handled decisions of this nature believed that it was better to take the time to answer faculty concerns and questions, to allow faculty to discuss problems, to watch one another to learn more about teaming so that they could embrace this innovation as a whole school rather than to forge ahead with less support and risk losing their common goals. Once teams were in place across the faculty, they began the same process of careful and lengthy deliberation to break the school into houses. (For more information about the move to smaller learning communities, see Chapter Five.)

In all of these situations, the teachers struggled with feelings of defensiveness and emotional turmoil—anger, sadness, hurt, and, at times, jubilation. Eventually, however, they were better able to make the connection between rigor and innovation, and as a result, they strengthened the connection between their efforts to improve their schools and student achievement.

Chapter Five

Scale and Discourse

Forest Park was in the midst of dividing the student population into mini-schools. Too many students in this poor community were dropping out. Attendance rates were low and violent incidents high. The central office believed that by breaking high schools into mini-schools, teachers would know their students better and would be able to work with families more closely, thus ensuring that more kids would stay and finish high school. As discussed earlier, these mini-schools were created by groups of teachers who banded together with a common philosophy to form an independent four-year school, located in the old, larger school building. In Forest Park, there were now three schools in one building. Each smaller school had a head teacher and shared a single principal among them.

Mr. Chapman had been teaching at the school for eighteen years and had watched conditions in the community worsen. He was deeply committed to helping the kids who attended this school: "These kids are black, they come from poverty, many of them live with guardians, and their neighborhoods are tough. Still, given half a push and a little confidence, they are so bright. Our job is to figure out how to push them. When they get hooked in, connected to school, they really shine!"

Tanya was seventeen, tall, big-boned, thin. Her hair was impossible, she thought, and she was always trying new contortions to bring it under control. She lived with her parents and brothers and sisters. For many years, Tanya, the eldest, had had to take care of her siblings because both her parents were drug addicted. In a kind of storybook miracle, as she neared the end of high school, her parents moved from rock bottom to recovery and were now providing decent support for her and her siblings.

As one might imagine, school for Tanya had been up and down. Still, in the last few years, as her school and her family rearranged themselves, she found herself in the business and science mini-school. The teachers who had come together to build this mini-school had agreed to give kids more support in building the kinds of skills they would need to get a job. For a long time, Mr. Chapman's students had done well in the tristate science competition. His colleagues asked him to join them in their mini-school because the science projects that he had students do were more like real business projects, and they felt that together, they could help provide even more support for his students. The collaborative promise proved invaluable to him in that the English teachers took on the teaching of research writing, and the math and technology teachers worked with Mr. Chapman and his students to do the needed mathematical calculations and to find appropriate and accurate means by which to display the data.

Mr. Chapman taught a yearlong course in which students learned the rudiments of scientific research, which led them to an independent project to be completed by the end of the year. Tanya had worked in a fast-food place and was interested in bacteria in food products. Eventually, she began experimenting with ultraviolet irradiation of various kinds of meats, keeping track of what happened to the bacteria and noting any variations in the meat that occurred. (Their school had been given an ultraviolet light chamber by the National Science Foundation.) While conducting her research, she contacted the Department of Agriculture for information over the Internet. Interestingly enough, they responded that they were involved in a similar research project, but they were experimenting with alpha and gamma irradiation.

During the course of her research, Tanya was in frequent contact with them, sharing data and findings. Her findings indicated that ultraviolet radiation did kill bacteria, but it rearranged the molecular structure of some of the meats so that the products were less suitable for consumption. Because her work was original, useful, and thorough, she received an award at the tristate science fair, where representatives from the Department of Agriculture gave her a second award and invited her to run her study again in their labs using alpha and gamma rays. At the end-of-the-year awards ceremony back at school, her parents were given the Best Parent Support Award by the staff—the first award either had received—for helping their daughter and encouraging her. The accomplishments were grand all the way around. That summer, she worked at the agriculture department for two weeks, using all of their more sophisticated equipment.

Mr. Chapman's colleagues suggested that although he, as a lone science teacher, had long done wonderful things with kids in science, their collaborative effort in a smaller setting made more opportunities possible for students and for their families. They were able to gather and plan more readily, and they got better at talking and working with one another. For them, scale and discourse were connected.

Students in other settings talked about issues related to scale and discourse. "Our school is so small, everybody knows everybody and our teachers know us really well, which is good I guess, except that you can't get away with anything. I mean anything!"

Sergei said, "Our teachers disagree a lot. They tell us about it in class, like my English teacher this year said that he wasn't going to baby us anymore like we had been in English for the last two years. Everybody knows that he doesn't like the Coalition. And like, some of our teachers are not really into teaching. One guy uses charred, I'm serious, charred lecture notes—they are so old—and he parachutes out of the building at three o'clock! He avoids talking with the other teachers about anything. And he doesn't want to talk to us about anything either."

Another kid agreed: "Our teachers argue a lot about whether to change or not. In fact, it isn't the kids that don't get along in our school, it's the teachers. I think it all comes down to the teachers deciding whether we really need to understand what we're learning or whether we just want to go ahead and do the work. That seems to be the issue, and the teachers don't always agree. One of my teachers told me he hasn't changed a thing. Another teacher told us, 'I'm only putting you in groups because the Coalition says I should.' We'd like to learn more about it."

Hakim was thoughtful. "In our school, it isn't the teachers in Overland that don't agree; they get along real well and it helps that there aren't very many of them. They fight more with the teachers who are in other mini-schools and with the principals. They can't agree on nothing."

As we watched Tanya's work in her mini-school unfold and listened as students shared comments like these, it occurred to us that success was greatly influenced by another essential connection—the connection between small scale and civil discourse. All of the schools were struggling with how best to assure that the benefits of reform accrued to all students, not just to ones taught by select teachers or groups of teachers. (Of course, though there was general public agreement, there were also outliers who were critical.) Many in the faculty agreed that the whole school needed to be involved in the changes they were trying to make at each site. That meant that the adults in the school had to have the discourse skills to work continually toward agreement. When faculty were able to join these two conditions—small scale and civil discourse—into dynamic interplay, they created a favorable context in which each of the connections discussed in the preceding chapters could flourish. Without small size and the ability of the faculty to engage in constructive discourse, the likelihood that they would connect caring and expectations, routines and repertoire, rigor and innovation diminished substantially.

In this chapter, we discuss the relationship between small scale and civil discourse by offering first a definition and then examples of each. The chapter concludes with three examples that demonstrate the importance of the interaction of these conditions.

Small Scale: What Does It Mean?

Hakim and his friends in the Overland mini-school were hosting some of the students and teachers from Oak Hill and Forest Park. (As mentioned earlier, Forest Park is in the same city as Marshall High School, which houses the Overland mini-school.) One of the common practices in Coalition schools is visiting one another in order to get ideas and to enable teachers and students to see other possibilities. A small group of kids gathered in Hakim's advisor's room to talk about their schools and to compare notes. Hakim talked with pride and enthusiasm about their mini-school at Marshall High, explaining the differences between Overland and the rest of the school. In Overland, teachers had the same high expectations for both behavior and academic performance. Students had better show up with pencil and paper, not be wandering the halls, and more important, they had better have done their homework and be prepared for the major projects based on the essential questions that guided their learning.

Hakim's friend Shardawn went to Forest Park, also divided into mini-schools, and she reinforced Hakim's description when she talked about her math teacher: "I have Miss Young. She don't play any games. When she gives an assignment, she means for you to do that assignment. And if you're like, 'Ah, man. I ain't doing that stuff,' she's going to put it back in front of you. Oh yes, you are going to do it. She is relentless."

Hakim believed that elsewhere in his school, expectations were lower: kids could not get the courses they needed to go to college, many roamed the halls rather than attending class, teachers argued over priorities, or, more often, simply worked by themselves without much attention to or from the rest of their mini-school. Students did not feel they were known—in some instances, not even when they had been assigned to mini-schools with structural characteristics similar to those of Overland.

Tommy, from Oak Hill, noted that his school was smaller than the Overland mini-school. Sally rolled her eyes, "It's small all right!

It's so small that you know everybody by the time you get through first grade! And the town is so small. There isn't even a movie theater! There is nothing to *do!*" She whined as if such deprivation would be unbelievable to Shardawn, Hakim, and their friends who lived in a big city.

Tommy countered, "I like it. It means that our teachers know us and we know them. They are willing to help us, and our classes are smaller than they would be in a big school. I hated school in my freshman and sophomore year, but some of my teachers kind of pushed me along." He continued with an example of how the school's small scale had had a very profound influence on him: "I had a wreck this fall, and the principal and my English teacher were at the hospital before my mom! What Shardawn said about not being able to slack off—when I got back to school, I was so far behind in everything, I didn't ever think I could catch up. My health teacher made me stay after class and study while she watched me. Then she made me take the test I had missed. She just made me do it; I had no choice."

The kids compared notes about the changes that had been made in their schools. Oak Hill had a student congress in which the Marshall kids were interested. The Marshall kids were doing very interesting work in science and math, which had been integrated. Sally was excited about this: "At our school, there is less going on in math and science than in other classes. Everybody says that math is a class you can't use Coalition methods in; you have to teach it in the traditional way. I don't agree. I feel that it is important that we look for new ways to teach math because it is the one class that a majority of kids have problems with, and everybody seems to blame their teachers for the problems they have. Math seems to be a class that you have to understand your teacher's train of thought, otherwise you can get lost even on simple things. I like the idea of time being allocated to work with another person in class, one-on-one."

Both schools had new graduation requirements. The seniors compared their projects. Hakim was thinking about a social service project, and Tommy was making a short advertising film. Sally did not know what she was going to do, but Shardawn was entering the project she had done for the tristate science fair. Their conversations turned to whether they agreed with the kind of changes their schools were making on their behalf. Hakim and his friends noted that they had a choice within their school. They could have picked any of the three other mini-schools but said that it was well known that the Overland teachers pretty much agreed with one another about what kids should be doing, so they got a better education there.

As students from Marshall, Forest Park, and Oak Hill emphasized, scale—specifically the limited size of the unit working directly with students—was the first factor that made a difference for them. In small schools and small units within larger schools, change advanced beyond the capacities of the innovating individual teacher or administrator to affect the whole school. They noted, accurately, that the smaller their school, the easier it was for the faculty to make changes. Personalization—knowing individual kids and their families well, which is so critical for today's kids—seems likely to occur only if the basic unit serving students is under four hundred students.[1]

In recent years, the wisdom of the creation of large schools has been challenged on several grounds. Architects and planning specialists have suggested that the large schools may be unwise because of extraordinary costs of supervision required when large numbers of students are gathered in a single setting. The assumed savings based on having only a single building have been challenged—especially when student learning is added into the equation.[2] The effects on students of large, factory schools are now well documented: too many kids slip through the cracks without any meaningful adult-student interaction and as a result, graduate with limited skills and poor preparation.

In addition to their promise of savings for local taxpayers, comprehensive high schools were developed to offer students educational choices. Though an expanded list of courses, emulating college, was considered a bonus at the time, many now consider it a weakness. Ernest Boyer, the late U.S. commissioner of education, observed that when it comes to the expectations Americans hold for high schools, "Quite simply, we want it all."[3] In order to offer students the majority of courses they want to take and—more important, some would suggest—to give teachers a chance to teach every course they want to teach, the list of classes available to students is expansive at most contemporary American high schools. For example, we noted 201 offerings for students during our first visit to Crossroads. By the early 1980s, one study concluded that the most apt metaphor for American high schools was a shopping mall.[4] In the middle of the mall, many "unspecial" students wandered in and out of specialty shops where they could stay if they wanted, leave if they chose. As a result, many were lost in the large, impersonal, academic fashion–conscious institutions that had emerged under the guise of providing more opportunities for students.

Now, as efforts to reform these institutions move ahead, educators and community members alike are more aware than ever that many schools are too large for teachers to have personal interactions with students around their work and that the influences of contemporary peer cultures can be problematic. Further, it is difficult for adults in such schools to communicate with one another. Adult energies have been expended to control students rather than to teach them.[5] Given these problems, the five schools and many others in the country have turned to the creation of small units in order to support student learning better.

Creating Smaller Learning Communities

When students talked about how teachers had made their schools smaller and more personal, they suggested the following options—mini-schools, interdisciplinary teams, and schedule changes. Each is a means of getting to smaller scale.

> *Hakim:* We get assigned to mini-schools. By being part of Overland, I've learned that it's like a family. Cause people come

around and talk to me and try to help me out. Everybody is friendly. We really help each other out.

Sally: For the last couple of years, my teachers have been working on interdisciplinary teams. It was good because if you can relate fiction to history and make connections, that is a very good way of learning. And that's what it's been like—like two teachers teaching one class instead of two teachers teaching two classes.

Alicia: That's a little like the team I was on last year. I loved the Keystone team.

Diego: Our Pathways program is really family oriented, and we spend more time in those classes than we do in others. If you have a problem, there is always someone here to talk to. I'm not sure, though, if everyone knows they can talk. But I know that I can be heard. I have a voice here.

To get to a smaller scale, scheduling changes were common in all the schools. The faculty typically rearranged their schedules for two reasons: teachers wanted to see fewer students each day, and they wanted longer blocks of time in which to get kids involved. Most students were relieved when the schedules changed so that they met with only half of their classes one day and half the next in a rotation. They had less homework each night; their classes were less harried; there was less rushing around.

The Coalition of Essential Schools advocates that, if teachers are to help students learn to use their minds well, no teacher should have more than 80 students. (In most high schools, teachers see between 120 and 180 students per day.) Other Coalition schools, many new schools in particular, have put this principle in place. In the study schools, however, four out of five managed to modify their schedules to reduce the number of students a teacher met on a given day, but they had not taken steps to reduce a teacher's overall load. The fact that they saw fewer kids every day was helpful. Both students and teachers talked about feeling less rushed and about being able to work in greater depth. However, this change did not reduce the number of papers teachers had to grade or the number of kids they needed to get to know well. Nor did it help with the task of getting to know students' families better, and it certainly did nothing to help those who were not "special."

Why did the schools not address the student-teacher ratio issue more seriously? Most faculty first perceived that the solution was simply to add teachers so that they could maintain the existing number of programs and that it would cost too much money to add the number of teachers they would need. The thought of reducing course offerings as a second way to get to smaller class size seemed perilous; some were unwilling to reduce course offerings or to simplify the curriculum so that they could get to the desired ratio. Either they believed parents would not tolerate such a change, or they believed it was too difficult a staffing decision—that some specialists would have to be let go.

Even though the schools did not push beyond reducing a teacher's daily contact load, they did attempt to create more intimate learning circumstances by instituting teaming—teachers forming interdisciplinary groups to work with cohorts of students—and by breaking the larger schools into smaller units.

Teams

To some extent, Oak Hill, with its 350 students, was already a small community, but it also sought through team teaching to create even smaller units within the school. Such efforts to create teaching teams for students were not new, as exemplified by Mr. Warren, one of Oak Hill's most beloved teachers (described in Chapter Two), who had been teaming for seventeen years. Oak Hill and Crossroads both developed interdisciplinary teams for English and social studies.

Lincoln championed smaller scale as their primary reform strategy by moving their entire faculty to teams. It was a long haul—six years. Their efforts to ensure that teams would provide students with better, more personalized attention met with mixed success and support. Still, they were clear that it takes time to generate successful teams but that the time is worth the effort. A Lincoln parent accurately reported that anything worth doing takes time and that students as well as adults get better at it over time: "My oldest said teaming stunk. The next year, I heard that it wasn't wonderful, but my second child lived with it. Now, I hear great things from my youngest."

Individual teams took different tacks and had different strengths. Some teams made progress in integrating instruction for students. The English and social studies teachers at Oak Hill created a two-year humanities program that was well coordinated from ninth grade through tenth and that was designed to give students the kind of practice they needed in project work and independent work. At Lincoln, a focus on the environment helped one team. Another Lincoln team concentrated on American studies by incorporating a range of activities, such as making masks, researching family trees, interviewing local citizens, acting out book reports, and hearing guest speakers.

In successful teams, teachers did know their students well. Teachers in such teams were able to talk in more detail about individual students. They conducted increased numbers of parent conferences, and when several teachers conducted such conferences together, parents obtained a more complete picture of their children's progress. Assistant principals reported fewer referrals to the school office for discipline once students were assigned to teams.

Some teams attempted to determine the effects of their efforts on student accomplishment. For instance, a team leader at Lincoln tallied her former students' grades in math, English, and science in the year after she taught them and was thrilled with how well they had done. She also discovered positive results when she tallied how many of the students from her ninth-grade team became school leaders in subsequent years. At Crossroads, Pathways teams in English and social studies used comparisons of student writing at the beginning and the end of school years to demonstrate that their teams were helping students learn to write. (Pathways is the interdisciplinary social studies and language arts program then required of students from their freshmen through their junior year.)

Smaller Units

In addition to creating teams of teachers, the large high schools tried to capture the benefits of smaller scale that occurred more readily in Oak Hill by generating smaller units such as houses, or schools-within-a-school, or mini-schools. At Lincoln, teachers soon discovered that teaming was not sufficient for the kind of learning context they wanted for their students. They engaged the faculty in painstaking, lengthy deliberations about the possibility of dividing the school into three separate units so that three teams of teachers would carry a third of the students throughout their high school years. It took them four years as a whole faculty to begin the move to houses.

Marshall and Forest Park were part of a districtwide effort to get to smaller scale. They worked over six years to move from large schools to smaller schools in which all students were assigned to a mini-school of 250 to 350 students, so that there might be three to four mini-schools in each building. To support the schools as they undertook this change, the district formed a new support unit called the School Reform Collaborative (SRC), which functioned like a reform agency. It provided professional development, raised money, worked on curriculum, developed new assessment strategies, sought to change the central administration, negotiated changes with the union and city officials, built partnerships with neighboring universities.

One of the most successful of these was the Overland mini-school at Marshall High School, where teachers who had long been a part of the National Writing Project were supported by a principal who was willing to take risks as they developed the prototype mini-school for Marshall. Teachers and administrators began building their mini-school with the help of the Coalition of Essential Schools and the foundation-funded SRC. The teachers and administrative leaders of Overland found the agenda of the SRC and the Coalition of Essential Schools to be compatible after their own efforts were well under way. They joined the Coalition to gain support for their efforts rather than as their initial inspiration. It was not uncommon for these schools to be involved in more than one reform initiative, and many of them had additional foundation support. For instance, Crossroads was involved with the Matsushita Foundation prior to its involvement in the Coalition. They designed their community on an evolving notion of what students need to know and be able to do, using a process the Coalition calls the "planning backwards process."[6] This process asks teachers, administrators, and other stakeholders to plan for change by first establishing what students should know and be able to do when they graduate. SRC money and technical assistance helped Overland teachers during summer retreats as they built curriculum in English, social studies, science, and mathematics around such essential questions as: What does it take to make a community? and What is the meaning of power in human relationships? These questions, defined by the teachers and their students, eventually helped shape final student exhibitions. Funds also helped teachers participate in ongoing teacher-as-researcher workshops with nationally recognized university faculty who are experts in developing teacher capacity to engage in reflective practice. In addition, they attended summer institutes provided by the Coalition, which helped them grapple with how to provide and build internal leadership. From these workshops, they built on the notion of student exhibitions and planning backwards, which they picked up during the CES seminars. They joined community mentors with faculty mentors to assist students in the development of these exhibitions. They added these new tools to skills and concepts they had developed during their participation in earlier curriculum-based reform efforts, then incorporated what they had recently learned about student learning. Although some of the other mini-schools failed to produce appreciably different learning experiences for students, Overland, with its focus on curriculum and thoughtful reflection of the Nine Common Principles, combined with the staff's skill in communicating with one another, resulted in Overland's being described as an exemplary high school program for urban students by Tom Brokaw in a national television broadcast.

Overland teachers also designed procedures for mentoring new teachers within their mini-school. This enabled them to help those teachers understand the philosophy that was guiding their efforts and to develop the skills required to teach the highly interdisciplinary curriculum. To assure a coherent program for their students, they took over a wing of the school and assumed responsibility for student scheduling. As a consequence of these efforts, they created a setting in which students were performing well—exhibiting the "habits of mind" that good Coalition schools are able to develop.[7] (Habits of mind are presented to students as questions thoughtful adults would be prepared to ask and to investigate: What's the evidence? From whose point of view? How is this connected to others? How else might it be considered? What difference does it make—so what?) Ms. Posada, an Overland teacher, attested to the contributions of that mini-school and to the CES principles it embodied: "I know it works. I've seen it work. I've seen it have a profound effect on a large number of students. My teaching, the program, it works. It changes lives of students; it gives them other options. It helps them see larger pictures, gives them skills and keeps kids in school who wouldn't have stayed. It makes socially unfit kids more socially fit; it can do remarkable things."

However, personal testimonials were not the only source of data about the effectiveness of the mini-schools. At Marshall and Forest Park, outside evaluators reported that being in a mini-school proved a statistically significant indicator of a student's increased success in English, history, mathematics, and science; promotion from grade to grade; and improved attendance. In the school district of which Marshall and Forest Park were a part, evaluators concluded that "despite uneven and incomplete implementation of the mini-school approach, there remains evidence that participation in such smaller units yields a net statistical benefit on student performance."[8]

Those smaller units that were successful fostered success by using past reform experience, incorporating outside stimulation for innovative thought, and having administrators and teachers whose focus was on the particular needs and interests of their students. Other small learning communities failed because fewer resources were devoted to them or because one or more of these conditions was absent. Jealousy played a role as well: some faculty in the other small schools envied the recognition that Overland gleaned.

Problems with Scale

Reducing the size of the school was not without its drawbacks. In spite of gains made by students, some students expressed concerns about working in smaller units. They complained that they missed seeing a broader range of students.[9] Others complained that they interacted with fewer teachers. However, most resistance to smaller units came from teachers rather than from students once the kids got used to seeing fewer of their friends. Nearly all teachers are trained to and have experience in working alone. As a result, some resented the lack of personal freedom they experienced working in teams and in mini-schools. Sometimes, teachers in teams planned curriculum together. Sometimes, they joined their classes for viewing films or for participation in a simulation. In still other teams, several teachers worked together in the same classroom with a larger number of students, taking specific instructional roles on which they had agreed in advance of the class session. This kind of teaming was the most unnerving. Some teachers feared exposure as their peers learned more about their individual capabilities, practices, and beliefs. Being a star in a one-man show does not necessarily prepare one to be an integral member in the cast of a larger production.

As Lincoln moved every teacher onto teams, personality conflicts adversely affected the decision-making process around team membership. Further, teachers felt hampered by a lack of time. They were not able to relinquish their daily responsibilities in order to learn new skills and approaches. Critics of the move to smaller units within the schools pointed out the failure of many such efforts in the past, especially schools-within-a-school in the 1960s and 1970s.

Further, some suggested that dividing up faculty and students only created more competition.[10] It was true, as was demonstrated in several of the schools, that unhealthy as well as healthy competition developed among the smaller units. It is also true that as teams and houses developed, their interests narrowed so that they became more self-interested and more self-protective, transferring their primary allegiance from departments to teams. Structural changes such as teams, houses, or mini-schools, or new schedules can be helpful components leading to significantly higher levels of student accomplishment. By themselves, however, they are insufficient. Teachers need new strategies for engaging, challenging, and supporting students. They must attend to critical issues of curriculum, instruction, and assessment as well as scale. To do this, they must engage in tough-minded civil discourse.

Recognizing the Need for Civil Discourse

All five schools experienced disruptions in their reform work when divisions among the faculty occurred. Divisions were engendered by many of the innovations each of the schools was interested in attempting—new schedules, advisory programs, teaming and graduation requirements, among others. Rigorous examination of different points of view is a necessity in any healthy community. Too often, however, the teachers and administrators were unable or unwilling to examine various perspectives on controversial issues because they could not see how to resolve their differences. As we pointed out in Chapter Four, it was highly unusual for teachers to develop shared understandings of rigor and innovation. What prevented or vitiated their ability to move through to resolution was often not related to the issue itself but rather to their lack of skill in dealing with controversy and, ultimately, their incapacity to engage in civil discourse. Overland teacher-leader Ms. Sherlock struggled to figure out how the staff might work through difficult issues so that they could get beyond resistance to change. She said, "So we are wondering how to spread this fever to the whole staff. Communication is the major thing. You sit down and talk, but it can't be done in faculty meetings. If there's no time for honest dialogue, we can't go on. We have to pay attention to people's fears. If teachers don't have the right to question and talk through it, then you will just get resistance."

Students, teachers, parents, and administrators identified the need for civil discourse. They often felt frustrated by stalemates and yet, more often than not, did not have the skills to guide people to better possibilities. And they acknowledged the difficulty of obtaining those skills. Certainly, schools are not alone in this regard.[11] Before considering the difficulties, however, civil discourse deserves clarification.

Defining Civil Discourse

By definition, civil discourse is *civil* in two senses.[12] Discourse should be conducted so that participants exemplify mutual respect; the participants are civil toward one another. It should also be conducted so that the group makes decisions that are in the best interest of the greatest number of people, so that the group succeeds in achieving the civic good. For instance, when Forest Park and Marshall and Lincoln High were working to get to mini-schools or houses, the administrators made decisions to support that move knowing that it might erode their power base, and change or complicate their roles. They did so because they believed new, smaller structures would better support students. In addition, *discourse* connotes more than simple conversation. It requires thoughtfulness and attention to procedural guidelines that allow for a thorough investigation of a given topic.

Too often, faculty in the five schools drew a distinct line down the middle of an issue and decamped to their own sides, embarrassed one another, or refused to come to the table, reflecting how difficult it is to engage in true civil discourse.

There are four prerequisites to practice civil discourse:

1. A set of skills
2. Shared values
3. Strong individuals to sustain civility
4. Participation of all stakeholders

Let us examine the importance of each of these elements in arriving at meaningful and effective discourse.

A Set of Skills

The skills needed to carry out such discourse include the steadfast willingness to put difficult, potentially controversial issues on the table. Participants must have the ability to confront, to be direct, to solve disputes, to listen carefully, and to imagine alternative possibilities from those originally conceived. Those involved begin to learn from and value conflict rather than being destroyed by it. Groups engaging in civil discourse must have the analytical capacity to uncover various viewpoints and perspectives and to weigh positive and negative ramifications of any decision. They must have facility in the deliberative processes—problem solving and using evidence and logic. Members of a community carrying out civil discourse do so with politeness, grace, and respect for and sensitivity to the needs, feelings, and aspirations of others.

Shared Values

Moreover, civil discourse requires that the group understand the importance of shared values and work toward them at all times. They must understand two aspects of shared values that seem potentially contradictory—the value of differing opinions when in pursuit of shared understanding and the necessity of common values to the preservation of the whole community. For example, without fairness or justice as common values, members of a community are apt to focus, as many in the schools did, on promotion of individual interests rather than on those of the community.

Of course, all individuals within a community have values of their own. One consistent problem in schools' efforts to develop common values among the members is that people fail to examine or be explicit about their own values. For many, that discussion seems far too abstract; others believe naively that such values should simply be understood. In part, it may be that many people are afraid to explore the significant differences in values that exist. Unresolved differences that illustrate the importance of shared values included the following:

- Whether race, class, or gender determines capacity to learn
- Whether there is a percentage of children for whom there is no hope of success
- Whether decisions should be made by those in authority or through democratic means
- Whether professionals should have exclusive control of school practices or should include the public
- Whether children are inherently good or bad
- Whether punishment or reward is more apt to produce desired behaviors
- Whether the aim of the school should be to control students or to develop their capacity to discipline themselves
- Whether learning is a passive or an active process
- Whether knowledge of the traditional disciplines is essential for each student
- Whether learning some subjects, such as foreign language, mathematics, or science, is beyond the ability of many students

As an example, in a number of instances, students suggested that teachers seemingly unconsciously let gender biases slip out.

Tommy had a teacher who frequently addressed all her comments to the girls in the class and made casual references to the fact that girls were so much more conscientious about their work. Sally and her friends offered opposite experiences: "My teacher said to me, 'Don't worry. Girls aren't supposed to be good at physics.' Can you believe that?" Diego and his friends bore the prejudice of Hispanic teachers who were prejudiced against recent immigrants. Special education staff who were working on inclusion noted that the biggest question staff had was about the capacity of students with learning disabilities. They wondered whether it was helpful or torturous to mainstream kids, wondering if the kids could understand what was going on around them and if it was a waste of teacher time trying to work with them. In the instances in which the schools grappled with these issues, there seemed to be a better chance that the faculty might learn from one another, that they might eliminate unfortunate biases and build policies and practices to support their students better.

Strong Individuals to Sustain Civility

Civil discourse also requires individuals who are confident and strong. If their own needs are great—if they are insecure, frightened, have low self-esteem, feel incompetent—individuals are rarely able to consider the greater good of the group. The need for strong participants does not pertain to leaders alone, though it is critical that leaders are strong and secure as well. All participants need this kind of security and strength to work toward school practices that better serve students. Too many of the teachers we observed felt overburdened and undervalued. Too many were expected to teach so many students that they had a hard time learning all the names, let alone knowing the students well. Too many of the teachers felt physically unsafe in their school setting. Too many felt unappreciated by their local communities or besieged by parents. All of these problems inhibited successful discourse in the schools.

Participation of All Stakeholders

Civil discourse must also be inclusive. The common good cannot be achieved when interested parties have been excluded from the decision making. In the five schools, in-groups too often dominated the planning, and parents and students were often included in inauthentic ways.[13]

At one of the schools, as the faculty were involved in change, the principal designed a seminar series for parents, which enabled them to grapple with the same questions the faculty were encountering: What do we want our students to know and be able to do? How would you know?[14] As teachers worked with the principal at these meetings, they were astounded to note that the parents' answers to these questions were very similar to their own. Parents felt that they understood the school's work and stood firmly behind the redesign process. When parents and teachers talked together, they had some common ground to discuss, which facilitated their mutual discourse.

The schools we observed that demonstrated a high level of civil discourse became a better place for young people to learn to become members and leaders in a political democracy. These schools included students in critical decisions on matters ranging from expectations concerning student behavior to curriculum and instruction in individual classrooms.

Faculty at Oak Hill worked hard at building their own skills and those of their students. Faculty members took responsibility for their bimonthly meetings. They set the agenda and facilitated these meetings. As their capacity for handling dissension grew, they got better and better at putting difficult issues on the table. They grappled with whether discipline policies were likely to improve student engagement, something any number of faculty felt strongly about. They discussed whether it was appropriate for teachers to discuss with students disagreements or controversies among the faculty. They worked on building a set of agreements about professional behavior in light of controversy. They questioned whether responsibilities like advisories were extra responsibilities or part of their professional duties. With each issue, their skill and their resolution to deal with tough issues grew. At the same time, their capacity for understanding and respecting various viewpoints expanded.

Students at Oak Hill ran a "fairness committee" to which students could bring any perceived injustice for a fair hearing. Over the course of several years, students debated such issues as the fairness of teachers, the fairness of the student-faculty congress, and the fairness of the eligibility policy, which required that students be in good academic standing before being allowed to play in extracurricular sports. The staff grew in their ability to acknowledge students, and students grew in their ability to challenge staff. At first, the staff developed an eligibility policy, and students complained bitterly. Then staff asked students to revise it. They did, and the staff roared that it was far too lenient. The students told the staff to redesign the policy, and then it was their turn to roar. A mutual respect grew and gradually moved away from staff versus students to staff *and* students who wanted more sophisticated policies that required responsible behavior, as opposed to staff and students who wanted rule-based policies. In one after-school meeting, a student appealed the athletic eligibility policy with great eloquence. Mr. Warren, who felt that the policy should be upheld, represented the congress's position. He was passionate in his delivery. Nearly a hundred students and teachers attended the meeting, during which the issues were presented to an interim committee for their adjudication. It was an exciting, complicated exchange over a difficult issue. Students debating faculty over issues like eligibility developed their capacity to analyze a stance and to learn appropriate ways to challenge traditional authority structures.

Lincoln was similarly skilled at including people. Because Lincoln's staff had been working on issues of reform for so long, a significant cadre of people were adept at running meetings, getting organized, and making decisions collectively. When their principal announced that she was leaving, the staff developed a process, led by staff members, that enabled them to build a job description for the new principal and included significant and inclusive participation for the staff. In the past, the district leaders had hired principals, but in light of the staff's ability to agree and convince others of the inclusiveness of their efforts, their process was used. As a result, they hired a principal who they were assured would not derail their efforts.

Difficult First Steps

As with the eligibility policy at Oak Hill, gaining proficiency at civil discourse did not come easily or instantly. It required patience, practice, a willingness to revisit what had gone well and what had gone poorly, and then the commitment to try again. All five of the schools experimented with new governance structures, which many believed would redistribute power in the schools, making interactions more inclusive and more civil. Many of these newly developed councils were plagued by insubstantial issues, lackadaisical follow-through, avoidance of difficult issues, and undermining by administrators who could not accept the council's authority. At Oak Hill, a student said, "We got all excited about building this new governing body—better than the old student council that never did anything. The congress gave kids and teachers both a say about how the school should be run. Then, as soon as we tried to put issues on the floor that mattered to us—like about classes and stuff—we learned that we couldn't make any decisions that would conflict with the State Board of Education—whoever they are. So now we're wondering what we can make decisions about."

In addition, some participants, students and teachers alike, were troubled because they believed that the new structures gave the appearance of legitimate civil discourse but really were only serving the predetermined ends of the leaders.

In all of the schools, developing a culture of civil discourse was difficult. So much history, so many traditional factors militated against it—notably, isolation and authoritarian decision making—that it took enormous time and effort to develop. Every now and then, in all of the schools, teachers' attempts to extend civil discourse to students were problematic in much the same way that the innovations teachers tried were not perfect when first implemented. An illustration of one such incident reinforces how important including students is but how necessary and crucial the accompanying skills are. The following is an excerpt from a teacher's journal:

> Mike, a special education student at Lincoln, was selected to attend a district-wide student council meeting. He and Alicia went, and heard the superintendent talk. The super urged students to think as consumers: "Are you getting your money's worth? What grade would you give your teachers? Are you shopping at Wal-Mart or at Nike? Are you getting the best you possibly can? You need to go back to your schools and speak to your student council and to your teachers about your concerns about your education." Mike described his feelings, "I had been thinking about the lack of discipline we have here. I had some ideas, but he just opened my mind to even more. He got me really emotionally involved. And we were at Washington High School. When the bell rang, you didn't see anyone in the halls; they were all studying. We went to a freshman math class and they were there paying attention. No one was in the hall unless they had a note, it was an emergency or something. Then when we were waiting for our ride, I talked to a couple of recruiters who were there. They were from two big Ivy League schools. I asked them if they were coming to Lincoln and they said, 'Where's Lincoln?' I was really upset. I told my counselor that if I knew in my freshman year that Princeton, Cornell, Harvard, Yale were to come to my school interested in A students, I would have tried that much harder. So I was pretty upset and I asked the principal if I could speak to the faculty and she put me on the agenda for the following week."

During the intervening week, the principal, the vice principal, and Mike's advisor met with him and tried to coach him about what he might say to the faculty. They tried to get him to think about his audience, and his evidence, to caution him not to be either overly dramatic or to generalize so that his claims were dismissed as a complaining student. They cautioned him to soften his language and to be well prepared. Mike admitted to them that he could get pretty fired up sometimes.

One of my colleagues described the faculty meeting: "Mike came just imbued with this rage of what he had been denied as a student." The rumor mill was going full tilt, with teachers talking about what the kid would say. One of the teachers was pretty upset. He was saying things like, "Does this young man realize that he's speaking in a public forum and that I'll be there filming everything that he has to say?" When Mike came into the faculty meeting, it was really kind of painful. So much of what he had to say was inaccurate. His tone was accusing—that none of us had ever brought good recruiters to the school. He had done a survey of his classmates about who would be interested in that kind of school, but we didn't make those kinds of opportunities available to them. Then he talked about what the superintendent had said and about grading the faculty. You could tell that people were getting angrier and angrier. At one point he accused us of not spending any time outside of school—that we were too anxious to get our paychecks and leave and at least we could show that we cared by coming out to school events. Finally a teacher walked out. Others stayed but had smoke coming out of their ears. The principal sensed that Mike knew the crowd was turning against him and his reaction was not to pull back but to attack. He pointed his fingers at us and said, "I'll be watching you, every move you make—look over your shoulder because I'll be out there watching you." The principal jumped up and took control, thanked him and he sort of backed down. After he left, the principal made the point that one of the many things that Mike doesn't realize is that he is a prime example of what Lincoln is about. He's a special education student included in all activities and welcomed to speak to the faculty. She pointed out that he had represented the school well when the superintendent asked him whether he was getting a good education. Anyway, people were furious and in the long run there was a kind of split. Some people just laughed it off but others were just furious. Several teachers decided they'd grieve the whole thing but couldn't because Mike is a kid. Someone slipped a note to the kid anonymously giving him heck. Then one of the teachers put a video tape of Mike's speech in the most upset teacher's mailbox. I told the principal and she went off like a rocket. She got both teachers in her office and reminded them about the legal ramifications of filming a kid and disseminating it. Anyway, it was not a good situation. We felt like we'd been great to let him speak and felt terrible afterwards.

Although the faculty were clear that they wished to have a more participatory and involving discourse in the school, their newfound willingness led Mike to unload, and the experience turned out to be troublesome. Because his responsibility was huge—to communicate his concerns about the school—and because his experience was not equal to the task, the outcome was hurtful. The teachers were angry at both the superintendent and the student. This incident reveals that like some teachers, whose inclinations are to swing from total control to little control, kids, when practicing new forms of discourse, can swing to extremes as well. Given some helpful feedback and another opportunity, Mike may well have been able to provide the faculty with useful information.

Developing civil discourse requires moving beyond polite conversation to developing the kind of inquiry that fosters significant learning. Students sometimes resisted the push to this kind of inquiry. We heard complaints from students unfamiliar with new techniques. Some preferred less demanding, more familiar methods. The following exchange between Marshall students and a teacher illustrates how confused they were when teachers asked them to learn differently:

Ms. Winters: This is a question that doesn't have a specific answer.
Hakim: How can you come up with the question if you don't know the answer?
Rashid: Why would you ask the question if you knew the answer?
Barnett: I don't know. The teachers make us do it.

Still, when students were developing better discourse skills, teachers commented. At Marshall, a teacher reported on an essential characteristic of her mini-school. "The kids are in on the adults' conversations . . . it's not like the teachers live in one world, and the students only get to be meager participants." Another teacher agreed, "The kids are what I see that tells me that something different has happened here. They carry themselves differently. They act as a community."

An Overland student expressed the same idea. "We process stuff together," he said.

At Oak Hill, one student showed insight into the complicated nature of developing inclusive discourse: "Some students feel that congress is a farce. It hasn't really clicked for everyone . . . until that happens you're not going to get the changes. So, you know, it's kinda a circle . . . if we change we could get student interest, we could get changes, but we can't get that interest until we get that change."

For the most part, adults in each school were struggling to develop the needed skills and to engage everyone in the discourse. The significant hope was that these skills would transfer to their students. One of the outcomes of building civil discourse was that shared values evolved, as people in the school community continued to grapple with common topics or ideas like the Nine Common Principles of the Coalition of Essential Schools. The challenge was to move individuals from feeling themselves in positions of weakness to positions of strength.

Connecting Small Scale and Civil Discourse

Small scale and civil discourse must work together in mutually reinforcing ways if the benefits are to be realized. Like all simple but simultaneously complicated relationships, each affects the other. A small learning community affects discourse by assuring that the members are familiar with one another. Change becomes easier as members of the community become familiar with one another's point of view—when they know who is apt to support a proposal and who can be counted on to raise the important, tough questions. In addition, in a small community, there is an inescapability factor: participants cannot hide. And when people know one another well, they are more likely to ask for the participation of the naturally reticent or the quiet.

These schools, involved in reform for some time, were clear that they intended to push for schoolwide change rather than settling for the participation of a small group of interested supporters. It was the interaction between small scale and civil discourse that made it possible for the schools to make progress on all the connections suggested in earlier chapters—caring and expectations, rigor and innovation, routines and repertoire. When students like Sergei were cared for but asked to perform to the very best of their ability, it was because the faculty had argued and revisited and revised the details. They could only do this when they were a small enough group to come to some agreement, and when they had the discourse skills to persist. Without the connection between small scale and civil discourse, all other efforts were more complicated, fraught with difficulties, and fragile.

The following two examples illustrate the connection between small scale and civil discourse. The first shows adults dealing with schedule changes in two schools with very different results.[15] The second shows three ways in which one of the larger urban schools and one of its mini-schools involved students in problem solving.

Changing Schedule at Oak Hill

Shortly after her arrival, the new principal, Dr. Brenner, suggested that the high school should be examining its long-held traditions to ensure that they promoted what was best for kids. She described these investigations as "good work" and a good way for faculty to get to know one another. The teachers rolled their eyes; they had known one another for years.

Still, she was determined and began by asking whether the teachers were satisfied with the schedule. They believed they were—had not changed it for seventeen years—not perfect, of course, but not bad either. "Schedules are hard, you know," said the teachers, "can't please everyone, but we're pretty satisfied."

She pushed: "What would you change if you could and why? What does our schedule say about our priorities? What does it tell us about what we think about how learning best takes place?"

Over the next three years, the faculty grappled with these questions in lengthy, often tiresome, and repetitive discussions. Eventually, they determined that they would change the schedule in order to rotate class time so that no one, neither teachers nor kids, would have to suffer after-lunch slump or end-of-the-day rowdiness in a single class. After the change was made, the principal prompted them to examine whether the schedule got them what they wanted. After the initial confusion of keeping track of which day and what class, they got used to the rotation. The faculty agreed that, in fact, they liked it. It seemed fresh to them, refreshing. What was refreshing to staff was how differently students behave at different times of the day.

Having gained confidence, some teachers wanted to push further: What about an activities period? What about time for teams of teachers to meet? The counselor, who did the schedule, rolled *his* eyes, "It's not simple to change, you know. Very complicated, *very* complicated."

"We just changed it!" exclaimed others.

"Let's try this one out for a while. It's complicated," said another, "I really have to concentrate on which day it is and what I have when. What's the rush?"

Still, a small band continued to push, to ensure that discussions about the schedule reoccurred on the faculty meeting agenda to ask whether the schedule might not be able to solve other kinds of problems. With relentlessness, the faculty next built a schedule that gave longer periods in English and social studies (science teachers already had extended periods for labs), provided an advisory period so the staff could do a better job of keeping track of kids' progress in school, and established an activities period to accommodate the new student-faculty congress. The new schedule accommodated the English and social studies departments, those interested in the new government, and those who wanted to break Oak Hill into even smaller communities by establishing advisories. Still, those who were not interested in these measures were not affected and had protected their forty-five minute daily period schedule.

As more teachers were affected by the schedule, more became interested in further possibilities. They moved the conversation to learning and time: How was it possible for kids to learn deeply in forty-five minutes? What kind of teaching opportunities were they simply unable to try because of the schedule? What kinds of these opportunities would they like to try? More teachers from various departments suggested ways in which they might benefit from longer classes. For instance, the home economics teacher longed to be able to prepare, cook, eat, and evaluate all in one session. The humanities teams wanted to be together for their planning periods. The band and the art teacher thought it would be helpful to have longer periods because so much of their time was spent getting equipment out and putting it away. The French teacher, right in the middle of preparing for the French students' visit to Oak Hill, thought the extended time would be marvelous. The math teachers and the physical education teachers continued to express their skepticism but eventually agreed to try it. So, another rotating schedule was devised that gave everyone extended periods a couple of days a week and a couple of days of shorter classes. Most people liked it, though the students found some classes particularly trying.

The support of the head of the local teachers union was obtained gradually. The new head of the scheduling committee was Mr. Renzler, a well-respected teacher who was skeptical about change and asked tough, important questions. The committee was given feedback by Sally and other students through the school's congress and through their advisory periods. When asked, students made astute comments, such as, "We are watching more movies now than before. Given how much TV kids watch at home, I wonder whether this is really better?"

The math teachers' worries about how to use the time well were acknowledged, and faculty tried to make helpful suggestions, rather than making negative comments. Students suggested that it was not helpful when math teachers simply did two lessons in the space of one class. As a result, several of the math teachers began to explore how they might expand their repertoire. One extended her work to include exhibitions, which changed classroom interaction. She got students working in groups to defend and compare the answers they had gotten. Another math teacher started trying to find real math problems—things he found on cereal boxes, heard on the news, found in the newspaper—to teach the kids about real applications. The principal supported the teachers' desire to vote on the change and accepted their condition of a trial period and a requirement that it be approved by a two-thirds majority on a secret ballot.

After the proposed new schedule passed and trial runs had been judged successful, the task of designing a new master schedule and scheduling students fell to the counselor, who was conscientious but who worried about the limits of his own scheduling expertise. In the spring prior to the planned implementation of the new schedule, he still had reservations, commenting:

> Our new scheduling endeavor takes on added significance as an instrument for new changes. I've almost come to the conclusion that no one is helping me because no one really wants to take any responsibility for it. The head of the scheduling committee has at least been curious about what I am doing, but there is certainly ambiguity of feeling by staff and students about the whole venture.
>
> I did get a trial schedule together to run in the computer. We are just six weeks behind last year, and I don't feel at all confident. We'll know this week whether we can do all this interdisciplinary and extended-period scheduling within the confines of my "expertise," in a small school setting, while trying to provide all the offerings and

electives that we have in the past, even though our enrollment is increasing and our staff is dwindling.

In spite of his worries, when school opened in the fall, almost everyone, faculty and students, liked the new schedule. It rotated and provided two days of double-blocked periods; one day which provided for congress, for special activities, and for seminars; and two other days of regular forty-five minute periods. They still had not managed joint-planning time for the teams, and these teachers were becoming more certain about the need for this and were willing to work on the schedule to get it. So the entire faculty assumed that this schedule was not the last, but it was a good one. The school community was small enough, the formal decision-making structures well-developed enough, and the climate of mutual trust solid enough that this innovative effort could move ahead.

Since then, they have made modifications to their schedule nearly every year. The scheduling committee got a new member when the experienced counselor retired but otherwise remains constant. In April of each year, the faculty is asked to write what characteristics they are looking for and what in the current schedule should be eliminated or adjusted. The committee comes up with a couple of schedules for mutual consideration and a couple of readings about schedules. Both students and faculty anticipate a couple of weeks during which they will pilot new schedules proposed for the next year. Most significant, they no longer see the schedule as the behemoth that could not respond to their needs or those of kids, that could only be managed by the principal, the vice principal, or the counselors. Now, they see it as a tool to accomplish a variety of instructional goals as these emerge.

Despite productive changes over time, however, the schedule still is not perfect. The committee has been unable to get the planning time that teams of teachers want, and the faculty complain that their discussions about the schedule continue to be sometimes tedious, sometimes very volatile. Admittedly, the Oak Hill faculty took a fair bit of time to get to these issues, but they did get there eventually. As a result of the lengthy and persistent process they used for examining the schedule, coupled with their examination of other aspects of school life, the very culture of the school itself changed. Factors such as the size of the faculty (thirty-five teachers who could all fit into the band room for discussions), their growing skill in civil discourse, their skill at organizing a smaller committee to continue working on the schedule, and their ability to listen to and problem-solve with reticent teachers aided their efforts and moved them toward a shared understanding about the schedule that they did not have before.

Oak Hill's story is not unusual, but it is not commonplace either. Observations in a number of other schools suggest that because schools tend to be large and unable to carry on civil discourse, they commonly change their schedule once and leave it, because it seems too difficult and too challenging to undertake again so soon. It is more common for faculty to go looking for a schedule to adopt, one that another school has found successful, than it is to stay home and study what it is in their own existing schedule that thwarts their ability to work with kids to optimal advantage. It is more common for teachers to build a schedule that responds to adult concerns rather than student learning issues. It is far less common to find a faculty that checks with those for whom the schedule was designed—students and their parents—to see if the kinds of changes they have made are having the impact for which they had hoped.

Exhibiting their skill at civil discourse, the small faculty at Oak Hill developed shared values, which enabled them to agree on essential questions related to the schedule. They expanded their skills in conversing about it and other reform issues. They included everyone in the discourse, and given an administration that had the same expectations of faculty as faculty had of kids, the faculty in the school acquired sufficient confidence as individuals to tackle difficult issues. In situations that are too large or ones in which the capacity for civil discourse has not been adequately developed, progress in improving schedules is more difficult to achieve. Crossroads, unfortunately, was such a school.

Changing Schedule at Crossroads

Many members of the Crossroads faculty also wanted a new schedule. Crossroads had a student population of eleven hundred students and some sixty teachers. One spring, the faculty voted by about a two-to-one majority to implement a new schedule involving two-period blocks. However, the principal, new that year, rejected the vote for a new schedule, suggesting that "too many teachers had trouble with one period and would not know what to do for two periods with the same students." He also explained that the proposal caused problems because a number of teachers, mostly coaches, came to the school to teach at the end of the day, and a block schedule would interfere with their work. In addition, there would be problems coordinating with other schools to which vocational students were sent for classes.

The debate over the schedule continued throughout the second year, but it continued mostly in the faculty room and hallways because there was no effective forum with legitimate authority in which various voices might be heard. Some of the teachers who participated in the Pathways program already had their schedules arranged so they could have two-hour blocks when they wanted them. Many of the science teachers were particularly eager to have the longer periods for the labs. Eventually, a year after the initial vote, the school's governance committee crafted a compromise, permitting the beginning of the day and the end of the day to continue as short periods all five days a week, short periods to be provided one day a week for all classes, and then other classes to meet every other day for longer two-period blocks. Students and parents had little awareness of the planned change nor any understanding of why it was being attempted. After this revised schedule was implemented, differences of opinion about the schedule changes were evident throughout the next year. Students shared stories with us of teachers complaining about the new schedule. The student paper featured its own survey of student and faculty opinion, concluding that, even though students were unclear regarding its intended aims, there was more support for than opposition to the change. Unfortunately, the continuing deliberations were still hindered by the absence of effective decision-making processes and by the large size of the faculty.

Finally, in January, staff from the state organization affiliated with CES facilitated a day-long review with the high schools in the city and helped the Crossroads faculty decide to work on the problem and other reform issues as a committee of the whole. This inefficient structure seemed the best that could be developed given the atmosphere of distrust that prevailed. After numerous faculty meetings and many proposals, the proponents of daily class meetings and the supporters of block schedules reached a compromise. Surprisingly, an intern from a nearby university helped craft the agreement, which was grudgingly accepted after the principal laid down a set of criteria for faculty decision making, which excluded the possibility of eliminating block periods altogether. By becoming more assertive as a leader and by calling for help from critical friends, the principal had facilitated some growth in the faculty's ability to consider the needs of the school as a whole. The size of the school community still militated against the development of consensus concerning the direction the school should take on its schedule, so the school lurched forward with much less commitment to continuing its reform than did Oak Hill.

The differences between Oak Hill and Crossroads have much to do with their capacity to engage in difficult discourse over time and to sustain civility throughout, and these abilities are very much influenced by size. Oak Hill was a much smaller community, so subversive voices were easier to call out in public meetings. Crossroads was too large for people to feel that they had either legitimate responsibility or reasonable authority.

Attempts to Change at Marshall

Small scale and civil discourse affected more than school schedules. The schools that made the most overall progress successfully developed interactions between adults and students that reflected the same elements of civil discourse that facilitated reform work among adults. Scale influences the capacity of a school to develop such dis-course with its students and in doing so, enhances the school's abil-ity to build the skills youngsters need to participate in a democratic citizenship. Nowhere was this more clearly demonstrated than in the large urban schools.

Marshall, like most American high schools in the 1990s, worried about violence, drugs, and other inappropriate student behaviors at school. Entering this huge school, students, teachers, and visitors passed through metal detectors, signed in under the watchful eyes of security guards, observed that many exits were locked in violation of safety codes, and proceeded to a crowded office, where a uniformed police officer often worked with harried school officials to deal with the latest discipline infractions. One spring, school officials tried to deal with problematic student behaviors in three very different ways. One reflected awareness of the advantages of small scale and civil discourse; the other two did not.

Although the students at Marshall were assigned to mini-schools intended to give them the advantages of small, personal communities, the administration chose to call them to assemblies by grade level. One morning, two hundred ninth graders, many of whom did not know one another, were called into the cavernous auditorium to be reminded of appropriate behavior. After a series of speakers, most of whom were poorly received, a speaker identi-fied himself as the school ombudsman. "I am, like, the school lawyer. This is your school. The only way it's going to work is if you make it."

To which comment a student shouted, "Shut up!"

Struggling to maintain his composure, the ombudsman contin-ued, "A lot of you females won't have a husband because there won't be any black men around."

The girls cheered loudly.

He muttered, "Think about it," and strode angrily off the stage.

As if surprised, a student turned to another and said, "Look at him, he's mad."

An assistant principal, Ms. Holmes, chided the students, "When you are older and more mature, you will think back on this moment." Then Ms. Holmes introduced a speaker from the school district's Antidrug-Antiviolence Network, telling the noisy, inattentive students, "He did not have to come here today. This is not his job. I will not introduce him while there's talking. He's a guest! You treat him like one!" Then, first to the teachers sitting in the audience and next to the students, Ms. Holmes exclaimed, "I want the name and book number of students who are misbehaving. Remember, you are not anonymous!"

The final speaker told the students that his aunt had died that morning and began an emotional recital about his personal history as a drug dealer, gun runner, and prisoner in the state penitentiary. The students laughed inappropriately as he described foul practices he had witnessed in the prison. The speaker went overtime until finally, the assembly was over. The ninth graders, school security staff, teachers and speakers filed out past the police officer stationed at the back of the auditorium.

Later that week, students were shown a televised movie designed to convince them not to use drugs, another whole-school activity. Students noted that the characters in the movie showed little respect for their mothers, something they said did not characterize their own behavior. More obviously, the producers of the film demonstrated little respect for African Americans, depicting them as the hoods who caused trouble for a thirteen-year-old white girl featured in the film. In any school, this should be offensive, but in a school where 99 percent of its students are African American, it was a blatant example of racial bias and highly disrespectful of the students. Naturally, given that the connection between small scale and civil discourse was again not in evidence, students did not see this activity as a helpful or thought-provoking intervention, resented it, and rejected it.

In a third incident at Marshall, the advantages of civil discourse among students and teachers and the contributions of small scale were evident as Hakim and his friends led a peer connections seminar for a younger group of the Overland mini-school students. The peer connections seminar was organized as another measure to help ensure that students remained in school, by providing older student mentors to younger students. Overland faculty worked with a group of seven seniors to prepare them for their first meeting with a group of ninth graders from their small learning community. Previously, the seniors had participated in a peer counseling retreat with young people from many different schools.

As they prepared an agenda, figured out who would do what, and what they hoped for from the session, the students commented on some of the recent changes at Marshall. They liked the new principal and spoke favorably about a new small learning community that had been created for students interested in teaching or medical careers. All in all, they felt that Marshall was "what you make of it." Some worried that too many students were "just playing around," and others said the school was "too violent." But all were committed to making the most of their mini-schools and to helping younger students take advantage of it.

The day after their planning period, the seniors met with twenty-five ninth graders in the school's community room. Ms. Winters and two other Overland teachers were also present. While some of the senior counselors set up sodas, bagels, and assorted junk food on a table in the back of the room, the ninth graders trickled in. They picked up some food and sat in folding chairs, which had been arranged in a circle. The seniors, some with food still in their hands, moved into the middle of the circle and began to speak.

One said, "I'm here for you. If you have any troubles in your classes, feel free to speak to me."

Another added, "I'm like a shoulder you can lean on. This is my partner, LaTesha."

After others had introduced themselves, Ms. Winters encouraged the seniors to tell the younger students the purpose of the session. They got right to the point, "The purpose is to help you get your act together in class. Some teachers feel you're too wild."

Ms. Winters expanded on their comments, "With the violence outside, we want to keep Marshall a peaceful learning environment. Some of you will need special loving care."

The seniors then told the freshmen that they had been trained as peer counselors to help the younger students. Some of the seniors shared the troubles they had experienced as ninth graders and then attested to the way Overland, like a family, had been helpful to them. The seniors exhibited impressive maturity in their ability to engage in civil discourse within their small community. They made it clear that they knew they were not perfect but that talking things out would work for the ninth graders as it had for them.

There were no put-downs among or by the younger students. The young students were not passive, as they recognized the genuine invitation for dialogue. The conversation proceeded as students engaged other students in talking about issues related to school life that were bothering them. Faculty advisors chimed in as needed to contribute depth to the conversation.

The power of Overland's small community worked to develop appropriate behaviors, attitudes, and skill in civil discourse that would never emerge from mass meetings or ill-conceived broadcasts. In the mass meetings, the rudeness of the students to the adults mirrored the lack of respect for the students communicated by the adults. In the broadcast, the lack of respect for the students produced student reactions that ranged from blatant rejection to sleepy disregard. The interactions in the Overland peer counseling activity were more caring, respectful, and thoughtful, as staff worked with students to build their skills. As such, they led to the desired kinds of student attitudes and behaviors, whereas the other approaches, which dealt in large groups without an emphasis on civil discourse, did not.

Progress

In spite of the real difficulty experienced by the five schools in trying to create schools of workable scale and to advance the quality of civil discourse, there were instances where progress was evident.

We observed small learning communities where all students experienced new forms of internships during their senior year; where each student participated in small, personalized seminar settings; where students joined actively with adults in challenging the fairness of various behaviors on the campus and in setting policies that affected both students and adults; where African American urban students were outperforming white suburban students in creative-writing projects and in math and science. Several connections contributed to these successes. In addition to those discussed in previous chapters, we found that progress was facilitated because in such small settings, teachers, students, and parents practiced discourse that was respectful and productively thoughtful. Rather than casting aspersions, taking sides, disparaging one another, they listened and worked to their mutual benefit. They focused on the best interests of the group as well as the interests of the individuals. Substantial numbers of people in these learning communities became convinced of the need for change and of their power to make it: they shared values and confidence in themselves. They developed the skills needed for civil discourse, learned how to take feedback from critical friends and analyze it thoughtfully. They challenged assumptions made by these critiques and sought modifications if the need for change made sense. They confronted one another but in a respectful manner.

As school communities began to practice civil discourse in more effective ways, there was a consistency between the way adults worked with one another and the way they worked with students. In the peer mediation sessions in Marshall's Overland mini-school and in the family groups at Forest Park and the seminars at Oak Hill, we could see growth in student skill—heightened analytical capacity, better listening skills, more respect for divergent opinions. In the congress and fairness committee at Oak Hill and in student committee work at Lincoln, we saw signs that students were beginning to engage in the same kind of dialogue that enabled adults to see more evidence of their own growing capacity.

Our research indicates that progress occurs when members of a school community demonstrate that they are able to step outside their more typical individualized concerns and engage collaboratively to determine new directions. It occurs when individuals treat one another with respect and when they push one another to participate. Even then, knowing how and wanting to collaborate are insufficient by themselves: civility and small scale must be joined.

Chapter Six

Kids, Connections, and Commitments

In the last spring we spent in our high schools, the halls were no less deafening than they were in the fall when we had first arrived, three years ago. In fact, if anything, the pitch was up, higher—a kind of burst of energy that synchronized with sap rising in trees, with leaves and natural greening, with budding, with sprouting up, with breaking ground, with birds squawking and chittering. High schools always feel a little wilder in the spring. More slamming, more whirling, more screeching, more crying, more angry exchanges, more exuberance, more, it seems, of everything. It is the time when adults wonder silently if the kids know how little control adults really have in schools: Are the students going to strike? Simply refuse to do any more work? the teachers wonder from the inner sanctum of rattily comfortable faculty rooms. Or maybe they'll smash the windows and leap out into the newly regenerating trees, streaming, flying out of the school.

It is also a time when teachers gather sweet rewards, "You nearly drove me nuts, Mr. Warren, but I really learned a lot in your class." "Thanks for sticking with me, Ms. Tommich. I see now what you were trying to get us to do during the year. My mom and dad think you are one of the best teachers around after seeing all the varied things you tried. I know I was a pain sometimes. But thanks."

As we listened to the increased pitch, we no longer felt like ancient aliens or lost adults afloat on a turbulent, youthful, blue jean sea. We knew a lot of these kids by this time. Many of them yelled and waved. We did not hear much swearing, as they moderated their language because they knew and liked us. We had listened to them talk about their school experiences, their families, their trials, and their dreams for three years, and they had enjoyed it, found it stimulating. Several bounced or swaggered over to chat one more time, to talk about plans: "So what are you doing for the summer?" they asked us, as if we too got a couple of months off.

Their plans varied. One student, eager about a summer job, told us: "Work at the local pool. It's the greatest job, because I can go to work in my bathing suit and cutoffs, and all I have to do is talk with people while they come in, take their tickets and work on my tan. I've done it for three years—so cush!"

Another very eager kid said, "My family is going to France. My dad is taking a course there, and so my brother and I will be loose in the streets of Paris. *Regardez-vous, les petites filles de France!*" Absolutely no embarrassment about turning a French phrase. We remembered how halting he was as a sophomore and grinned at him. He continued, "Then off to college. I can't wait. The college is trying to impose a curfew on kids during the week because there is too much partying, but I don't think they'll manage to pass it. My dad went there, too. He said they had a curfew, and it was really quiet after 9:00 P.M. Could you stand that? Why go to college? I'm hoping to do animal medicine."

Another, with a different outlook: "I'm working at the drugstore. It's a complete drag, but it's better than nothing."

We had seen and learned so much in these halls that we have not discussed here—like the principal whose husband died while she was on her way to work on Monday morning and who, in her grief, asked herself, "If I could have all the extra time back that I spent trying to change this school, would I take it? To spend more time with Sam while I could? Has it been worth it? I just didn't know."

Or the teacher whom the administration and the police suspected was using and possibly dealing cocaine, who went to his car in between too many classes. But was too smart to get caught.

Or the kid who was so bright, who started bringing her work to us so that we could have examples of the points she wished to make about when school worked for her and when it did not. She brought an aphorism for us at each visit, which expressed her current feelings about school: "School is for the mindless," or "Teachers hold the key to students' intelligence." She was now in a rehab hospital for alcohol abuse and attempted suicide. Her father had cancer, and her early admit to Yale seemed somehow overwhelming to her. In the spring she had quit track, quit the newspaper, and said she just wanted time out. She would not be at graduation. We, like her teachers and her parents, had not understood the clues she had dropped before her collapse.

And there were so many positive stories of the kids who had done well and were off to do exciting things—the young woman who would be interning with a famous theater company this summer; the young man who did not get into the school of architecture that he had wanted, so he grabbed the plans he had drawn for his senior project, flew out to the university, and made an appointment with the dean. His plans so impressed the dean that the university admissions office reversed their decision. He flew home and did not touch down for weeks after landing!

As graduation neared, we felt the buzz, the pump, the reckless wild hooray of their impending conclusion. They shimmered in their own three-year physical metamorphosis that mirrored their intellectual growth. All of their schools were trying to make a difference in their lives, to assure that the kids transcended previous intellectual boundaries. Had it worked? Was there a difference?

We had set out on this journey asking ourselves, Are greater gains for kids in evidence in these changing schools, and if so, what are they? To ask and answer these questions is difficult, complicated, which we believe is precisely why they are not asked or answered very often. All of the gains we hope for kids—higher levels of competence, better skills, justified confidence, authorized opinions—require change of some kind in schools. To get *more* than schools traditionally get from students necessitates different routines, approaches, structures, practices. Greater results for kids must first be conceptualized by teachers and administrators, who then bring their ideas to bear on students through strategies, projects, or other concrete changes in their work. Such changes require time, analysis, critical feedback, and continuing work to assure that these gains accrue to kids.

Further, as our small group of students reminded us so clearly, kids come with their own histories, beliefs, difficulties, and expectations. Home life and family interactions continue to vie with even the most determined, ennobling, and enabling school experiences. Regardless of the relationship schools and parents had, it was undeniably true that for most kids, family life as they were growing up was different than it had been for many of the adults who surrounded them. More kids had to work to support their own needs. More lived with one parent, or a relative. More carried the scars of their parents' marital wars. So as we searched the halls for the six students we had met when they were mere sophomores, we wondered again: Who are these students specifically? What do they represent in light of the larger group?

They are not simply the kids who made the greatest gains, though some of them did very well. We could have chosen to include only students who were positively affected by their schools (something many of our colleagues suggested would provide better learning for them); however, kids who had made great gains were not the only kind of kids we got to know well. There were those who benefited to be sure, and there were students who would have done very well no matter what the system. And there were those who did not do well despite the school's best efforts to change. Our six students' experiences represented the real range of gains, misses, and complications and the real challenge that school reformers face.

Sally

Sally had grown from five feet seven inches to five feet nine inches. She was now a full-force beauty, resplendent with long, thick red hair, tall, diffident confidence, a gorgeous figure. She could have been anywhere from twenty to thirty-five, but few would have guessed she was a mere eighteen. A bombshell—in more ways than one. Her personality was still mercurial. At times, she looked surly. At other times, she was rude. She had developed a harder, pricklier persona to cover her vulnerability, her insecurities. And she was full of confusing contradictions: she was passively resistant at school—not a big troublemaker, but an occasional skipper. She was angry about school, which she still claimed to hate, and she was passionate about some of the issues she was studying and worked hard at them: "I have learned so much in social studies and history. I have really been following politics, and I've been reading the newspaper every day and watching the news to keep up. My stepdad and I have been arguing a lot, and the best part about it is that I am better informed than he is, so I don't have to back down anymore. It's really terrific, even though we get pretty heated every now and then." She has a new job in a local dentist's office, which she likes: "I make good money and I get raises a lot. I'll be working there for the next two years to save money to go to college." The brightness and enthusiasm fades instantly, "I'll probably have to go to the local community college to get my grades up."

In an instant, she was down, depressed, the anger gone. We asked why. Her language changed when talking about disappointment:

Well, I wanted to go to a local college in the city, but I called the other day and I was really sad. I didn't get in. Because I thought the guidance counselor told me that my GPA [grade point average] was eighty-one, so I was like, okay, cool, they require an eighty, so maybe I'll just make it. If I'd known it was lower, I wouldn't have even bothered. So I had no idea. The woman at the college was like, "No, I'm sorry, your grade point average is a seventy-seven." And I had no idea. It's really annoying. Or if they just messed up. But I don't know. It's just bothering me. I want to go into advertising, but that's like marketing and I stink in math so I don't know. I guess for the first two years in community college, I'll just take liberal arts to find out really what I want to do, and then the next year I'll focus in on what I want to do and hopefully get a scholarship.

She had had a boyfriend in her junior year, and he had been all-consuming then. Now, according to Sally, he felt as uncertain about his life as she did about hers. "I don't know. He wants to go to college, and that's like hard because he needs to make money. So I don't know what he's going to do."

This year, Sally had taken Mr. Warren's economics class, business math, computers, adolescent psychology, humanities. "They're all really annoying. Humanities is all right. It's a lot of reading, like a book a week. But it's fun because it's more discussion than lecture. I like economics, but I'm not very good at it. Like I think I'm good at it but then I get my report card and I'm like, oh, okay. I don't do homework. My mom says, 'You don't study and you get like eighty-fives and nineties. Just think what you could get if you studied.' I'm like, yeah, whatever. It's true." When we look at her assignments and grades, we see that she has done better in the more difficult classes than in the easier classes. In several of the latter, she has flunked or gotten D's. Further, she is ill informed about what she needs to do to get into college, what classes count for what credits, and so forth. She has what seems like a normal drive for difficult tasks and a kind of lethargy for things she is not particularly interested in. On the other hand, she lapses into depending on others to help her, even when things really matter: "I want to go into advertising, so for my senior project, I want to intern at an agency. My advisor is supposed to arrange it for me. I don't know. It's sort of hanging." One wonders whether this is in fact the case, or whether she skipped the days when other students learned what they needed to do, or whether she goes just so far and then retreats because she is scarred by her relationship with her father, and she wants not to expect too much either of herself or of others. Sally herself expressed real disappointment:

> And it was so funny because I was totally thinking about it the other
> day when I called to see if I got accepted. And it was so right. Like I
> wish I'd listened to my mom and really studied. I totally wish I was
> like a nerd and a bookworm. I really, really wish I was. It's so bad. I'm

so mad at myself. Because I always thought average was okay because my mom, she's always told me that "there's five hundred million average people in this world. You don't have to be above average." I was like yeah, right. I don't know. I'm very mad at myself lately.

It's like I just didn't know. Like this year, I have top-level classes, and they are hard, and you have to know what you are talking about. My other classes, well, they've been lower level but they are so boring, and I don't know how. . . . And then Mr. Warren. It's like he only has goals for the smarter kids. That's who he calls on, and it makes me feel embarrassed and intimidated. I don't know. I just wish I'd worked harder. My boyfriend and I, last weekend, we went over to see some of his friends who go to the university. It was such a cool place. We both really liked it. But, you know. We could never get in there. Why did my mom tell me it was okay to be average? It isn't!

Sally drifted on through the rest of her senior year. Of all the senior projects we watched, hers displayed the least effort. It was barely adequate. The panel asked her to redo some of her work before they would accept it. Although she finished high school, she left feeling disappointed in herself and ill prepared to make decisions about her future.

Sally was one of the kids for whom the changes in the school made little difference. She became prickly to protect herself against any kind of disappointment—and so was not pleasant to deal with, nor did she allow adults to come close. She was alternately vague, haughty, confident, irritating, honest, perceptive. Sally's definition of average was problematic. She may have believed that her mother's claim that she need only be average was exemplified in the performance of her friends who only did some of the work required for their classes. Sally's interpretation of "average" may have required less effort than her mother meant to suggest.

Staff efforts to get to know her better were either shunted off or were not rigorous enough. In her school, teachers were not as used to pushing kids out of personal, idiosyncratic difficulties and into solid academic performance as were the teachers at the inner-city schools, Marshall and Forest Park. Teachers in these urban settings were practiced at ferreting out kids' perceptions of themselves, looking into kids' personal histories to discover what prevented the kids from pushing themselves.[1]

Perhaps Sally's advisor needed to be tougher with her about what she needed to do and what the consequences of her actions would be. Perhaps her teachers needed to be in closer contact with her family so that they might have developed a mutually sustaining message for her. Teachers' efforts to engage her academically were accepted by her sometimes but rejected at other times. Our observations in her classrooms corroborated what the experts in tracking have been suggesting for some time: students in lower-track classes encounter less powerful teaching, less engaging curriculum, less demanding assessments.[2] Typically, the connections between and among rigor, innovation, routines, and repertoire are weak in these lower-track classes. At the same time we observed Sally's poor performance in the easier classes, we watched her do well in the more difficult classes, but not consistently. Somehow, her understanding of consistent effort had been short-circuited. Overall, we were left with the impression that she pulled back from thoroughly investing herself and fully displaying her capabilities in order to avoid further hurt and disappointment. The school's efforts, remarkable in many ways, were not yet aimed at correcting her individual problem.

Hakim

Hakim had a fabulous senior year. In three years, he had grown nearly a foot in height and was now a big, imposing young man. He was cheerful, but commanding, solid, muscular. Someone to be reckoned with. His confidence was way up from where it had been when we first met him shortly after his mother had died and he had been transferred into this school involuntarily. He told us, "I've been real involved in peer counselors. It's been good for me, good for the younger kids. I didn't have anybody there for me when I was their age. And I am graduating and I am going to college." In his sophomore year, he had been selected to be part of the Horizons program: a former district official had promised 116 kids in Hakim's class that if they graduated from high school, he would help them with college tuition. As part of the program, a stockbroker with a local firm visited Hakim regularly and helped him complete work like the homeless project on which he had done so well in his sophomore year.

Currently, he was finishing his final exhibition, a new graduation requirement. His commitment and enthusiasm were unmistakable:

I am revitalizing a house on my block. It's next door to me. Once it had a lot of copper on it, but the drug addicts in the neighborhood ripped all that off and sold it. Now it's nothing but just the wood and it's boarded up. I want to buy it, and then we'll use the first floor as a place for homeless people to gather. I have talked to the deacon at our church, and he'll come every week to talk and to try to help them with their problems. And the second floor will be used by teenagers.

His mentor, the stockbroker, had agreed to come in and talk about sexually transmitted diseases and AIDS and HIV with all the teenagers in the neighborhood. Hakim explained, "The teenagers will work on having different brochures to pass out in the neighborhood, like on teen pregnancy, so that they'll learn about it while they are developing it for other kids. The third floor will be for little children. Someplace really safe for them to play with table tennis and video games."

Hakim figured he would need to raise $32,000 to match the funds guaranteed as part of the assignment, so he contacted a variety of possible sources and found several willing to help with his dream. As part of the assignment, he had to do a budget, a description of the community, a management plan for the project, an environmental impact statement. He had to answer eight questions that asked him to reflect on the assignment after it was complete. Finally, he had to prepare a typed paper that summarized the project, and he had to defend it before a panel in June. The panel included a parent, a junior student, two teachers, and another adult from the community. When he did his presentation, Hakim enlisted the help of a friend, and they played the roles of the deacon and the winos on the first floor of the shelter and the children on the other two floors, demonstrating the various activities that would take place there. It was a creative, effective presentation. In it, Hakim talked about how his local church had helped him out with his project and also had gotten him involved giving out doughnuts and coffee for the homeless on Saturdays.

Hakim felt involved and hopeful about his neighborhood:

> We're having a block party this Saturday. Things are coming back. We didn't have that for the last two years cause there was too much fighting on the street. But now the lady that was block captain, she wants to do it again, you know, get the street together. We were out there two weekends in a row cleaning. I feel good about it.
>
> I feel good about school. My school, Overland, it helped me grow up, you know, instead of just going to class and doing nothing. In Overland, we got into groups, or we worked as one big group. We read sections of books out loud so that everybody got what we were doing. And I know it might sound childish, but it really prepares you for college. It got me in cause I like to read now. And I read now even if it's just a health book or something. I'm reading around the house now.

Hakim's grades had increased steadily. He had been accepted into four colleges and planned to pursue sports medicine: "I'll also play a little football there. I'm an athlete here—I play quarterback. I'm excited I'm the first one in my family to go straight to college from high school. My sister is at Temple now, but she went in the Marine Corps first. I'm going to do okay, and I think I'm going to get straight A's on my last report card! The best yet!"

Hakim, involuntarily transferred into this big neighborhood school, found the smaller Overland mini-school within Marshall to be a haven for him. Through it, he located a mentor and the promise of college support, a powerful incentive. He participated in English classes that helped students build basic skills and demanded rigorous analysis of literature, from *Hamlet* to contemporary works; chemistry classes that challenged him to think beyond memorization of formulas; and social studies classes that constantly demanded that he and his fellow students interpret today's world in light of historical precedents. The overarching themes around which his course work was built, themes like power and community, helped Hakim develop an understanding of the connections between ideas that would exceed the grasp of most freshmen entering higher education from more traditional school settings. Further, his teachers devised activities that helped him no matter what his skill level—from reading complicated text out loud to pursuing his own interests on his own street, such as homelessness and urban neighborhood renewal. Small scale, repertoire, caring, rigor, high expectations—these were intertwined to strengthen his experience in school.

Alicia

When we saw Alicia near the end of her senior year, she had lost much of her bubble. She had blond, teased hair and wore a little black dress with white polka dots, shoulder straps, and black stockings, a more sophisticated image. As always, she was quick and insightful. Her life outside of school had become more difficult. Over the last couple of years, she had struggled with manic depression and had been hospitalized four times. She suggested that it was hard for her to get a handle on her relationship with her mom, who was deeply troubled, "If I was not in this school, I would be in a group home right now." She was tired. She worked two jobs, was a cheerleader, and had a boyfriend who complained that he never saw her. "It seems like I just wake up, throw my hair back, and barely make it here on time. It's just go, go, go, sleep, get up, go." Some of her grades had slipped, including math, but she had not lost her sense of humor: "Well, we don't really have gangs but, well, this guy and this girl were having this big argument. And this other guy started dating the girl. And then the first guy got mad. And he came here to school and he shot off his gun, straight up in the air. I heard it, but I didn't see it because I was stuck in a room with six math teachers! That would have been too much—if it'd been my last day because math is my worst subject. To die with six math teachers!" She felt anxious about graduating and leaving Lincoln. She felt as if the school kept her straight, steady, and coping. It provided her with both fun, like games and proms, and thoughtful, caring adult supervision. During and after her hospitalizations, her teachers kept track of her and reassured her, "We won't let you flunk." She was worried, though, because her grades were not high enough for scholarships. "My dad makes too much money for serious financial aid. And they [her parents] don't seem gung ho on my going to college. They don't care. I guess I'll have to work for a year."

When we first had met her, she was convinced that she wanted to be a teacher and that she would, of course, teach at Lincoln. Now those plans were not so firm in her mind, but she concluded by saying, "My kid will go to Lincoln. For the fun stuff like games and proms and homecomings and getting your report card and knowing you brought this grade up a bit and being happy about it. And having teachers that are so caring that you think the world of them. I wouldn't want my kid to miss out on all that. I mean, *the child will go to Lincoln*. I've made up my mind, even if I have to drive her here from the next state!"

Alicia had missed school due to illness. Her teachers cared about her, let her know it, and kept her from succumbing to her own depression. They gave her an alternate image of adult support, and she knew even before she left that she would miss it. Teachers like Ms. Murray showed her what caring meant when it had an academic focus, when she was pushed and prodded to understand what numbers and formulas meant. She also learned from teachers who were developing a repertoire, who were trying new things and whose enthusiasm spilled over to her. As her parents were not interested in college for her, the likelihood that she would go on was diminished, but she had found a place that believed in her, where she gathered significant experiences, pushed herself, and came out stronger for it.

Tommy

Tommy was one of those kids who shot up in height from his sophomore year. As a senior he was over six feet tall, very thin and lanky, and much more confident and cheerful. His mother described the kinds of things that had happened to him: "You remember how worried his father and I were about whether he would make it here? Well, I have to credit the school. They did so much for him!"

Near the end of his sophomore year, he had been in a terrible car wreck. While he was driving a bunch of students home from practice, a bus ran a light in the rain and they collided. Several kids were seriously injured, and he injured a disk in his back. His mother explained what had happened:

His father and I were terrified that it would send him right back into his old depression. He had just finished therapy. But the kids were just great and so was the school. The principal and his teachers visited. He passed all his subjects, which was a miracle because he fell way behind, but his teachers pushed him. His English teacher, with whom we thought he was going to have a full-scale war all that year, discovered that he liked being a DJ [disc jockey] or an announcer, and so she let him rearrange a few assignments so he could explore that. She let others in the school know of his interest too, and pretty soon, he was the DJ for private parties and announcing at school assemblies and at games. He put together all of the sound and music for the junior talent show. He loved it! Somehow or another, it made him feel like he fit, and he really just took off from there. That is not to say that he didn't struggle in English. He still hates to write! And he continued to struggle in math, but he got so involved in the events at school that his complaining nearly dried up. He joined in all the drama stuff, had the lead in the play this year. And he did a lot of the sound work. He really wants to be a sound engineer. He was invited to a leadership symposium in the city to represent the school. I judge the quality of the school based on his involvement and his ability to articulate ideas he's learning about there. While he wasn't an academic star like his sister, he was another kind of star. I do feel like that involvement is happening, that the staff has really hooked into Tommy's strengths. And they work around his weaknesses. He got lots of recognition from teachers and kids for his work.

And he decided to go to college. We didn't push him, because we didn't know whether his confidence would be high enough. He applied to Emerson—it's a great communications school in Boston—which was a stretch, and he did a great portfolio of his work for them. They loved it and called him and told him that he was the kind of person Emerson is about but they'd have to see his grades come up so that they could see that he could do the work. You should have seen him study! And he got in! He got a ninety in English and an eighty in physics. It's a miracle! He's not doing better work than, say, his sister did two years ago, but he is doing top-quality work for him—much more rigorous than we ever expected!

We attended his senior exhibition. He had made a ten-minute advertising video on the Senior Options program—which was the new graduation requirement. He made the film for the school to use with parents and community groups and with younger students so that they would know what to expect. He narrated the film and then interviewed six students about their projects. One got an internship at a laboratory that did research with chimpanzees. Another wrote a script and then directed a cast of volunteers in her own play. Another volunteered in an early childhood classroom. Two brothers did an architectural landscape project. Sergei built the scale boat (see Chapter Four). Tommy interviewed all of them about the scope of their work, what they had gained from it, where they had run into problems, what they might recommend for others. To add depth to the film, he had spliced in short segments from movies about school and to add humor, he spliced in cartoons.

During his exhibition, he first explained his interest in video production and in advertising. Then he showed the film. Afterwards, he showed a series of the outtakes that had been problematic. These were humorous, but they also showed the precision with which he had worked. Then he stood for questions. On the panel were two teachers, a returning graduate, a parent, and a community member who had some experience in advertising. They asked him tough questions: "Were you satisfied with your video?" "What would you do differently?" "How did your experiences in school during the first four years connect to this project?" "The research component of your portfolio [which the committee had in advance as part of his exhibition] is slim. You didn't do as much as other students have done in terms of background work. How do you explain that?"

Tommy answered without hesitation:

Anyone who has known me over the years knows that reading is really a struggle for me. I basically don't like doing it. I prefer to try things myself, to *do* things over reading about them. I think that reading clouds my own sense of what I can do. It's like depressing because when you read about it, everything has been done before, and it kind of squelches your enthusiasm. I am going to a college that emphasizes doing things. I know that I'll get a job in a place that is more interested in what I can do than how much I've read. That's just me. It's not like I'm opposed to reading. I did what I felt I had to do in order to get ready, but I was more interested in spending the time getting the filming right, getting it just where I wanted it.

When he left the room, one of the teachers was quite concerned about his answer. Unfamiliar with video production, she suggested that although the film was good, it did not look as if it had taken much effort. The community member who had done television advertising exploded, "That was a first film, and I'm telling you it was nearly top quality. The precision, the message, the flow . . . all were perfect. Sure, he could have had better equipment, but it held my interest and it educated me at the same time. I've paid thousands for less quality from professionals. That kid must have spent hundreds of hours on that piece." A lively debate ensued and in the end, his exhibition was unanimously deemed excellent. Tommy, in a Michael Jackson imitation, moon-walked off to Emerson with another piece to add to his portfolio. Here was an entertainer in the making.

Tommy's "teachers looked to his strengths and worked around his weaknesses," said his mother. He moved out of special education and into regular classes at a time when all the kids in the school were mainstreamed. Although he struggled with his sophomore English teacher, who admitted to wanting to pull her hair out while working with him, she pushed him, watched him, learned about him, and helped other people understand him. Together, the teachers pulled him into the school through his interest in sound technology. Perhaps because he became more likable and less depressed as he found a place in the school, perhaps because his parents were involved in the school's life, he was pushed by more of his teachers than Sally was. He was not allowed to slip to average or below. Teachers prodded him along as they sought ways to make school pertinent to him. As a result of his work in the school, he gained concrete experience in a field of interest to him and developed confidence as well.

Diego

Diego continued to do well in school. When he had arrived fresh from Mexico in his freshman year, he knew virtually no English but learned extremely quickly and worked hard in school. He was an able math student: "My dad would always teach me math when I was in elementary school. Now I have taken algebra and calculus, I am helping him." (Diego's father did not go beyond the fifth grade.) "I like to be ahead of other people. Like this girl in my class, I teach her too and it makes me feel good."

Diego's English teacher encouraged him from the time he arrived to think about college. In his sophomore and junior years, he intended to go to the local community college and then to a four-year college. He also fell in love, which he shyly announced with a grin—for him an important personal milestone.

Over the three years, he continued to love industrial arts: "This year, we learned how to build a cabinet, and the teacher told us to pick the kind of cabinet we wanted to make, and then he taught us the kinds of joints we needed. I did a good job. I like working with my hands. He also taught us about engines, gas engines, and welding where this was needed for the cabinet. Then he showed me how to make the joints stronger. He had books we could learn from too that illustrated how to put them together." In his junior year, he designed a two thousand square-foot house. He explained modestly that he would, of course, never live in such a fancy house. He had a different teacher every year for drawing, and each year, the teacher either did not understand the material in the book, or did not know how to use the computer software that was available, or did not know how to discipline the class, but Diego slogged through on his own, uncomplaining, and made good progress.

As a senior, he became interested in working with computers, joining with some other students who were successful in a computer class. They worked to master some animation software, which a teacher had ordered. "We learned just by messing around with it." And then they taught the teacher and the other students.

Diego won the Bootstrap Award, given to the two students who had done the most to pull themselves up and succeed academically. Although English was his second language, Diego ranked seventh in his class when he finished. He was also selected for the Sterling Silver Award, given to about 10 percent of the seniors with outstanding achievements. Students are nominated and then present portfolios, which are used as a basis for selection. Some of the teachers thought that he had not made broad enough contributions to the school to qualify for the Sterling Silver Award. He was active in the Spanish Club, Aliente con Todos, but otherwise did not participate in extracurricular activities.

As school was drawing to a close, Diego was saddened: "School has become a lot funner. It is fun to come. Now that I am getting out, I want to stay in school. But my girlfriend wants to get married. I will graduate in June, and then one of these days I will go to the community college to see their programs. I will need a job to pay for that school. When I graduate from school, that will be a big step in my life. I will go out into the world where I want to succeed."

When we asked his counselor about the kind of help Diego had received in looking for scholarship opportunities, given his impressive high school achievement, the counselor said, "There isn't much we can do with the kids that come from Mexico. It's likely that one day they'll go back. You know, they slip back and forth across the border all the time."

Diego did well in school, and he seemed to be one of the students who would have done well in almost any setting. Though he got significant support from his English teacher, the math teacher, and the Spanish teacher, he was left on his own by others. Diego accomplished levels of education previously unachieved in his family. Indeed, he did better than all but six of his classmates, finishing seventh in his class of approximately four hundred students. He was one of those fortunate kids whose family valued what the school had to offer and supported his efforts. Indeed, Diego's achieving a high school diploma was an important milestone for them. Unfortunately, despite his success in school, Diego could not escape what seemed to us a devastating local bias against newly arrived Mexicans from some of the adults in the school and in the surrounding community. Diego was at the top of his class; there surely must have been some way to help him make further progress. He did not want to leave school, he told us, but was not familiar enough with higher education possibilities to pursue them on his own. As recent immigrants with little formal education themselves, his parents may have been unaware of the possibilities that lay beyond high school for their son. Where might he be today if he had received the helping hand that Hakim got?

Sean

By his senior year, Sean was still working at the country club and, on the side, he was installing sound equipment in cars, something he had become very skilled at from his electronics classes. In the summers, he was a roofer. Things had happened, though, to sober him. A young cousin had been killed, and Sean had broken up with his girlfriend. He did not have much time to get out to his grandparents' farm anymore, and he realized that he probably would have to move away from his family because the area did not have enough high-tech industry, which he intended to pursue.

Electronics was truly his favorite class. It was in this class that he really dug in, connected past to present, connected what he was learning in other classes like English, physics, and math. And he gained valuable skills. It was the electronics work that kept him plugged into school. In the fall of his junior year, he described their electronics project:

> Now we're building a TV. I mean the technology's so high that we're working on specific parts of the TV. We're not learning about the whole thing; we're learning about one little component that does a big thing. You know what I'm saying, that's hard to swallow, but that's what it is really. Like I don't know how much you know about computers, but you've heard of Intel? Well they developed the microchip, and that chip has a copyright on it. And every computer in the world needs that chip to run. So it's like that one chip, you know, runs the whole thing. And it's just like blossoming. It's like the medical field, there are just so many different things you can do in telecommunications. We are really deep into it right now.

In his senior year, Sean had made a robot at home and with other kids had built miniature, radio-controlled cars. He made the decision to apply for the two-year electronics program at a nearby community college. He got information from the counselors, set up an appointment to visit, and applied all on his own. When he got in, he announced it to everyone, but not before he announced, "I'll be the first in my family to ever go to college, besides my grandma, she went to nursing school. I'll make it, I know I will!" When we first had met him, he was etching a printed circuit board. By his senior year, he was talking about the mathematics and the physics of it: "Well, a printed circuit board with resistors, capacitors, all that stuff's in there—math and physics and electronics and computers. And it's just microscopic. Unbelievable, isn't it?" As a senior, Sean was as enthusiastic about what he was learning in electronics as he was on the day he had begun. Full of wonder.

He was interested in what lay ahead for him, and he had come to appreciate the school almost as much as Alicia:

> I think about the last four years and what I've gotten here at Lincoln. Mostly, it's the opportunity to go further. I want to get into a communications company like the phone company, and then I want to start my own business selling cellular phones. You know, I had my own business for a long time already. Me and a buddy have been hooking up stereos in people's cars. The newspaper came out to do a story on teenagers who start businesses. For us, it was just word of mouth. Anyway, I know I can do it—start a business. And I learned a lot about how to do things here. For all the idiocy and imbecility that goes on here, I learned a lot.

Sean was hooked and held in school by the smaller-scale electronics magnet adopted as part of this school's strategy to hold kids. He was a kid who liked to do things, who liked to see the connections between things, and so the school's efforts to create smaller focused houses worked to his advantage. The opportunities provided by the magnet and by his other classes built his self-esteem by virtue of the real skill he built and the experience he gained. By the time he was a senior, he had become less a critic of the school and more of an advocate, fuller of enthusiasm for his own possibilities. He did not mention the scoliosis with which he had learned to live, but he did mention Mr. Thornton as a positive force in his life.

Gains for Kids?

As we watched our young friends move back into the river of students in each school, we asked ourselves again: Any gains? If so, what are they? What is the evidence? And are these gains greater than what they might have accomplished in more traditional settings? Yes, there were gains, we believed. Not for every student, but for many. The gains were important: perspicacity, perseverance, academic enthusiasm, growing skill, and increasing confidence. They were the gains that parents had expressed hopes for early in our discussions with them.

Evidence of these gains came from several sources—from our examination of actual student work; from questions asked of students about their work; from conversations with parents, students, and teachers. We saw young people like Tommy, Sean, and Hakim discover topics of interest and develop them over time so that they built legitimate skill, recognized by adults and other students— recognition that would not have been easily obtained had the school not changed its requirements. We saw evidence that students understood important concepts thoroughly and could apply them in new circumstances: math in building boats, data gathering and analysis in forecasting weather, electronics in wiring car radios. We noted gains that were embedded in students' abilities to work on a particular topic over time. They demonstrated persistence— an important ability in nearly all walks of life. Tanya, whose parents were recovering addicts, ran her data over and over again in order to make sure her findings were correct, and then she ran them again with a new set of variables. Sergei sanded and sanded and sanded and sanded because it was necessary, important. He worked alone and then went to the Hobby Shop for advice or the shipbuilder's office for guidance. Then he went back home, incorporated the advice, and worked again. We saw papers, videos, speeches that were rehearsed and nearly errorless, because students had developed a consciousness of audience and of correctness. The gains, and evidence of them, were there. We listened to students' descriptions of themselves as skilled, curious, enthusiastic.

When we asked ourselves whether these gains were greater than the gains made in schools that are not involved in change, the answer was both no and yes. No, because over the years each of us has seen student work that rivaled that of the kids we were watching. All over the country, exceptional teachers in traditional American high schools have pushed some of their students to remarkable accomplishment. However, we could also answer yes, because these schools were trying to get more from a far greater number of kids, from all kids. Had they succeeded yet? Not entirely, but our sense was that they were asking for more from a wider range of kids and getting it more often than most expected. Tommy, Sean, Hakim, Diego were less tracked than they might have been in more traditional schools.

Further, when we asked parents the same question—whether their kids were getting more—they frequently traced specific gains made to changes in the schools: "Tommy's sister was in the top track. She was in the school really before it got involved in trying to get better. She did very well. Tommy is not doing better work than his sister, but he has been pushed by the school, and he is a different kind of student. This school has been every bit as rigorous for him as it was for her—different but as challenging. We are not at all sure that if the school had not been involved in change, that it would have pushed a student like Tommy."

"Hakim has not stopped talking about this urban renewal project he is working on. He's giving us a lecture every night at the dinner table about what's possible and how it could be done. We can't turn him off—not that we'd want to!"

"All my wife and I really want is for our kids to be interested in school. To come home and talk about it at the dinner table instead of the old routine, 'What did you do in school today?' 'Oh, nothing.' We've heard a lot of that and when kids say that, it just makes school seem like such a waste of time and energy. We've had two daughters go through Oak Hill in recent years, and as the teachers develop more active techniques, we've noticed that our second daughter is talking about school more than our first. She gets assignments to bring topics up at home, to figure out what we think, to push us to think about it differently. We are pretty astounded at how she's blossoming. Our second daughter has always been the quieter of the two and in the shadow of her older sister. Not anymore!"

"My son did not waste a second in his senior year. No senioritis in this high school. And he didn't complain at all when building that boat, even though he worked on it night and day. It was as if he was putting everything that he learned together. I am grateful to that school. The changes they are making are good."

Thus, we believed that some of the kids were making identifiable gains, that we could find evidence of them, and that the gains were traceable to the school's efforts. That led us to reflect on the conditions that made these gains possible.

The Nature of Connections

For Hakim, Alicia, Tommy, Sean, Tanya, and others, the connection between one set of conditions and another seemed to make the difference. Connectivity. Linking one goal to another. Fighting to make one condition pull more weight by placing it in relation to another. We discussed these connections and weighed their respective importance.

One of us would say that Alicia was helped by all the people who cared about her—her math teacher, her ninth-grade team of teachers, the guidance counselors. But what about the time that they made her finish her work even though she was in the hospital? Caring isn't enough by itself, another would counter. When her grandfather died, her math teacher allowed a low level of participation in class but did not excuse her from the work.

The routines that Mr. Renzler built helped his students gain important skill in analytical reading. He pushed them to understand the symbolism in Ethan Frome and then went further in My Ántonia.

But what about the kids whose enthusiasm remained high, and their efforts increased every time Ms. Tommich expanded her repertoire, tried something new? She tried to integrate English and social studies. She also used a variety of teaching strategies from role playing to new assessment techniques like exhibitions.

Parents described with interest the new things their kids were trying *and* they valued the rigor of Mr. Renzler.

Sean did well because his electronics teacher had solid routines in place. But his teacher also had a fine repertoire that he could draw from depending on kids' interests. He helped students figure out how to apply the concepts they were using in ways that interested them. Sean and his friend grew in sophistication about car sound systems. They could explain the implications of various speaker locations, of different amplitudes, of different manufacturers.

When the schools demonstrated attention to the connections—routines and repertoire, caring and expectations, rigor and innovation, small scale and civil discourse—these kids' efforts pushed beyond ordinary, traditional accomplishment and into the realm of more. Unfortunately, however simple the connections sound, they challenge the existing secondary educational system to its core.

Each of the schools was engaged in reshaping long-standing structures that had fostered disconnection, separateness, specialization—faculty divided by departments, the school day chopped into six equal parts, students grouped by ability, graduation by credit collection, teachers working alone. All of these practices prevented the adults in schools from sharing powerful ideas about how to make schools better. Further, it kept the adults from collaborating to build a coherent, connected set of skills for the students. In the face of the historical tendency to fragment and isolate people and their ideas within high schools and to discourage common commitments, it was when our school communities attended to connections in the midst of their reform work that the greatest gains accrued to their students.

Working on connecting two dissimilar, unrelated, or different dimensions of schooling was essential to these schools and to their students for a host of reasons. Connecting things helped people avoid oversimplification. Too often, reforming schools resemble water bugs, with long, extended legs. They skim the surface of every new technique, every new trend, but do not go below the surface to explore the full potential of those techniques and trends.

To concentrate only on a repertoire would have led to inattention to the routines that Tommy needed to develop in order to watch snippets of film—interviews, cartoon clips, narration—over and over and over until he could see how to build a coherent whole. To pay attention only to the routines in math left Sally uncertain about the utility of it and did not provide her with a range of ways to approach the problems, which only worked to convince her further of her own ineptitude.

To connect two things makes explicit the complex nature of the endeavor, thus illuminating the real challenge, the importance and significance of the undertaking. Working on serious and important central issues fueled teachers' interest in their own profession, adding a freshness to it that is sustaining. Though the topics of investigation might have been different, working on fresh and new techniques was every bit as energizing for adults as fresh approaches were for the kids. To check to see if the Socratic seminar is helpful in expanding students' skills connected the technique to one of the most important motivators for Mr. Landon—evidence of his own personal efficacy. At the same time, the kids moved into the poem "If We Must Die" with new interest because the technique required that they attend closely.

To work the connections between various dimensions of teaching and learning provided balance and helped prevent the pendulum swings for which educational reformers are all too infamous. For Mr. Dobbs to get better at teaching physics concepts through projects, he needed to learn how to build more rigor into the assignment itself. Doing so will prevent him from another free-for-all, two-week session during which kids simply roll paper, roll paper, roll paper.

To look from one dimension like rigor to another like innovation helped people clarify what they were looking for in terms of quality. As they learned more about the quality of their efforts, they moved closer to providing convincing evidence that what they were doing was working. For example, when their goal was to ensure that kids would graduate only after giving evidence of their accomplishments, the teachers' strategy was to require a final month-long internship, a report on the internship, and a defense of it. By doing so, the faculty then had a product that they could use to determine whether the strategy had provided sufficient evidence of the goal. At Oak Hill, Marshall, and Lincoln, teachers made adjustments in these assignments to get to heightened quality, and eventually, they became more confident in their own efforts. Simultaneously, they got better-quality work from students. Oak Hill videotaped every student exhibition and each year had a community-staff review to see whether there was enough rigor in the innovation. Over time, the quality of students' work grew, as did the quality of the teachers' work in preparing students to undertake such tasks.

Our schools were different from one another. It was their differences in socioeconomic make-up, their location in this country and in their communities, and their academic standing that made them such an interesting cross section of American high schools. One colleague who visited the schools suggested that the most striking thing about them was how very different they were, one from the other. Despite their differences, all were either struggling to make these connections or were struggling because of the lack of them. Thus, it seemed to us that making the connections between various aspects of schooling paved the road to the *essential connection between school reform efforts and real gains in student achievement.*

Commitments That Encourage Connections

As it became increasingly clear that making the right connections was central to making important gains for both schools and students, we wondered and argued about them. What exactly were they? What is the nature of the connection? What are the parts?

What makes them so important? Each set of connections combined different goals of the reform movement: caring with expectations, rigor with innovation, routine with repertoire, scale with discourse. Identifying these goals emerged from many observations and critiques of secondary schools: too many kids pass through the halls of large high schools unknown. Too many students are tracked into classes that ask too little of them. The work students are doing has been watered down over the years; it is no longer demanding enough for our students to compete with students from other nations. Teaching techniques are too narrow—the lecture still predominates. The size of many schools is too large to ensure careful guidance. Faculties are too separate in interests and goals to collaborate on important problems.

In addition, each pairing of two goals suggests characteristics of good teaching. Good teachers believe that each of their students can learn and that the teacher's job is to care for their academic development. Good teachers are both innovative and rigorous. They establish productive routines and work toward an interesting and varied repertoire. Good teachers know about the dynamics of scale and have the skills to engage in important discourse on behalf of their students' learning.

To bring each of the sets of connections to life, faculties had to translate the goals of reform into strategies, projects, structures, and activities: professional development for teachers so that they could expand beyond routines to a broader repertoire, routines embedded in new techniques to make a repertoire more manageable, advisories and new graduation requirements as a means by which to get at both caring and expectations, smaller units within the school to facilitate more manageable discourse.

When we watched one connection in relation to another, we did observe that the schools tended to emphasize one dimension over another. Faculty put more strategies in place for caring than for higher expectations. They focused more on routines than on repertoire. More on innovation than on rigor. More on scale than on discourse. When we thought about why this might be so, there seemed to be a variety of explanations. Strategies for one were often more readily available than the other. For instance, innovations were easier to locate and define than rigor, structures for improving scale more obvious than strategies for improving discourse. Routines were easier to establish than a meaningful repertoire. The ease of implementation influenced which side of the equation school faculty emphasized more.

In addition, however, for each of these connections to work, the adults in the community also had to make personal and mutual commitments. They had to commit to examining personal beliefs about teaching and learning in order for any of the connections to be charged with their full potential. They had to commit to the idea that building a repertoire is in fact important; that high expectations and caring should extend to all children regardless of race, color, or gender; that smaller schools offer deeper opportunities for academic gains; that innovations alone are not enough. These commitments were the bonding agents that joined both ends of the connections together, that held them together, that fueled the relationship between one characteristic of good teaching and another.

Without these commitments, new strategies were easily undone by old beliefs. A new grouping technique in math did not eliminate a biased belief that boys are more competent in that subject. Public discussions of a faculty's commitments to its student body were rare. Private discussions among individual teachers about the nature of their commitment were equally rare. When the teachers in these schools began to team, they frequently talked to us about the differences they perceived between their commitments and those of their colleagues, but seldom were those conversations public.

As we studied the connections, it seemed that four kinds of commitments were central to the development and maintenance of the connections:

1. Commitment to ideas
2. Commitment to bias-free schools
3. Commitment to teacher growth
4. Commitment to evidence

In illustrating each of these commitments, we hope to suggest both why they were necessary and why they were so difficult.

Commitment to Ideas

The first commitment was to a philosophy or a set of ideas to undergird the work these schools were attempting. To have such was to assure a kind of centerpiece around which they could anchor their work and check it for accuracy and appropriateness. All of the schools had voluntarily joined the Coalition of Essential Schools and in so doing, agreed to put the Nine Common Principles of the Coalition into place (see Appendix A). The principles embody Sizer's belief that each school must be responsible for its own redesign work and that the adults in schools must grapple with and come to some agreement about the philosophical underpinnings on which they are creating changes. Basing the Coalition's work on a set of ideas established a reform movement around a set of mutual commitments that adults might make together to guide their work.

Confirming Sizer's belief that a philosophy provides one of the important commitments that adults in schools must make, Cuffaro recently examined the necessity of an undergirding philosophy to her own teaching.[3] It is the clarity of her progressive philosophy and her commitment to it that allow her a theoretical basis for explaining her actions with children. Her commitment to this philosophy provides another tool she uses to measure quality work. All too often in the reform movement, teachers adopt strategies and techniques without the necessary philosophical underpinnings that would enable them to explain their commitment to a particular approach, to support it, to share it. It is in these circumstances that schools can justly be accused of undertaking change for its own sake.

When we asked individuals in schools why they thought their community joined the Coalition, they frequently said that the ideas made sense, and they liked the notion that they were responsible for interpreting the ideas in their own contexts. It was around these ideas, however, that we saw some of the greatest controversies in the schools.[4] It was in committing to the ideas that staff found themselves most divided and blocked. Even though it was the ideas that bound these schools in common goals, the strategies, such as block scheduling, were much easier to commit to than the ideas themselves. When faculty began to examine some of the ideas together, deep-seated feelings about how teaching and learning take place emerged, making it difficult for people to proceed in their mutual explorations. For instance, the statement "less is more" in principle two engendered very strong emotional responses: "Less is never more. We have worked for years to build a curriculum that gives kids what they need in order for them to be successful in college. If we cut that down, do they get more? No! They get less!"

Others thought differently: "I love 'less is more.' I imagine a history course where instead of covering all the wars in chronological order, we'd pick one recent skirmish, one that is in the newspapers every day, and let the kids explore that and then trace in it the roots of all the world's great wars. We try to do too much, we have too much information to cover, so we have to find new ways to get at the curriculum."

Discussing ideas was difficult because it required a particular kind of professional intimacy that made many uncomfortable. It meant that individual teachers revealed to their colleagues what they believed about their students' capacities to learn, about their own responsibilities in guiding students. Few teacher-training programs support emerging teachers as they grapple to build a personal philosophy. The immediacy of the daily exigencies in schools overtook the opportunity to have such discussions. Because faculty did not have adequate time to delve into deep controversy, and partly because their discourse skills were still developing, the schools invariably chose those ideas from the Nine Common Principles that were the least controversial and avoided dealing with the whole set as they were intended. Although there was evidence of the ideas in all of the schools—graduation by exhibition and student as worker, for example—commitment to the ideas as a whole was not always in evidence.

Part of the value of the ideas is their capacity to engender controversy and important discussion. Such discussions are critical for clarifying what teachers in a community believe about their students' capacities, about the nature of teaching and learning, about their role in facilitating for their students. To have an undergirding philosophy that teachers can use to examine the strategies they have selected provides them with the compass they need to stay on course, to make steady progress toward their mutual destination.

Commitment to Bias-Free Schools

A second commitment was to providing a bias-free environment for the children who attended these schools regardless of socioeconomic background, race, religion, gender, or ethnicity. Diego's case was one of many that provided clear evidence in our five schools that neither wealth nor poverty was the determinant of a student's academic ability. Nor was race, ethnicity, or gender. Some black kids in deeply impoverished circumstances equaled the academic capabilities of some wealthy white kids in the suburbs. Some recent immigrant Mexicans did as well as some long-established American Hispanics, the most privileged African Americans, and Caucasians. Some girls did every bit as well as some of the boys in math and science. One of the key determinants of their success seemed to be whether or not the adults in their schools believed in the kids and then helped the kids believe in themselves. When the kids were hampered, they were often hampered by the unchallenged biases of their teachers, whose job it was to nurture them.

We were quite certain that the adults were, for the most part, unaware of the damaging nature of their biases. They did not hear the bias embedded in their own statements, such as "Don't worry. You're not supposed to do well. You're a girl" or "You'll probably want to get married soon, won't you? Your people marry young." We also believed that none of them would claim any of these biases if challenged. Without the kind of direct feedback that illuminated specific instances, we could not see that conditions would improve. No problem perceived, no solution required.

Unfortunately, we saw the worst offenses, not in the inner city schools, where race and bias were issues faculty and kids grappled with daily, but in the other schools, where kids were mixed together and where race or ethnicity or gender was not publicly claimed as an issue or an agenda by the faculty.[5] Despite rhetorical platitudes in mission statements about all kids being able to learn, these faculty had not grappled with their commitments to all kids. Teachers admitted in interviews that things had been better for them before these "other kids" came to the school. They seemed unaware that comments like these were evidence of their own biases, their own lack of commitment to some of the kids in their school. Again, the issue was too sensitive, too politically incorrect, too emotionally charged actually to talk about publicly. However, though the adults did not reveal their individual beliefs to one another, scores of young people heard messages from their teachers loud and clear: "You probably won't do much more than this because you are a girl," or "Your people don't do well in school," or "The fact that you learned Spanish first is probably making it hard for you to learn," or "It's hard for boys to express their feelings."

Commitment to Teacher Growth

Another commitment was to teacher growth. In order for these essential connections to flourish, adults in schools and in their communities had to commit to teacher growth. Teachers, like the children they teach, gain skill, competence, and wisdom over time if they are in a culture that supports such growth.

Nearly every notable report and study in recent years has suggested that teacher growth is key to what our schools are able to accomplish. Our own data show clearly how complicated and demanding it is for experienced and competent teachers to develop a broader repertoire and to connect it to the rigor they hope to gain from their students. They need time to watch one another. They need time with experts who can point out what is missing in a new strategy. They need much more specific feedback to enable them to examine what they are trying to do.

Despite the centrality of the commitment to teacher growth to the goals of the reform movement, little has been done to make teacher growth a substantial priority. The schools we watched all made progress, and all had access to additional resources to support their efforts. Oak Hill and Marshall had substantially more than the other schools, which may account for their positive achievements, but even in these schools, more support for teachers was needed. Most of our teachers were expected to learn about new strategies outside of school time. Frequently, they had to pay out of their own limited resources to attend seminars and courses that taught new approaches. To get feedback when trying new techniques, they were expected to arrange their schedules to watch one another teach and to give up the only planning time they had each day. Most had little or no time to practice giving and receiving feedback in the company of knowledgeable experts who could facilitate their growth.

In the best of circumstances, teachers in these schools had an hour a day to work with team members, four early-release days a year to work with school colleagues to build discourse skills and tackle difficult issues that would enable them to establish strong mutual commitments, plus an occasional foray out to a conference where they might meet with other teachers. In the worst of circumstances, they got no time or support at all.

Without a strong commitment to teacher growth from both teachers and the surrounding educational system, faculty were more likely to be defensive, protective of familiar strategies and approaches, less willing to scrutinize their own work, more critical of the work of others, and more reticent to work more closely with parents and community members. Without a substantial commitment to teacher growth that translates into time and support to learn and develop, the incentives for change are lacking.

Commitment to Evidence

A final commitment was to the search for evidence of gains for students. When adults in the schools were committed to searching for concrete evidence of gains for their students, two things happened simultaneously. They gathered the data they needed to self-correct— to ensure that the strategies they were developing were moving toward legitimate gains for students. And they were able to convince one another and their surrounding community more readily of the soundness of their endeavors.

When a group of adults—Ms. Tommich, Ms. Mosback, the special education teacher, the two ninth-grade teachers, and the parents from Oak Hill who were invited to join the review of the tenth-grade exhibitions—saw work that showed children exhibiting skills that they all agreed had not been in evidence previously, the entire effort was propelled forward like a rocket booster.[6] When Brian completed his senior exhibition on weather and everyone from family members to teachers registered the depth and breadth of his growth, everyone was encouraged to pursue both inclusion and exhibitions further. When Ms. O'Leary listened to her students as they worked in groups to compare their findings on tidal action, when she heard them slowly begin to speculate as to why their findings were different, she said that she saw a transformation in the kids—her students talking and behaving like scientists! When Mr. Dobbs read the excerpt from Brian's journal describing what Mr. Dobbs had thought of as a worthless activity as one that had helped Brian see the fun in physics, it helped convince Mr. Dobbs that this kind of innovation was worth pursuing.

Each of these examples suggests that teachers were compelled to do more when they saw a piece of evidence that they considered legitimate. Far too often, teachers have been asked to locate evidence of their success by measures they do not deem legitimate.

When teachers were committed to the search for evidence, we saw renewed commitment, enthusiasm, and energy on their part. To build assessments that required legitimate demonstration of understanding, to focus on the work kids produced, to look for real evidence of legitimate skill and competence are some of the very best sources of standard-setting available. Teachers engaged in these kinds of activities produced the only kind of standard-setting that improved work inside of schools that we've seen. In the long run, it is that work that will convince the broader community of the viability of our public schools.

Final Glimpses

We believe that over a period of three years, the connections between kids and school reform could be traced through the efforts of the adults in the schools. When schools were involved in translating the various goals of school reform into action, and when they placed these goals in dynamic tension, one with the other, greater gains appeared to accrue to students. Further, when the adults were able to grapple with and then make the kinds of commitments necessary to fuel these connections, they were clearer about what to do and how to do it. Neither of these things—making connections or making commitments—was simple or quick. None of the schools felt that they had arrived, finished, completed their redesign work. But the act of doing it was teaching them a great deal and left them with solid direction for continued work.

As we left the halls of each of these high schools, we could hear our friends Hakim, Sally, Tommy, Sean, Diego, Alicia, and many others jamming lockers shut, hustling out into the world with their friends, making plans, making their own connections, making their own commitments. We strained to catch final glimpses, to listen as long as we could. We felt so hopeful for them. Such wonderful kids, green hair, pierced belly buttons and all, and such promise when undergirded by powerful educational experiences. We hoped that these school faculties, parents, and community members would keep pushing to build essential connections. We hoped they would push themselves to make the critical commitments that would enable important connections to be made. And we hoped that these students had taught us well so that the lessons we share here will help the next round of students to graduate from schools better prepared to face the challenges that our world offers every day.

Appendix A:
Nine Common Principles

The Coalition of Essential Schools defines the Nine Common Principles as follows:

1. *Focus*. The school should focus on helping adolescents learn to use their minds well. Schools should not attempt to be "comprehensive" if such a claim is made at the expense of the school's central intellectual purpose.

2. *Simple goals*. The school's goals should be simple: that each student master a limited number of essential skills and areas of knowledge. While these skills and areas will, to varying degrees, reflect the traditional academic disciplines, the program's design should be shaped by the intellectual and imaginative powers and competencies that students need rather than necessarily by "subjects" as conventionally defined. The aphorism "less is more" should dominate: curricular decisions should be guided by the aim of thorough student mastery and achievement rather than by an effort merely to cover content.

3. *Universal goals*. The school's goals should apply to all students, while the means to these goals will vary as those students themselves vary. School practice should be tailor-made to meet the needs of every group or class of adolescents.

4. *Personalization*. Teaching and learning should be personalized to the maximum feasible extent. Efforts should be directed toward a goal that no teacher have direct responsibility for more than eighty students. To capitalize on this personalization, decisions about the details of the course of study, the use of students' and

teachers' time, and the choice of teaching materials and specific pedagogies must be unreservedly placed in the hands of the principal and staff.

5. *Student as worker.* The governing practical metaphor of the school should be student as worker, rather than the more familiar teacher as deliverer of instructional services. Accordingly, a prominent pedagogy will be coaching, to provoke students to learn how to learn and thus to teach themselves.

6. *Diploma by exhibition.* Students entering secondary school studies are those who are committed to the school's purposes and who can show competence in language, elementary mathematics, and basic civics. Students of traditional high school age who are not yet at appropriate levels of competence to enter secondary school studies will be provided with intensive remedial work to help them meet these standards rapidly. The diploma should be awarded upon a successful final demonstration of mastery for graduation—an "exhibition." This exhibition by the student of a grasp of the central skills and knowledge of the school's program should be jointly administered by the faculty and by higher authorities. As the diploma is awarded when earned, the school's program proceeds with no strict age-grading and with no system of credits earned on the basis of time spent in class. The emphasis is shifted to the students' demonstration that they can do important things.

7. *Attitude.* The tone of the school should explicitly and self-consciously stress values of unanxious expectation ("I won't threaten you, but I expect much of you"), of trust (until abused), and of decency (the values of fairness, generosity, and tolerance). Incentives appropriate to the school's particular students and teachers should be emphasized, and parents should be treated as essential collaborators.

8. *Staff.* The principal and teachers should perceive of themselves as generalists first (teachers and scholars in general education) and specialists second (experts in one particular discipline). Staff should expect multiple obligations (teacher, counselor, manager) and feel a sense of commitment to the entire school.

9.   *Budget.* Ultimate administrative and budget targets should include, in addition to total student loads per teacher of eighty or fewer pupils, substantial time for collective planning by teachers, competitive salaries for staff, and an ultimate per-pupil cost not to exceed that at traditional schools by more than 10 percent. To accomplish this, administrative plans will inevitably have to show the phased reduction or elimination of some services now provided to students in many traditional comprehensive secondary schools.

Appendix B: Methods

This book derived from the School Change Study, developed in 1990 by Patricia Wasley for the Coalition of Essential Schools (CES) and funded by the Exxon Education Foundation, the DeWitt Wallace–Reader's Digest Fund, and the Pew Charitable Trusts. When we began our work, Muncey and McQuillan were finishing a major study of eight of the original Coalition school sites.[1] They focused on the initial steps and first stages of reform. In contrast, we wanted to study high schools further along in their transformation. How did they sustain the momentum of change? How did they move from isolated pockets of innovation to involving the entire school? In what way did they use the ideas set forth by the Coalition to undergird their new practices? We hoped these three questions would help us answer our major question: What changes made by the adults altered and enhanced the educational experiences of students?

To select schools, we interviewed CES staff and other researchers and then contacted six schools to ascertain their interest. We visited each of these schools, talked with their faculties, and recruited three of the six schools to participate. With increased funding, we added two more sites in 1992 for the remaining two years. (See Appendix C for more information on the five schools.)

We had teams of three researchers for each of the schools, with another investigator concentrating on state policy setting for each school. We wanted researchers who offered varied perspectives, so we hired associates with different ethnic and professional backgrounds. Some of our colleagues came from universities, but most had substantial experience in schools. We hired a director of secondary education; a former assistant professor who had returned to teaching; and a former special education teacher. Although none had worked in a Coalition school, each had been connected with various innovations, pilot projects, and national reform networks. Prior to the first school visits, a weeklong orientation-training session helped assure common approaches by this diverse group. The entire staff reassembled for a week following the second year of data gathering.

Each author served as a team leader (with Richard Clark coordinating the field work in the two sites added in 1992), and we each joined the other teams on one visit in order to see all five sites firsthand.

Each team went to its site twice a year, once in the autumn and again in the spring. The visits began in October 1991 and ended in April 1994. A faculty member in each school served as our local coordinator. Before each site visit, researchers and school coordinators collaborated to develop interview protocols of six to ten questions for hourlong sessions with the "primary subject" students, teachers, administrators, and parents. Each of these individuals was interviewed in all six visits. Each researcher also had two-hour meetings with focus groups of students, teachers, and parents. In addition, we observed our primary subjects in many of their classes and focused on the teaching therein. (Approximately one-third of the researchers' time was devoted to classroom observations.) Two teachers and two students at each school were paid to write weekly journals.

From the start, we sought an interactive and collaborative relationship with each school. The method we relied on to build the partnership featured "snapshots" of each place. After each researcher finished lengthy but not verbatim field notes, the team leaders triangulated the data into twenty- to sixty-page snapshots, which detailed the experiences of students in the school and presented the multiple perspectives of staff, parents, and administrators (using pseudonyms for all people and places). The snapshots differed in style from site to site, but they all included information on classroom work and described major issues facing the school. Although these reports usually explored the protocol questions, they also often concentrated on what particular issues were facing the schools at that time. Various teachers and administrators read drafts of each snapshot, pointing out errors, omissions, and questionable interpretations. Once negotiations were completed—we never reached an impasse on the final draft—the snapshot was distributed to every adult in the school and any outsiders with whom the faculty and administration wished to share. Students read excerpts from the snapshots that presented their views.

Our hope was that the schools would use the snapshots as analytical tools to help them determine for themselves whether they were on or off track. By reporting change as it was happening, the snapshots provided a mirror to the school communities about the progress made and the distance yet to go. As a result, we, the researchers, held overlapping roles: as we were studying the schools, we were also trying to support the very changes we were studying.

After the school visits ended and the last snapshots were circulated, the three authors reread the entire database. In addition to the 26 snapshots, we possessed 140 field notes on interviews with administrators and counselors, 218 with teachers, 170 with students, and 93 with parents. From classroom observations, we had an additional 192 notes. The aggregate field notes constituted approximately sixteen thousand pages. As we read, we drafted outlines of the book, identifying the dyads (the essential four connections as we saw them) featured in Chapters Two through Five and the individual students profiled in Chapters One and Six. Then each author reread the material from his or her research site to select the interviews and observations that bore most directly on the theme of each chapter. After the authors exchanged notes, Wasley wrote Chapters One, Two, Four, and Six; Hampel wrote Chapter Three; and Clark wrote Chapter Five. Revisions followed, with Wasley doing the final "write-over" of the entire manuscript.

To provide advice (to us and to the schools), we had an advisory board from 1990 on. Ann Lieberman, Arthur Powell, and Seymour Sarason not only read our work but also visited each of the sites from 1991 through 1994, writing field notes with their observations about the schools' progress and how our research was affecting the schools.

For more discussion of our methodology, see "Creating CES Schools Through Collaborative Inquiry" and "Collaborative Inquiry: A Method for the Reform-Minded."[2]

Appendix C: The Schools

We started in 1991 with three schools in three states and in 1992 added two inner-city schools in a fourth state. The schools represented a kind of cross section of American high schools—suburban, rural fringe, urban, small town. None of these schools was new to school reform—all had been involved for seven years or more, and all were members of the Coalition of Essential Schools. All recognized that they had completed the first stages of reform work—new schedules, cross-disciplinary teams, site-based councils and new governance structures, advisory programs. All of the schools believed that they had strong support for change but that whole-hearted agreement was still remote. Brief descriptions of the schools will help illuminate their differences and will give a context for our findings.

Oak Hill High School

Located in a suburb in the Northeast, "Oak Hill" (all the school names are pseudonymous) has served its community for over a hundred years. The town is small, quaint, scenic. Over the years, the community has changed from blue-collar to a more upscale commuter suburb, raising both the level of income and the interest in education.

The school houses 350 students, the majority of whom are white; however, minority populations are growing quickly. The number of students going to college has risen steadily in the past twenty years. Currently, between 89 and 93 percent of the students go on to some tertiary institution. The school is a safe place—no gangs, no metal detectors. Staff turnover is low, and staff members joke that they really come to Oak Hill until retirement. The mean number of years of experience on the high school staff is eighteen.

The Oak Hill staff have had three principals in the past five years. (The first left to become superintendent of the district.) All social studies and English teachers are on teams. Most teachers work with an advisory—a small group of students—for four years. All sophomores and seniors are required to complete final exhibitions prior to graduation. Special education students are mainstreamed with side support from the special education teachers, who attend classes with their students. Faculty in nearly all disciplines have been working on curricular, instructional, or assessment revisions. Some of the staff continue to debate whether the vote they had taken to join the Coalition had been a legitimate one.

Lincoln High School

Built at the outer edges of a midwestern city, "Lincoln" feels both rural and urban. Buses bring in minority kids from projects on the other side of town, but neighborhood kids walk to school. It is part of a larger district that has magnet programs, which skim the most academically able and artistically talented students. Once known primarily for athletic success, the school has, since the mid-1980s, joined and led several district and state reform initiatives, so it is now recognized as innovative. However, low scores on new statewide tests almost categorized Lincoln as a school "in crisis."

Lincoln has 1,120 students, many attracted there by a public safety magnet program housed in a spacious building at the back of the campus. Approximately 40 percent of the graduates continue their education, most in-state. Slightly more than half of the students qualify for free lunch, and special education teachers work with 45 percent of the students. Despite an occasional fight, gun, or drug deal, the school is relatively safe and orderly.

Recent retirements and transfers lowered the mean years of service on the Lincoln staff from twenty-one to sixteen. A long-term partnership with a nearby university provides the school with interns and student teachers and a steady supply of researchers. Lincoln has had two principals in the past five years.

The school has focused on teaming as its central reform strategy and has demonstrated enormous patience as it has carried on discussions for years at a time, waiting until a significant majority of the staff could agree. Two-thirds of the faculty are currently on teams. Believing that this is insufficient, they are moving toward breaking the whole school into four smaller units or houses, again working on whole-school agreement.

Crossroads High School

Located in one of the nation's most beautiful cities, "Crossroads" High School looms against bare hills in a striking southwestern landscape. A relatively new school, it struggles to overcome the community's tendency to consider it a second-rate place in comparison with the other, long-established high school in town. Crossroads does draw more of its 1,100 students (73 percent Hispanic) from low-income homes, single-parent families, or recent immigrant families.

Teacher salaries at this school are below average in a state that is below the national average. Because the city is so popular, teachers have trouble affording housing and are feeling the pinch as the city's property values skyrocket beyond their capability to afford. As a result, teacher turnover is a major challenge each year.

During its short history, Crossroads has developed a statewide reputation as a leader in school reform. All ninth-, tenth-, and eleventh-grade students enroll in the Pathways program—originally designed as multi-age, interdisciplinary humanities classes. The school also has a governance council led by a teacher chair. The council involves teachers, parents, administrators, and students. The faculty is currently struggling to institute new block schedules, advisory programs, and graduation exhibitions. Despite its reputation as a reform leader, the school has consistent difficulty reaching consensus on how to fulfill its own dream to be a very different kind of high school. Crossroads has had two principals in the past five years.

Marshall High School

"Marshall" is a large urban high school with a faculty of 150 people. Because the district has hired few new high school teachers in the past decade, the faculty is very senior. About 45 percent of the staff and roughly 99 percent of the student body are African American. There are about 2,060 students enrolled. With an average attendance of slightly less than 60 percent, there are between 1,000 and 1,500 students present on any given day.

Marshall is a comprehensive neighborhood high school. As such, it serves the students who remain after others have chosen to enroll in magnet programs designed to respond to federal integration mandates. In an attempt to serve their students better, a principal successfully lobbied to create a nursery for infants and toddlers. Young mothers, who otherwise would be at home caring for their babies, bring them to school, where two large former laboratory spaces have been converted to child-care facilities.

Marshall was identified four years ago as one of the schools to receive intensive attention by the foundation-funded School Restructuring Collaborative (SRC). The main thrust of the SRC has been to break down large urban high schools into smaller units, or charters, to enable the teachers to know students better by working with smaller groups over time and to create safer, smaller learning communities. The SRC has offered numerous seminars, frequently in connection with the district and local universities, and has promoted site-based management. As part of its work with the SRC, Marshall has paid attention to student transitions from the eighth grade on, from Marshall into the world of work or higher education. One of the four charters in the school, the Overland Charter, used its affiliation with the Coalition of Essential Schools to guide its reform efforts. The Overland Charter staff came together because they shared similar views and goals. Although they find it easy to agree, it is much more difficult for them to establish clear agreements with the other charters in the high school. Marshall has had four principals in five years.

Forest Park High School

"Forest Park" is another comprehensive neighborhood high school in the same city as Marshall. Located in a neighborhood in which 98 percent of the families are on some form of public assistance, Forest Park includes an elementary school, a middle school, and a high school in the same sprawling brick structure. When we first visited the high school, it had about 800 students enrolled, mostly African American. In addition to its affiliation with its state's Re:Learning effort,[1] the school identified more than twenty special programs in which it was participating as it sought to improve student attendance and reduce a high failure rate. Like Marshall, Forest Park is receiving intensive attention by the SRC. Staff created a special program for ninth graders, in which teams of teachers concentrated on offering pre-school-year transition programs, knowing students well, and providing personalized instruction. During the course of our study, the SRC helped Forest Park organize all ninth-through twelfth-grade students into three charters. The school had particular success in working with science and mathematics, in which strong teacher leaders headed innovative programs. As we complete our study, Forest Park has been selected by a new superintendent as a lead school for his major reform initiative. This school now has its third principal in five years.

❖

Table C.1 provides a demographic summary of each of the schools. Tables C.2 through C.6 represent, for each of the three academic years of the study, the phase (either implementation or planning/debate) that each school was in regarding its efforts to bring about reform in specific areas, such as team teaching, mainstreaming special education students, creation of small learning communities, and so forth.

Table C.1. Demographic Composition of Schools.

School	Setting	Enrollment	Minority Students	Principals, 1988–1995	Featured Adults	Featured Students
Oak Hill	Northeast, suburban	350	9%	3	Ms. Bishop	Sally
					Dr. Brenner	Tommy
					Ms. Capraro	Brian
					Mr. Dobbs	Tony
					Mr. Garland	Sergei
					Mr. Hodgkins	Melissa
					Ms. Mosback	
					Ms. North	
					Ms. O'Leary	
					Mr. Renzler	
					Mr. Santamaria	
					Mr. Timar	
					Ms. Tommich	
					Mr. Tydal	
					Mr. Warren	
					Mr. Weiss	

Lincoln	Central South, urban fringe	1,120	30%	2	Mr. Dee Mr. Gordon Mr. Landon Mr. McCarthy Ms. Murray Ms. Norton Mr. Thornton	Alicia Sean Mike
Crossroads	Southwest, small city	1,100	73%	2	Ms. Donnette Ms. Sherlock	Diego
Marshall (contains Overland Charter)	East, urban	2,060	99%	3	Ms. Fried Ms. Holmes Ms. Posada Ms. Winters	Hakim Rashid
Forest Park	East, urban	800	99%	4	Mr. Chapman	Tanya Shardawn

Table C.2. Crossroads Reform Activity.

Reform Activity	1991–92	1992–93	1993–94
Team teaching	I	I	I
Mainstreaming	I	I	I
Integration of subjects	I	I	I
Block scheduling	P	P	I
Creation of small learning communities			I
Teaching strategies			
Cooperative learning	I	I	I
Socratic seminars	I	I	I
Kids teaching kids	I	I	I
STARS curriculum			
Simulations (for example,			
stock market)	I	I	I
Other			
Portfolio assessment	P	P	P
Student exhibitions	P	P	P
Detracking	I	I	a
Student advisory periods, family groups	P	P	I
Partnerships			
With universities	I	I	I
With businesses			
School clinics, social services	I	I	I
Child care for student parents	—	—	—
District magnet programs	—	—	I

Note: I = implementation; P = planning/debate.

[a]Initial emphasis on detracking gave way to renewed tracking by 1993–94.

Table C.3. Forest Park Reform Activity.

Reform Activity	1992–93	1993–94
Team teaching	I	I
Mainstreaming	I	I
Integration of subjects	—	—
Block scheduling	—	—
Creation of small learning communities	I	I
Teaching strategies		
Cooperative learning	I	I
Socratic seminars		
Kids teaching kids	I	I
STARS curriculum		
Simulations (for example,		
stock market)	I	I
Other	I	I
Portfolio assessment	I	I
Student exhibitions	P	P
Detracking	—	—
Student advisory periods, family groups	I	I
Partnerships		
With universities	I	I
With businesses	I	I
School clinics, social services	I	I
Child care for student parents	I	I
District magnet programs	I	I

Note: I = implementation; P = planning/debate. Forest Park was part of the study for just two years.

Table C.4. Lincoln Reform Activity.

Reform Activity	1991–92	1992–93	1993–94
Team teaching	I	I	I
Mainstreaming	I	I	I
Integration of subjects	I	I	I
Block scheduling	P	P	I
Creation of small learning communities	P	P	P
Teaching strategies			
Cooperative learning	I	I	I
Socratic seminars	I	I	I
Kids teaching kids	I	I	I
STARS curriculum			
Simulations (for example,			
stock market)	I	I	I
Other	I	I	I
Portfolio assessment	P	I	I
Student exhibitions	—	P	P
Detracking	I	I	I
Student advisory periods, family groups	I	I	I
Partnerships			
With universities	I	I	I
With businesses	I	I	I
School clinics, social services	I	I	I
Child care for student parents	I	I	I
District magnet programs	P	I	I

Note: I = implementation; P = planning/debate.

Table C.5. Marshall Reform Activity
(including Overland Charter).

Reform Activity	1992–93	1993–94
Team teaching	I	I
Mainstreaming	I	I
Integration of subjects	I	I
Block scheduling	I	I
Creation of small learning communities	I	I
Teaching strategies		
Cooperative learning	I	I
Socratic seminars		
Kids teaching kids	I	I
STARS curriculum		
Simulations (for example,		
stock market)	I	I
Other	I	I
Portfolio assessment	I	I
Student exhibitions	P	I
Detracking	I	I
Student advisory periods, family groups	I	I
Partnerships		
With universities	I	I
With businesses	I	I
School clinics, social services	I	I
Child care for student parents	I	I
District magnet programs	I	I

Note: I = implementation; P = planning/debate. Marshall was part of the study for just two years.

Table C.6. Oak Hill Reform Activity.

Reform Activity	1991–92	1992–93	1993–94
Team teaching	I	I	I
Mainstreaming	I	I	I
Integration of subjects	I	I	I
Block scheduling	P	I	I
Creation of small learning communities	—	—	—
Teaching strategies			
Cooperative learning	I	I	I
Socratic seminars	I	I	I
Kids teaching kids	I	I	I
STARS curriculum	P	I	I
Simulations (for example,			
stock market)	I	I	I
Other	I	I	I
Portfolio assessment	I	I	I
Student exhibitions	P	I	I
Detracking	—	—	—
Student advisory periods, family groups	I	I	I
Partnerships			
With universities	—	—	—
With businesses	—	—	—
School clinics, social services	—	—	—
Child care for student parents	—	—	—
District magnet programs	—	—	—

Note: I = implementation; P = planning/debate.

Notes

Chapter One

1. The names of the schools, those who work in them, and those who attend them have been changed to protect their anonymity.
2. Michelle Fine (1994) coined the term *charters* for these small units within schools, although the term soon came to describe schools established under various state authorizations as newly formed, independent public schools. However, many of the same notions of independence from the established bureaucracy were essential to her definition, which envisioned charters as small units with students in grades nine through twelve, heterogeneously grouped, pursuing a rigorous interdisciplinary curriculum in nontracked classes.
3. The resource room is where students who have been identified as having special needs are sent. Resource rooms are typically self-contained classrooms for students with behavioral problems or learning difficulties. This approach of separating special needs students from regular education students is currently being challenged in the interpretation of Public Law 94-142. It requires that students with special needs must be in the least restrictive environment possible so that they do not suffer from unwarranted stigma.
4. These were not the only questions we asked. In addition, we were interested to see whether these schools could move beyond pockets of change to whole school redesign. We explored the issue of whole school change in "The Puzzle of Whole School Change" (Wasley, Hampel, and Clark, 1997). We

wanted to know how the schools maintained momentum. We also wanted to know how the schools used the Nine Common Principles of the Coalition of Essential Schools to undergird their work.

5. For a complete discussion of the methodology used, see Appendix B. In addition, see Wasley, King, and Louth (1995) and Wasley, Hampel, and Clark (1996).

6. Despite our stance as advocates for the kids and their schools, we did not begin by positing a hypothetical answer. Instead, we applied the *grounded theory method* of research. Rather than formulating a theory that offers a potential answer to a question, which researchers then proceed to prove or disprove, grounded theorists go in search of answers without predicting. This enables them to consider a wide range of possibilities.

Chapter Two

1. Historically, the hope for a teaching repertoire has been present during much of the last century. Dewey believed that teachers should have a great enough range of skills to foster student explorations, as students pursued work that was of particular interest to them (Dewey, 1910, p. 205). In the 1960s, Taba (1962) developed an approach for curriculum development that matched educational goals to a particular philosophy of learning that required more intellectual process skills. Books like *Models of Teaching* (Joyce, 1972), still well used in methods courses, suggested to potential teachers that there were a number of intellectual approaches they might use with students. The rationale was that students learn in a variety of ways and therefore teachers need a range of classroom approaches.

In the 1970s, analysis of earlier attempts to reform schools suggested that teachers needed more support to grow professionally once they moved into teaching service. Enormous growth in professional development courses that encouraged teachers to develop a range of techniques took place. States like

California spent billions of dollars to provide teachers with more growth opportunities. At the heart of these efforts was the belief that teachers needed a significant repertoire (Warren-Little, 1986). In the three studies that fostered this current wave of interest in secondary school reform, all called for a broader range of experiences for students (Boyer, 1983; Sizer, 1984). In his major study of schooling, which is reported in *A Place Called School*, Goodlad (1984) indicated that teachers should have between twelve and fourteen techniques at their fingertips for working with students

More recently, Howard Gardner's work on multiple intelligences (1991) reinforces the notion that teachers need a broader range of techniques in order to engage more students. Current trends suggest that teachers should be helping kids construct their own knowledge and that teachers need a range of techniques to share with students so that students can actually apply what they are gaining in new and fresh situations (Cohen, McLaughlin, and Talbert, 1993).

Unfortunately, powerful research has indicated that much of the inservice and professional development work that is designed to expand teachers' repertoires has been ineffective in the face of the complexity of the task (Warren-Little, 1986). Teachers, working in isolation, lack the time needed to try new techniques, or the time and support needed to gather adequate feedback to make the building of a broad-based repertoire a viable proposition. Recognizing these problems, however, is a major step in correcting them.

2. For a fuller discussion of this topic, see Wasley, *Teachers Who Lead* (1991) and *Stirring the Chalkdust* (1994). During the research for this second work, it became apparent that teachers hold strong beliefs about their need for a repertoire. They talked about the need for a variety of techniques to get students involved and to maintain their own passion for teaching.

3. Sizer (1984) included exhibitions in the Nine Common Principles, suggesting that schools should encourage students to

prepare a culminating performance. This, he believed, would ask more of the kids and give the surrounding community, the parents, and the teachers more information about what the student has accomplished in school.

4. McKay (1986), p. 144.

5. Cohen (1990), pp. 327–346.

6. Loucks-Horsley and Siegelbauer (1991) described this in their work on beginning teachers, who tend to focus more intently on the content or the process than on their students. It is only later, when new teachers are more familiar with a technique, that they can look up from the text to make adjustments based on the reactions of the students. It seems likely that when experienced teachers try new things, they revert back temporarily to this same reaction, though they have more experience on which to draw.

7. Schön (1983).

Chapter Three

1. Lipsitz (1984); Noddings (1984).

2. Chaskin and Rauner (1995), p. 672.

3. Bosworth (1995), pp. 690–691.

4. Lewis, Schaps, and Watson (1995).

5. Fried (1995), p. 50.

6. Merrow Report/Learning Matters, Inc. (1995), p. 2.

Chapter Four

1. Craigie (1910), pp. 682–683.

2. McDonald (1996), pp. 155–242.

3. For a very thorough analysis of implementation considerations, see Miles and Huberman (1984).

4. For a thorough discussion about autonomy, see Shulman (1993), pp. 3–36.

5. Santee-Siskin (1994); Santee-Siskin and Warren-Little (1995).

6. In the middle of our study, Joe McDonald and colleagues at the Coalition began working on processes for examining student work as a means by which to help faculty build shared understandings about standards, expectations, and coherence. He worked in a number of schools, other than these five, while building these procedures. Oak Hill and Lincoln began experimenting with these procedures near the end of data collection. Since then, the Overland Charter within Marshall has used these techniques as a means by which to come closer to shared understandings.

Chapter Five

1. Two reports issued in 1996 suggested that high schools should be smaller than is common in most suburban and urban settings. The Commission on the Restructuring of the American High School recommended units of no more than six hundred students. Lee and Smith reported at the 1996 American Educational Research Association convention that "the ideal high school enrolls 600 to 900 students—no more, no less" (p. 10). However, our observations indicate that such units are still too large, particularly in urban settings or in schools where most students come from low-income families. Others agree that schools must be much smaller. For example, in a 1993 conference sponsored by the Philadelphia Schools Collaborative, Michelle Fine and Deborah Meier stressed the importance of engaging in significant discourse about student learning. Their experiences in New York and Philadelphia led them to advocate basic units of closer to two hundred to three hundred students (Meier, 1995). Excellent sources are Raywid (1996), Oxley (1994), and Meier (1996).

2. Sergiovanni (1996, p. 112) and Fine (1994) contain two recent discussions of the advantages of small school units.

3. Boyer (1983), p. 57.
4. Powell (1985); Sizer (1992, esp. p. 126).
5. This condition was described by Linda McNeil (1986). Her data illustrate how clearly a focus on control contradicts the central purpose of schooling—to educate students.
6. For a thorough description of the process CES schools have used to plan backwards, see McDonald (1992; 1993, pp. 1–13).
7. The Central Park East Secondary School faculty developed the "habits of mind" to direct their work. Many Coalition schools have adopted these or adapted them for use in their own settings. For a further exploration of these ideas, see Lear (1993) and Lieberman (1996).
8. McMullan, Sipe, and Wolf (1995), p. 15.
9. A student interviewed in another study said, "I thought my teachers were trying to stunt my social growth forever! I thought I'd never get a date hanging around with the same kids all the time" (Wasley, 1994, p. 151).
10. Kruse and Seashore Lewis (1995).
11. See, for example, Bellah and others (1991), Etzioni (1991), and Putnam (1993).
12. See Wasley, Hampel, and Clark (1997).
13. Mary Ann Glendon (1991) has suggested that excluding students from real participation is deeply problematic in light of the school's role as a place where kids learn democratic practices. She asks three pertinent questions: (1) Where do citizens acquire the capacity to care about the common good? (2) Where do people learn to view others with respect and concern, rather than to regard them as objects, means or obstacles? (3) Where does a boy or girl develop the healthy independence of mind and self-confidence that enable men and women to participate effectively in government and to exercise responsible leadership? (p. 129).
14. These questions were designed by Joe McDonald (1996) and colleagues as part of the process for examining existing programs for appropriate rigor, breadth, and depth.

15. For a more thorough discussion of schedule changes and their effects, see Wasley (1997).

Chapter Six

1. Arthur Powell's recent book (1996) suggests that teachers in private schools are more used to doing this for kids as well and that this is one of the aspects of private schooling that gives these students greater advantages.
2. Oakes (1985); Wheelock (1992).
3. Cuffaro (1995).
4. For evidence of these controversies, see Wasley, Powell, and Hughes (1992) and Muncey and McQuillan (1996).
5. Although we collected a number of anecdotes revealing racial, gender, and ethnic discrimination, because our study was focused on issues related to school change and school reform, we did not adequately pursue these incidents to find out what had been done in each setting to prevent such conditions and to educate teachers. We did not find out whether there were any steps under way to resolve these problems and what the repercussions were when such incidents were discovered. This, in particular, taught us that although a focus is important and helpful, freedom to pursue emerging issues should be given more careful consideration in the initial design phases of a study.
6. Joe McDonald and colleagues at the Coalition of Essential Schools and at the Annenberg Institute for School Reform have developed a series of tools for looking at student work. The first of these is the "tuning protocol"—a process for examining student work as a means for teachers to get feedback about how they might strengthen their efforts. Several of our schools were just beginning to use these at the conclusion of the study. Currently, McDonald and others have gathered some ten tools for examining student work, all useful in helping teachers determine whether the changes they are making are resulting

in gains for kids. See McDonald (1996); see also Darling-Hammond, Ancess, and Falk (1995).

Appendix B

1. Muncey and McQuillan (1996).
2. Wasley, King, and Louth (1995); Wasley, Hampel, and Clark (1996).

Appendix C

1. Re:Learning was a partnership between the Coalition of Essential Schools, the Education Commission of the States, and member states. Between 1988 and 1996, thirteen states joined Re:Learning to develop a policy context hospitable for Essential Schools. Re:Learning's subtitle—"From the Schoolhouse to the Statehouse"—signaled the interest in forging alliances to seek formal regulations and informal advocacy to sustain local reforms without dictating to or interfering with the innovators. For more information, contact the Education Commission of the States, 707 Seventeenth Street, Denver, CO 80202.

References

Bellah, R. N., and others. *The Good Society*. New York: Knopf, 1991.

Bosworth, K. "Caring for Others and Being Cared For." *Phi Delta Kappan*, May 1995, pp. 686–693.

Boyer, E. L. *High School: A Report on Secondary Education in America*. New York: HarperCollins, 1983.

Chaskin, R. J., and Rauner, D. M. "Youth and Caring." *Phi Delta Kappan*, May 1995, pp. 667–674.

Clark, R. W., Hampel, R. L., and Wasley, P. A. *Snapshots of the School Change Study*. Providence, R.I.: Coalition of Essential Schools, 1995.

Cohen, D. "A Revolution in One Classroom: The Case of Mrs. Oublier." *Educational Evaluation and Policy Analysis*, 1990, *12*(3), 327–346.

Cohen, D., McLaughlin, M., and Talbert, J. E. (eds.). *Teaching for Understanding: Challenges for Policy and Practice*. San Francisco: Jossey-Bass, 1993.

Commission on the Restructuring of the American High School. *Breaking Ranks: Changing an American Institution*. Reston, Va.: National Association of Secondary School Principals, 1996.

Craigie, W. A., *A New English Dictionary*, vol. 8. Oxford, England: Clarendon Press, 1910.

Cuffaro, H. K. *Experimenting with the World: John Dewey and the Early Childhood Classroom*. New York: Teachers College Press, 1995.

Darling-Hammond, L., Ancess, J., and Falk, B. *Authentic Assessment in Action: Studies of Schools and Students at Work*. New York: Teachers College Press, 1995.

Dewey, J. *How We Think*. Lexington, Mass.: Heath, 1910.

Etzioni, A. *A Responsive Society: Collected Essays on Guiding Deliberate Social Change*. San Francisco: Jossey-Bass, 1991.

Fine, M. *Chartering Urban School Reform*. New York: Teachers College Press, 1994.

Fried, R. L. *The Passionate Teacher*. Boston: Beacon Press, 1995.

Gardner, H. *The Unschooled Mind: How Children Think and How Schools Should Teach*. New York: Basic Books, 1991.

Glendon, M. A. *Rights Talk: The Impoverishment of Political Discourse.* New York: Free Press, 1991.

Goodlad, J. I. *A Place Called School: Prospects for the Future.* New York: McGraw-Hill, 1984.

Joyce, B. *Models of Teaching.* Upper Saddle River, N.J.: Prentice Hall, 1972.

Kotlowitz, A. *There Are No Children Here.* New York: Doubleday, 1991.

Kozol, J. *Amazing Grace.* New York: Crown, 1995.

Kruse, S., and Seashore Lewis, K. *Teacher Teaming: Opportunities and Dilemmas.* Brief to Principals No. 11. Madison: University of Wisconsin, Center on Organization and Restructuring of Schools, 1995.

Lear, R. "Developing Valuable Habits in ATLAS Students" in *ATLAS Atlas.* Newton, Mass.: ATLAS Communities Education Development Center, Inc., 1993.

Lee, V. E., and Smith, J. B. "By the Numbers." *Education Week,* Apr. 24, 1996, p. 10.

Lewis, C., Schaps, E., and Watson, M. "Beyond the Pendulum: Creating Challenging and Caring Schools," *Phi Delta Kappan,* Mar. 1995, pp. 547–554.

Lieberman, A. *Visit to a Small School (Trying to Do Big Things): A Guide to Central Park East Secondary School.* New York: National Center for Restructuring Education, Schools, and Teaching (NCREST), May 1996.

Lipsitz, J. *Successful Schools for Young Adolescents.* New Brunswick, N.J.: Transaction, 1984.

Loucks-Horsley, S., and Siegelbauer, S. "Using Knowledge to Guide Staff Development." In A. Lieberman and L. Miller (eds.), *Staff Development for Education in the '90s.* New York: Teachers College Press, 1991.

McDonald, J. P. *Steps in Planning Backwards: Early Lessons from the Schools.* Studies on Exhibitions No. 5. Providence, R.I.: Coalition of Essential Schools, 1992.

McDonald, J. P. "Planning Backwards for Exhibitions." In *Graduation by Exhibition.* Alexandria, Va.: Association for Supervision and Curriculum Development, 1993.

McDonald, J. P. *Redesigning School: Lessons for the 21st Century.* San Francisco: Jossey-Bass, 1996.

McKay, C., "If We Must Die." In P. Burnett (ed.), *Penguin Book of Caribbean Verse in English.* New York: Penguin Books, 1986.

McMullan, B., Sipe, C., and Wolf, W. "Update on Student Performance, Charter Development and Effects of Charters on Student Performance for 1993–94 School Year." Memorandum to the Pew Charitable Trusts, Apr. 26, 1995.

McNeil, L. *Contradictions of Control: School Structure and School Knowledge.* New York: Routledge, 1986.

Meier, D. "How Our Schools Could Be." *Phi Delta Kappan,* Jan. 1995, pp. 369–373.

Meier, D. "The Big Benefits of Smallness." *Educational Leadership*, Sept. 1996, pp. 12–15.

Merrow Report/Learning Matters, Inc. "The Fifty Million Dollar Gamble." In *The Challenge of School Change: Inside One Essential School*. Videotape produced in cooperation with South Carolina ETV and the Coalition of Essential Schools, 1995.

Miles, M., and Huberman, A. M. *Innovation Up Close: How School Improvement Works*. New York: Plenum, 1984.

Muncey, D., and McQuillan, P. *Reform and Resistance in Schools and Classrooms*. New Haven, Conn.: Yale University Press, 1996.

Noddings, N. *Caring: A Feminine Approach to Ethics and Moral Education*. Berkeley: University of California Press, 1984.

Noddings, N. *The Challenge to Care in Schools*. New York: Teachers College Press, 1992.

Oakes, J. *Keeping Track: How Schools Structure Inequality*. New Haven, Conn.: Yale University Press, 1985.

Oxley, D. "Organizing Schools into Small Units: Alternatives to Homogeneous Grouping." *Phi Delta Kappan*, Mar. 1994, pp. 12–15.

Powell, A. *Lessons from Privilege: The American Prep School Tradition*. Cambridge, Mass.: Harvard University Press, 1996.

Powell, A., Farrar, E., and Cohen, D. K. *The Shopping Mall High School*. Boston: Houghton Mifflin, 1985.

Putnam, R. *Making Democracy Work: Civic Traditions in Modern Italy*. Princeton, N.J.: Princeton University Press, 1993.

Raywid, M. "Taking Stock: The Movement to Create Mini-Schools, Schools-Within-Schools, and Separate Small Schools," ERIC Clearinghouse on Urban Education, Urban Diversity Series No. 108, 1996.

Santee-Siskin, L. *Realms of Knowledge: Academic Departments in Secondary Schools*. London: Falmer Press, 1994.

Santee-Siskin, L., and Warren-Little, J. (eds.). *The Subjects in Question: Department Organization and the High School*. New York: Teachers College Press, 1995.

Schön, D. A. *The Reflective Practitioner: How Professionals Think in Action*. New York: Basic Books, 1983.

Sergiovanni, T. J. *Leadership for the Schoolhouse: How Is It Different? Why Is It Important?* San Francisco: Jossey-Bass, 1996.

Shulman, L. S. "Autonomy and Obligation: The Remote Control of Teaching." In L. S. Shulman and G. Sykes. (eds.), *The Handbook of Research on Teaching*. Old Tappan, N.J.: Macmillan, 1993.

Sizer, T. R. *Horace's Compromise*. Boston: Houghton Mifflin, 1984.

Sizer, T. R. *Horace's School: Redesigning the American High School*. Boston: Houghton Mifflin, 1992.

Sizer, T. R. *Horace's Hope*. Boston: Houghton Mifflin, 1996.

Taba, H. *Curriculum Development*. Orlando, Fla.: Harcourt Brace, 1962.

Warren-Little, J. "Seductive Images and Organizational Realities." In A. Lieberman (ed.), *Rethinking School Improvement*. New York: Teachers College Press, 1986.

Wasley, P. A. *Teachers Who Lead: The Rhetoric of Reform and the Realities of Practice*. New York: Teachers College Press, 1991.

Wasley, P. A. *Stirring the Chalkdust: Tales of Teachers Changing Classroom Practice*. New York: Teachers College Press, 1994.

Wasley, P. A. "Straight Shooting." *Educational Leadership*, Apr. 1995, pp. 56–59.

Wasley, P. A. "Alternative Schedules: To What End?" *National Association of Secondary School Principals Bulletin*, Apr. 1997, pp. 44–50.

Wasley, P. A., Hampel, R. L., and Clark, R. W. "Collaborative Inquiry: A Method for the Reform-Minded." Paper presented at an American Educational Research Association symposium, Apr. 1996.

Wasley, P. A., Hampel, R. L., and Clark, R. W. "The Puzzle of Whole School Change." *Phi Delta Kappan*, May 1997, 78(9), 690–697.

Wasley, P. A., King, S., and Louth, C. "Creating Coalition Schools Through Collaborative Inquiry." In *NSSE Yearbook, 1995*. Chicago: National Society for the Study of Education, 1995.

Wasley, P. A., Powell, B., and Hughes, D. "Interpreting the Nine Common Principles." In *Studies on School Change* (Oak Hill No. 2a). Providence, R.I.: Coalition of Essential Schools, 1992.

Wheelock, A. *Crossing the Tracks: How "Untracking" Can Save America's Schools*. New York: New Press, 1992.

Index

Printed in the United States
86894LV00002B/253-273/A